Artery

Artery

RACIAL ECOLOGIES ON
COLOMBIA'S MAGDALENA RIVER

Austin Zeiderman

Duke University Press *Durham and London 2025*

Printed in the United States of America on acid-free paper ∞
Project Editor: Livia Tenzer
Cover design by David Rainey
Typeset in Portrait and Helvetica Neue
by Westchester Publishing Services

Library of Congress Cataloging-in-Publication Data
Names: Zeiderman, Austin, [date] author.
Title: Artery : racial ecologies on Colombia's Magdalena River / Austin Zeiderman.
Description: Durham : Duke University Press, 2025. | Includes bibliographical references
and index.
Identifiers: LCCN 2024025063 (print)
LCCN 2024025064 (ebook)
ISBN 9781478031406 (paperback)
ISBN 9781478028185 (hardcover)
ISBN 9781478060390 (ebook)
Subjects: LCSH: Shipping—Colombia—Magdalena River. | Globalization—Social
aspects—Colombia. | Globalization—Economic aspects—Colombia. | Magdalena River
(Colombia)—Commerce.
Classification: LCC HE655.Z7 M35 2025 (print) | LCC HE655.Z7 (ebook) |
DDC 304.209861—dc23/eng/20241217
LC record available at https://lccn.loc.gov/2024025063
LC ebook record available at https://lccn.loc.gov/2024025064

ISBN 9781478094371 (ebook/other)

Cover art: Illustration by Reno Inchenko.

This book is freely available thanks to generous support from the LSE
Department of Geography and Environment and the LSE Library.

For Eliseo

Contents

Preface

A Colombian nursery rhyme with the catchy title of "La serpiente de tierra caliente" tells of the misadventures of a serpent from the hot lowlands (*tierra caliente*) who travels to the cold interior (*tierra fría*). It visits the hairdresser—in vain, as it has no hair. It goes shopping for shoes—another failure, as it has no feet. Children laugh at the serpent's silliness, of course. Yet they probably miss the explanation stressed by the refrain: the serpent is drunk on plantains spiked with *aguardiente*, a potent firewater brewed from sugarcane. The delicacies of its tropical homeland have gone to its head: it is out of its mind, *demente*. In another song, an iguana grooms itself on the banks of the Magdalena River, as if to become more socially acceptable. But what's the point? Try as it might, the iguana can never fit in: it drinks coffee at teatime (*tomaba café a la hora del té*).

During my research, these tales lost something of their youthful innocence. The human target of their playful mockery was all too evident. That they appeared in nonhuman form was unremarkable. After all, the fluidity of the human/animal divide is characteristic of the early childhood imagination—only later do we begin to think of our species as unique. Yet tropes of animality have also been inseparable from racial ontologies and their entanglement with ideas of nature. In Colombia, these ontologies have geographical coordinates: lighter-skinned people from the cool, mountainous highlands are presumed intrinsically superior to the darker-skinned inhabitants of the hot, coastal lowlands. In the stories of the crazed serpent and gauche iguana, I could not but hear echoes of the entrenched hierarchies that govern Colombian society and the place of nature within it.

I encountered these regimes of naturalized inequality often in relation to the Magdalena River. Indeed, I began to sense the importance of the waterway in establishing and sustaining them. The more I focused on social and environmental orders in this place, the more I felt the need to understand race as an organizing principle of the modern world—what Sylvia Wynter, in "1492: A New World View," identifies as the new construct that came to take the place of prior ordering structures, such as religion and caste. The construct of race, she argues, buttressed the metaphysical order of the post-Columbian societies and polities of the Caribbean and the Americas, extending through the nineteenth-century empires of Western Europe and continuing into the present. The problematic under examination in this book—the intersecting regimes of difference that shape relations among humans and between humans and the rest of the world—emerges out of the shared history of disparate geographical locations—what Lisa Lowe calls the "intimacies of four continents."

Decades of critical scholarship have shown how racial formations structure social, economic, and political life. Less attention has been given to how race also structures ecologies and infrastructures, thereby underpinning exploitative relations, not only among human populations but also between humans and the planet. Increasingly recognized as unjust and unsustainable, these relations are undergoing profound change as climate crisis is radically transforming landscapes and waterscapes. Meanwhile, movements for economic, environmental, and social justice are emerging to challenge entrenched relations of inequality. There is now more reason than ever to think about the racial formations embedded in ecological and infrastructural orders as well as the conditions of possibility for their eventual undoing.

At this pivotal moment, *Artery* examines a flagship megaproject on Colombia's Magdalena River that aims to build a logistics corridor along the waterway through engineering works (mainly dredging and channeling). Focusing on this intervention reveals the centrality of racialization and other forms of difference-making to the contemporary global order, especially as they undergo major shifts in Colombia and indeed in the world at large. By ethnographic standards, the navigation project is large and the river basin vast. Their scale is dwarfed, however, by the magnitude of the issues at stake. In this sense, the Magdalena is a microcosm encapsulating a much wider problematic. *Artery* strives to enrich the nascent yet burgeoning field of critical inquiry centered on the shifting relationship between race, nature, and capitalism in the Anthropocene.

A book's title can only do so much. In selecting one for this project, I sought a word or phrase to bridge the gap between concerns that often run parallel: racial formations and infrastructural environments. In referencing both the circulation of the blood and a key transport route, *Artery* felt right. After all, the Magdalena is often referred to by anatomical metaphors: it is the nation's life force (*fuerza vital*) or spinal column (*columna vertebral*). As in the catchphrase "rivers are the veins of the planet," arteries carry oxygen from the heart, just as waterways enable other vital flows. However, I was never entirely comfortable with the analogy to the human body, as if it were a neutral abstraction. The history of scientific racism is itself a reminder that some invocations of blood are far from benign. Yet it was precisely these complexities that I hoped to examine, and *Artery* signaled that intention. This book engages with entanglements of race and nature while aspiring toward a future in which they might be undone.

Acknowledgments

A popular saying along the Magdalena River alludes to oscillations of fortune and misfortune: *el río le pone, el río le quita* (the river gives, the river takes away). I have heard people apply this expression to all sorts of situations concerning life along the waterway. In researching and writing this book, I thought frequently about the ethics of reciprocity, knowing that I was receiving from my interlocutors more than I could possibly return. I hope the gratitude expressed here, and in the footnotes, goes at least some way to redressing that imbalance.

My appreciation goes, first and foremost, to the men and women who power fluvial transport along the Magdalena River: riverboat captains and crews, but also the dockside workers of shipping companies, port terminals, and logistics hubs. Their knowledge was indispensable to this book, as their labor is to the economy. Despite their demanding workloads, Edinson Mercado, Eder Luna, and Aníbal Robles became confidants in matters both professional and personal, first on water and then on land. Corporate managers, government officials, and technical experts sacrificed less to speak with me but were often generous respondents. Daniel Posen and Diana Reyes were especially sympathetic to my interest in logistics. I also benefited from time spent with townspeople in Honda, Puerto Berrío, Puerto Wilches, El Banco, Calamar, Yatí, Mompox, and Magangué.

My relation to Colombia as a place from which to think is not uncomplicated. I have been conducting research there since 2006, yet I am acutely aware of my status as visitor. I have no authority or legitimacy based on birth, ancestry, or identity; my connections to places and people are entirely artificial, in that they have been made. My attention to race stems partly from my upbringing in the sharply segregated city of Philadelphia and partly from my own genealogical descent: southern Italian and Swedish migrants on one side and

Polish-Jewish refugees on the other who navigated structures of racial hierarchy to eventually become white Americans, with all the privileges and obligations that come with that position. My interest in nature, especially rivers, was sparked by my time spent working with the Western Water Project of the Natural Resources Defense Council. Though over twenty years have passed, I remain indebted to Hal Candee and Barry Nelson for starting me on this journey.

Although completing this book took longer than expected, my colleagues in the Department of Geography and Environment at LSE provided much-needed encouragement and feedback along the way. I'm especially grateful to Kasia Paprocki and Rebecca Elliot for creating space to think about the social life of climate change and the environment. Thank you to Sam Colegate, Lee Mager, and their team for making the department a pleasurable and productive place to work. A group of brilliant scholars near and far commented on parts of the manuscript or shaped the ideas contained therein: Rivke Jaffe, Matthew Gandy, Alejandro De Coss-Corzo, Rory O'Bryen, Sandrine Revet, Clive Nwonka, Alpa Shah, Laura Bear, David Madden, Suzi Hall, Gisa Weszkalnys, Pablo Jaramillo, Diana Ojeda, Ashley Carse, Robert Samet, Nikhil Anand, Sharad Chari, Asher Ghertner, Kiran Asher, Kevin O'Neill, Sergio Montero, Ananya Roy, Hannah Appel, Tariq Jazeel, Tianna Paschel, Sylvia Yanagisako, Niranjana Ramesh, Laura Pulido, AbdouMaliq Simone, and Diane Davis. I also learned valuable lessons from teaching Geographies of Race with a succession of superb graduate teaching assistants: Taneesha Mohan, Jeanne Firth, Dalia Gebrial, Zo Mapukata, and Line Relisieux.

I have been lucky to work with a stellar group of research assistants. At the London School of Economics, Kyle Kulmann, Leopold Schwarz-Schütte, and Lina Quiñones conducted background research in the project's early stages. A virtual collaboration with Melissa Martínez and Rubén Gutiérrez during the pandemic was a breath of fresh air. Sylvia Naneva helped prepare the manuscript for publication, and Mina Moshkeri lent it her formidable cartographic skills.

I could not have asked for a more capable and conscientious editorial team than Gisela Fosado and Alejandra Mejía of Duke University Press. They patiently guided this project throughout trying times, always on hand with judicious advice. Two anonymous reviewers offered invaluable insights that improved the book in ways large and small. My thanks also go to the press's editorial, production, and marketing teams for their commitment to quality.

Of the many whose love and friendship sustained me over the years, a few made concrete contributions: Jesse Watt, Hayden Thorpe, Paula Durán, and

Mike Day. Special thanks to Natalia Guarín for help with the title. Eeva Rinne was a paragon of calm, creativity, and care. Howard Zeiderman, Colin Thubron, and Stefanie Takacs were unwavering allies, while Margreta de Grazia's support is in a category of its own. This book is dedicated to my son, Eliseo, who fondly referred to it as *his* book. I hope it lives up to his expectations!

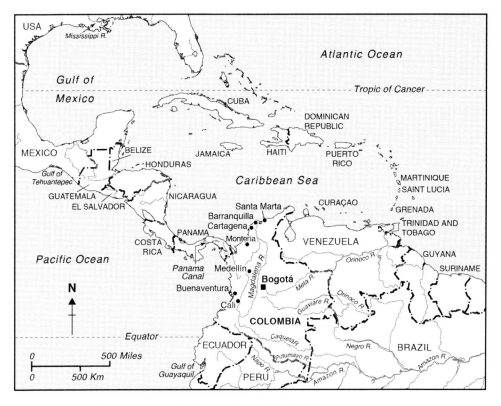

MAP 1. Colombia, between Latin America and the Caribbean.
Cartography by Mina Moshkeri.

MAP 2. The Magdalena River basin and its environs. Cartography by Mina Moshkeri.

Introduction

Race, Nature, and Logistics in Fluvial Colombia

The water was clear and cold. It even smelled good. I decided to trust my senses, ignore my apprehension, and take a long drink. Before embarking on this journey up the Magdalena River on a towboat-and-barge convoy (figure I.1), I had asked whether to bring my own water supply. The operations coordinator facilitating my trip, who worked out of the shipping company's Cartagena office, reassured me that the boat had a top-rate purification system, and I need not worry. "We test it frequently," she said. "It's cleaner than the water we drink here in Cartagena." And so I dropped the subject. After all, I wanted to avoid being the demanding guest, much less jeopardize the permission I had waited so long to get.

Having just boarded, I was now being shown around by the operations coordinator. She made a point of introducing me to the faucet, filling up two glasses, and downing one without hesitation. Standing before her with my glass in hand, droplets of condensation on its surface, I froze in one of those momentary flashes of uncertainty when conflicting thoughts collide. Her tour of the boat thus far had seemed like a performance—one designed to showcase the company's commitment to health and safety—and this stop felt contrived. But it could have also been a genuine attempt to assuage my concerns. Either way, there were no alternatives, so I gave the water one last look and gulped it down.

Later that afternoon, as we set off upriver, I found myself reflecting on that encounter by the faucet. I thought back to my suspicions—about the coordinator's reassurance, about the water's quality. It occurred to me that mistrusting the shipping company was a crude manifestation of my disciplinary training—anthropologists assume that the powerful always resist scrutiny and that we're too clever to be duped. But distrusting the boat's drinking water had more to do with my racial formation—the assumption that some bodies are more sensitive, even more valued than others, is integral to whiteness. I was struck by a pang of guilt. Though normally condemning presumptions of superiority, I had just succumbed to two of them simultaneously. "Fuck it," I thought to myself. "I'll just drink the water and like it."

Over the next few days, I did just that. In fact, I drank zealously from that faucet. It was as if each sip filled me with satisfaction for having identified and overcome pernicious prejudices. I vowed to rally my critical faculties, redoubling my vigilance toward civilizational hierarchies of all sorts. Trips to the kitchen to refill my water bottle even provided glimmers of that vaunted ethnographic virtue—recalibrating one's value system, to the point of feeling more camaraderie with "the field" than with "back home." Eager to document my heightened awareness, I remarked in my field notes on the water's appeal, extending the coordinator's comparison to the water in Cartagena: "It tastes better than the water that comes out of my tap in London," I wrote.

A few days later, I fell ill. My body ached, my head throbbed, my stomach churned. At first, I hid my suffering from the captain and crew, fearing mockery. Though I hardly knew them at that point, my head was full of stereotypes—about logistics workers, about Colombian men, about masculinity in general—and I was already self-conscious about being an effete academic among rugged boatmen. We had gotten along well so far, but in my vulnerable state I worried about triggering an onslaught of machismo. When I could no longer conceal my discomfort, what followed was instead an outpouring of care and generosity. It would certainly have been inconvenient if the gringo perished, but I doubted their compassion could be attributed to that alone. Coupled with the absence of stereotypical behaviors associated with seamen and their riverine counterparts (drinking, swearing, philandering, and so on), I felt my assumptions about the forms of masculinity inherent to riverboat life and labor start to dissolve.

In sympathizing with my condition, the crew repeatedly asked about the cause of my illness. "I think it may have been the water," I responded sheepishly to a group of deckhands on break. Looks of surprise and alarm spread across their faces as one exclaimed, "What, you're drinking the water from the tap?! *Está muy pesado* [literally, "It is very heavy," but with connotations of being hard on the body]. It may be filtered, but it's still sucked straight from the river." This is the same river that receives raw sewage from millions of upstream city dwellers, is polluted by mercury and other toxic chemicals discharged by mining operations, and just a few days before had absorbed the largest oil spill in Colombia's history. The fact that an office worker had assured

FIGURE I.1. Towboat-and-barge convoy ascending the Magdalena River.
Source: photograph by author.

me the water was fine to drink elicited a collective chuckle: "It may be fine for us, but it's certainly not for you," one responded. Although this echoed my earlier concern, I was taken aback by the sharp line drawn between their bodies and mine—this time by them—not to mention their downplaying the potential health risks of long-term exposure. In the conversation that ensued, my efforts to cast doubt on the physiological differences dividing us were repeatedly rebuffed.

We agreed on the obvious—that on the surface we look different. After all, most crew members were darker-skinned and would be categorized socially by terms connoting some degree of proximity to Blackness (*costeño* and *moreno*, perhaps Afro-colombiano or *negro*). My appearance and accent occasionally allow me to pass as a Colombian from Bogotá, but I am usually identified as a gringo (light-skinned foreigner, often North American or European), and while sometimes labeled *judío* (Jew) after explaining the origins of my surname, I am still classified as white. However, when I suggested that these racial taxonomies—despite their social, political, and economic implications—may not explain my intolerance of contaminated water, crew members insisted that the differences between us were more fundamental. I started to wonder what determined where the line is drawn: Was it because I'm not Colombian or because I'm white? Would someone from Bogotá be able to drink the water? These questions sparked a flurry of comments, but uniting them was a categorical order separating riverboat workers from everyone else. Their bodies, I was told, are uniquely suited for the ordeals of laboring along the river, and that was inherited, not acquired.

When put in historical perspective, this connection—between the peculiar qualities of riverboat work and the physical constitution of those who perform it—comes into sharper relief. From the early sixteenth century to the mid-twentieth, the Magdalena River was the primary artery of trade and travel between the Andean interior and the Caribbean coast (figure I.2). Those whose labor powered the watercraft moving people and goods along the river were known as *bogas*—a category that referred simultaneously to professional occupation, geographical origin, and racial extraction (figure I.3). Initially denoting enslaved Indigenous and African boatmen, and later free people of African descent from the lower Magdalena valley, *bogas* were typed as evolutionarily closer to tropical nature, and therefore genetically predisposed to the hardships of riverboat life. This category supported the exploitation and control of a racialized labor force, but it also enabled *bogas* to establish and protect their monopoly over river transport, much to the chagrin of elites from the interior. Though the term *boga* is uncommon today, the vocation of riverboat worker remains tied to the same river towns and their inhabitants, who are believed to be constitutionally fit for this demanding occupation.

Having read up on this history before embarking on my journey, I was unsure how to handle crew members invoking the very typologies once used to subjugate their predecessors. And it felt even more uncomfortable recognizing in myself some of the same prejudices that Spanish colonizers and criollo elites had leveled against them.[1] Despite their fundamental importance to both colonial and postcolonial regimes of accumulation, *bogas* were the target of harsh discrimination, which ascribed qualities to them such as bestiality, lasciviousness, and debauchery.[2] These racialized and gendered stereotypes are repulsive, yet they were not entirely distinct from my assumptions about the forms of masculinity I would encounter among the crew—assumptions quickly invalidated but nevertheless present.[3]

---

1 Villegas, "El valle del río Magdalena."
2 O'Bryen, "On the Shores of Politics."
3 For the argument that masculinity is deeply embedded in infrastructure, see Siemiatycki, Enright, and Valverde, "The Gendered Production of Infrastructure." For an insightful essay

Equally awkward is the recognition that my experience mirrored narratives written by travelers who had journeyed along the river centuries before.[4] Their accounts uniformly emphasized the hardships endured during their travels, with many describing illnesses similar to mine. Like the Spanish colonizers and their locally born descendants, who believed that they could only survive in the temperate climates of the highland interior, European and North American voyagers saw the exuberant tropical nature of the Magdalena River valley as hostile and unhealthy. Indeed, it was in such encounters with the region's suffocating heat, torrential rain, irrepressible vegetation, swarming insects, and unfamiliar animals that people who understood themselves to be "white" came to define the tropics as the primordial home of those whose labor they would exploit—who, in turn, would be made into "Blacks" and "Indians."[5] And here I was: a white researcher from London, on a boat powered by a racialized workforce, tormented by gastrointestinal malaise, entertaining the idea that I was anatomically unfit for life along the river. The parallels made me cringe.

With echoes of the past bouncing around in my head, I began to feel stuck in an endless cycle of racialized encounters with the human and more-than-human natures that make up the tropical lowlands of northern Colombia's Caribbean coast. For centuries, hierarchical relations between different categories of humans (races, but also genders, cultures, nations, and so on) have been entangled with hierarchical relations between people and the so-called natural world. The Magdalena River has played an important role in that history, and its social and environmental orders have been markedly transformed by it. I would find myself thinking about this again and again throughout my journey as I struggled to understand the peculiar world of a commercial riverboat. But the story would not end there, as entanglements of race and nature would continue to haunt my wider inquiry into this vital artery of cultural, political, and economic life.

* * *

<hr />

that questions "the very assumption of logistics' masculine character," see Peano, "Gendering Logistics." My thinking about the forms of masculinity among riverboat workers is inspired by feminist geographical scholarship on intimacy and care work. See Berman-Arévalo and Ojeda, "Ordinary Geographies."

4 Martínez Pinzón, "Tránsitos por el río Magdalena"; Nieto Villamizar and Riaño Pradilla, *Esclavos, negros libres y bogas*.

5 For a vivid account of this phenomenon, see Carby, *Imperial Intimacies*, 279.

FIGURE I.2. Map of Kingdom of New Granada and Popayán. Originally published in Joannes De Laet, *Nieuwe Wereldt ofte Beschrijvinghe van West-Indien*, 1625.

RACE AND NATURE are two of the most powerful organizing principles of the modern world. Their histories are deeply intertwined, and their influence spans a wide spectrum of cultural, scientific, moral, economic, legal, and political institutions. Together they structure our societies and environments, effectively drawing boundaries among humans and between them and their categorical others. However, both terms have been called into question of late as artifacts of earlier paradigms of knowledge. Decades of genetic research have debunked the scientific validity of race, and the Anthropocene debate contends that nature is no longer an independent realm beyond human activity. Yet even if dismissed as problematic or passé, these potent concepts continue to reassert themselves in both familiar and unexpected ways.

Troubled by this paradox, and building on a rich body of scholarship in anthropology, geography, history, and related disciplines, I situate myself at the intersection of race and nature to account for the work these interrelated ideas continue to perform in the world: how they regulate social and environmental

FIGURE I.3. Ramón Torres Méndez, *Champán en el río Magdalena*, ca. 1860.
Source: Banco de la República.

orders; how they divide the category of humanity and determine what (indeed, who) is excluded from it; how their meaning and materiality are made and remade in everyday encounters; how their historical legacy weighs on the present and shapes conditions of future possibility; how they enable and sustain relations of care as well as violence; how people navigate a world structured by these ideas; how they saturate the research enterprise; and why scholars still need to think critically and carefully about them.[6] The concept of *racial ecolo-*

---

6 Many studies have tackled the historical and ongoing entanglement of nature and race. For those influential to this analysis, see Cronon, *Uncommon Ground*; Wade, *Race, Nature and Culture*; Haraway, *Primate Visions*; Leal, *Landscapes of Freedom*; Moore, Kosek, and Pandian, *Race, Nature, and the Politics of Difference*; Stepan, *"The Hour of Eugenics"*; Brahinsky, Sasser, and Minkoff-Zern, "Race, Space, and Nature"; Ranganathan, "Caste, Racialization, and the Making of Environmental Unfreedoms"; Jazeel, *Sacred Modernity*; Hosbey, Lloréns, and Roane, "Global Black Ecologies"; Jaffe, *Concrete Jungles*; Ferdinand, *Decolonial Ecology*.

gies foregrounds the indisputable significance of race and racism to the ordering of both human societies and nonhuman environments.[7]

Impending climate emergency and resurgent white supremacy give these matters heightened urgency. Yarimar Bonilla puts it succinctly, urging scholars "to think more carefully about the relationship between notions of civilizational hierarchy and of human superiority over the more-than-human world, interrogate how these logics have operated in tandem, and explore how they can be tackled in unison."[8] Over two decades ago, Clyde Woods alighted upon the entanglement of extractivism and exploitation: "the settler worldview saw the ecosystem in all its biodiversity as isolable and exploitable parts: forests became timber, deer became fur, water became irrigation, and people became slaves."[9] Together, the logics of civilizational hierarchy and human superiority have been responsible for an unfathomable degree of violence and destruction in the past, and they may well be careening toward a catastrophic future. Yet these logics are also undergoing processes of profound change as new movements for racial and environmental justice emerge to pose radical challenges to long-standing relations of domination within human society and between humans and the planet. The biggest question of our time may be: Which of these two forces will ultimately prevail?

My encounter with this question is sited along Colombia's Magdalena River, the primary waterway connecting the country's Andean interior and Caribbean coast.[10] These coordinates are significant to the conjoined careers of nature and race, which have circulated globally over centuries of imperial domination, capitalist expansion, and scientific exploration.[11] No single location can claim to be the sole birthplace of such ubiquitous formations, but their history is inconceivable without the European conquest of the Americas, especially the greater Caribbean, including the archipelago of islands and

7 Nishime and Williams, "Introduction"; Ranganathan, "The Racial Ecologies of Urban Wetlands"; Pulido and De Lara, "Reimagining 'Justice' in Environmental Justice."

8 Jobson, "Public Thinker: Yarimar Bonilla."

9 Woods, *Development Arrested*, 43; cited in Hosbey, Lloréns, and Roane, "Global Black Ecologies," 2.

10 Bocarejo Suescún, "Lo público de la Historia pública." Several social and historical studies of rivers have influenced my approach to the Magdalena. Key examples are Raffles, *In Amazonia*; White, *The Organic Machine*; Mukerji, *Impossible Engineering*; Pritchard, *Confluence*; Bear, *Navigating Austerity*; da Cunha, *The Invention of Rivers*; Rademacher, *Reigning the River*. For river studies that examine the racial orders of fluvial environments, see Ballantine, "The River Mouth Speaks"; Johnson, *River of Dark Dreams*; Woods, *Development Arrested*.

11 Stepan, *Picturing Tropical Nature*; Grove, *Green Imperialism*.

adjacent coastal lowlands.[12] Indeed, the Magdalena River itself was racial slavery's conduit into mainland South America; it was also along its banks that naturalists like Alexander von Humboldt began their groundbreaking expeditions.[13] The river and its peoples again featured prominently in the racial imagination of republican Colombia, where the democratizing potential of *mestizaje*, or hybridity, was hotly debated.[14] During the armed conflict, lighter-skinned paramilitaries displaced darker-skinned peasants from the river's adjacent swamps, and the environmental controversies now roiling its waters reflect the stark inequalities engendered by enduring structures of coloniality.[15]

Yet the relationship between past, present, and future along the Magdalena River is marked by persistence as well as change. Here I follow recent studies pointing to the shifting relationship between race and nature in the sciences, extending their insights to the dynamic processes through which social and environmental orders are entangled with big development projects.[16] My focus is a project at the heart of the government's plan for postconflict Colombia: reactivating commercial shipping along the Magdalena River. While the river was once the country's primary axis of travel and trade, a combination of economic, political, and environmental forces precipitated its decline in the second half of the twentieth century.[17] In 2014, the Colombian government initiated the process of returning the waterway to its former glory by establishing a permanently navigable shipping channel and resuscitating fluvial transport through channeling and dredging (figure I.4). In highly unequal societies like Colombia, megaprojects like this one, which seek to harness nature through technology in pursuit of economic progress, inevitably intersect with historically entrenched racial hierarchies.[18] Focusing on this project allows me to examine how social and environmental orders structured by the articulation of race and nature are both reproduced and reconfigured through large-scale infrastructural interventions.

---

12 Thomas, *Political Life*; Wynter, "Unsettling the Coloniality of Being/Power/Truth/Freedom." On the Colombian Caribbean as a historical region, see Vanegas Beltrán, "Elementos para identificar"; Bassi, *An Aqueous Territory*.

13 Múnera, *El Fracaso de la nación*; Cañizares-Esguerra, *Nature, Empire, and Nation*.

14 Appelbaum, *Mapping the Country of Regions*; Wade, *Blackness and Race Mixture*; Restrepo, "'Negros indolentes.'"

15 Taussig, *Palma Africana*; Gómez-Barris, *The Extractive Zone*.

16 Fullwiley, *The Encultured Gene*; Wade, *Degrees of Mixture*; Hartigan, *Care of the Species*; M'charek, "Curious about Race."

17 Márquez Calle, "Un río difícil."

18 Benjamin, *Captivating Technology*.

Current efforts to remake the river into a logistics corridor, in the terminology favored by the Colombian government and industry groups, draw on what Sheila Jasanoff calls "sociotechnical imaginaries." According to Jasanoff, sociotechnical imaginaries are "collectively held, institutionally stabilized, and publicly performed visions of desirable futures, animated by shared understandings of forms of social life and social order attainable through, and supportive of, advances in science and technology."[19] As evidenced by recent national development plans, the Colombian state now envisions fluvial transport and the logistics industry as keys to future prosperity. Echoing earlier moments in which imperial or national fortunes were tied to the river, the plan to improve navigation and increase trade along the waterway now promises to advance Colombia forward to a new stage of history. Yet racialized inequality, as Ruha Benjamin notes, ensures that "the hopes and capacities of some are routinely discredited in popular representations of progress or completely written out of futuristic visions, a kind of temporal penitentiary that locks the oppressed in a dystopic present."[20]

In the case of the Magdalena River, the sociotechnical imaginaries invoked by the project's investors, planners, and technicians reflect deeply rooted taxonomies and hierarchies. The project to promote commercial shipping by engineering the river is part of an extensive process of infrastructure building following the historic 2016 peace accord, which aims to capitalize on the promise of *el posconflicto* (the postconflict) to promote not only political stability and economic growth, but also social equity and ecological sustainability.[21] The economic and political imperatives of dredging and channeling are evident: these interventions clearly underpin the expansion of extractive infrastructures in resource-rich areas, the integration of supply chains managed by the global logistics industry, and the establishment of sovereignty in territories once marked by the absence of the state.[22] The potential for social and environmental reform is less tangible, however, as nearly all the products currently moving along the river are fossil fuels, and riverine communities—who have been consistently disadvantaged by Colombia's racial and geographical

<hr />

19 Jasanoff, "Future Imperfect," 19.
20 Benjamin, "Introduction," 16n20. See also Benjamin, "Catching Our Breath." For a discussion of the need for attention to race and racism in STS, see Mascarenhas, "White Space and Dark Matter."
21 Zeiderman, "Concrete Peace."
22 For the political ecology of channel deepening projects, see Carse and Lewis, "New Horizons for Dredging Research"; Carse and Lewis, "Toward a Political Ecology."

FIGURE I.4. Dredge rig consisting of a tracked excavator mounted on a pontoon barge. Source: photograph by author.

hierarchies—are unlikely to benefit.[23] The regime of accumulation and sovereignty predicated on resource extraction and racialized subjugation, which has been in force for centuries and has long depended upon the river, may be difficult to undo. Yet people living and laboring alongside megaprojects like this one maneuver within their interstices, often in ways that hover somewhere between acquiescence and opposition.

The civilizational hierarchies embedded in large-scale infrastructure projects often go hand in hand with notions of human superiority over nature. Indeed, the logic of master/slave and colonizer/colonized that defined the labor regimes underpinning capitalist modernity also informed the modern construction of nature as wild, unruly, and in need of domination.[24] According to the paradigms of knowledge that have enabled capital accumulation on a global scale, certain human and more-than-human natures belong to an inherently inferior world that could be domesticated by force and whose productive

---

23 For another example of how climate crisis and related social initiatives translate into dispossession in the Caribbean coast region of Colombia, see Camargo and Ojeda, "Ambivalent Desires."
24 Heynen, Kaika, and Swyngedouw, *In the Nature of Cities*; Gandy, *The Fabric of Space*.

potential could be harnessed.[25] These violent acts of appropriation and exploitation were mediated by infrastructure. From the technologies of finance and shipping that enabled the Middle Passage to the hydraulic systems that powered the processing of precious metals and minerals extracted by enslaved workers, and from the human bodies converted into machines to the marvels of modern industry and engineering they made possible, infrastructures undergird the transformation of certain people and things into the raw materials necessary for the production of the modern/colonial world.[26] The persistent relationship between notions of civilizational hierarchy and human superiority is reanimated by this contemporary megaproject and its futuristic visions of social and environmental transformation.

Yet the project to remake the Magdalena River will inevitably do more than simply reproduce histories of dispossession and dehumanization. After all, while infrastructures have been instrumental in the racialized control of nature and labor, they have also been sites of insurgency and insurrection, as well as more minor acts of autonomous creativity and clandestine subterfuge.[27] From the network of safe houses and passageways that expedited the abolition of slavery in the United States to "service delivery protests" around electricity meters in apartheid South Africa and demands for tribal sovereignty along the Dakota Access Pipeline, movements seeking to disrupt the dual appropriation of labor and nature have continuously coalesced around infrastructures.[28] Although the Magdalena River project is explicitly designed to minimize potential disruptions to the flow of goods along the waterway, it inevitably provides a stage on which social and environmental injustice can be debated and challenged. Moreover, those whose lives and livelihoods have long depended on the river, such as the riverboat workers I came to know on my journey, regularly enact forms of knowledge and practice that disrupt the logics and optics—the ways of thinking and seeing—on which the megaproject depends.

* * *

25 Moore, *Capitalism in the Web of Life*; Johnson, *River of Dark Dreams*.

26 Aimé Césaire's concept of "thingification" has been influential among scholars of race, but less so his emphasis on its infrastructural dimensions. See Césaire, *Discourse on Colonialism*, 42. See also Heynen, "Urban Political Ecology II"; Roediger and Esch, *The Production of Difference*; Harney and Moten, *The Undercommons*; Derickson, "Urban Geography II."

27 Simone, "Urbanity and Generic Blackness."

28 von Schnitzler, *Democracy's Infrastructure*; Cowen, "Infrastructures of Empire and Resistance"; Mitchell, *Carbon Democracy*; Chari, "State Racism and Biopolitical Struggle."

MY APPROACH TO thinking about the conjunction of race and nature is large scale and long term, since this is how today's most pressing social and environmental problems are often framed. The geographical locus of this study is Colombia's vast Magdalena River basin and its fluvial and maritime ports, while its historical reach stretches from the colonial period to the present. This analytical frame, though capacious, is still limited: the transformations underway relate to economic and ecological processes that are planetary, and the river's human and environmental history goes back long before the Spanish arrived in the early 1500s. To give focus to this potentially infinite expanse of space and time, my account selects certain aspects of the river's past, present, and future. But I also make a bolder claim about how to engage with large social and environmental transformations: paradoxically, through a fine-grained analysis of situated practices, specific actors, and ordinary events. Tacking back and forth between the micro and the macro provides insights that neither scale in isolation possibly could.

Grappling with racial ecologies along the Magdalena River requires pushing beyond the categorical divides that have long structured the humanities and social sciences. This book is as much about the social and cultural life of the river as it is about the river's political and economic significance, and these human dimensions of the river frequently appear alongside its physical properties.[29] These ostensibly separate dimensions of "riverhood" are often inextricably intertwined, so much so that it often makes little sense to differentiate between the river's social and natural histories, its imaginary and material manifestations, its cultural and economic values, its human and nonhuman constituents (figure I.5).[30] However, while I steer clear of binary frameworks that separate the world into neat and discrete categories, I also exercise caution toward hybrid analytics that collapse such bifurcations.

Across the humanities and social sciences, the imperative to recognize the entanglement of humans with countless other living and nonliving beings has become orthodoxy.[31] While I agree with the ethical and political importance of

---

29 Camargo and Cortesi, "Flooding Water and Society."

30 Boelens et al., "Riverhood."

31 A substantial body of work on posthumanism, new materialism, multispecies ethnography, and the Anthropocene posits the hybridity of material processes and social relations, the entanglement of humans and other beings, and nonanthropocentric forms of agency as the ontological foundations of a renewed approach to the humanities and social sciences. For problems involved in ignoring race and racialization in these conversations, see Zeiderman, "Low Tide." See also Rosa and Díaz, "Raciontologies." Rosa and

FIGURE I.5. Cattle ranch along eroded stretch of riverbank, Tenerife, Magdalena. Source: photograph by author.

unsettling anthropocentrism and coloniality, I chart a path between humanist and posthumanist paradigms, for neither alone can capture environmental politics in all their complexity or account for the practices and performances through which ontological divides (such as subject/object, human/nonhuman, person/thing, being/nonbeing) are created and sustained, navigated and mediated, destabilized and reconstructed.[32] Inspired by the tradition in Black

Díaz ask and answer a key question: "How might the 'ontological turn' be disrupted if we understood that modern ontologies are profoundly anchored in race?" For efforts to foreground justice within multispecies studies, see Chao, Bolender, and Kirksey, *The Promise of Multispecies Justice*. For a persuasive argument for "nondualist" ontological politics that engages with racism and anti-Blackness, see Escobar, *Pluriversal Politics*. I share these concerns but also see the need to treat ontological indeterminacy, multiplicity, and pluriversality as empirical questions and to carefully and cautiously consider their political implications.

32 My emphasis on the practices and performances of ontological fixing derives from Frantz Fanon's discussion of "Look! A Negro!," in which he "found that [he] was an object in the midst of other objects." In my reading of Fanon's account, the "epidermal racial schema" that rendered his ontological status as less-than-human, while rooted in colonization, was constituted in that momentary encounter: "the Other fixes me with his gaze, his

studies of interrogating the human as the arbiter of being and belonging, my goal is to understand how articulations of race and nature come to organize lifeworlds and the role they play in the creation of unequal, and often unlivable, social and environmental orders.[33]

These inequalities reflect the river's place within the formations of racial capitalism underpinning the project of colonial modernity in the Americas.[34] With its insatiable appetite for cheap inputs—racialized labor, appropriated nature—fluvial transport and trade along the Magdalena River has been integral to Colombia's long, bloody history of resource extraction, human subjugation, and wealth accumulation. No doubt some things have changed over the years: Indigenous groups no longer predominate along the river; the abolition of slavery occurred over 150 years ago; alluvial forests are mostly gone; gold and silver are less plentiful; and the Spanish colonizers and white criollo elite are no longer the primary beneficiaries. However, accumulation still depends on the Lower Magdalena's racialized workforce; the carbon-based energy powering the riverboats is fuel oil rather than wood; the lucrative resources being extracted are now petroleum, gas, and other minerals and metals; and it is mainly multinational logistics, commodity trading, and infrastructure firms that stand to benefit. And the colonial and postcolonial geographical imaginary—in which the river was a racialized measure of civilization and a means by which to enrich predominantly white elites—continues to orient the models of development that attempt to restore the waterway's historical importance. Yet some visionaries foresee an alternative future for Colombia reflected in the river's surface. How, then, might histories of human exploitation and environmental degradation be redressed and overcome?

Focusing on this megaproject and its stated objective of making the Magdalena River into a "logistics corridor" puts me into contact with three key dimensions of the global economy: the logistics industry; the paradigmatic space of that industry, the supply chain; and the governing rationality of

---

gestures and attitude, the same way you fix a preparation with a dye." Fanon, *Black Skin, White Masks*, 89.

33 Weheliye, *Habeas Viscus*; Jackson, *Becoming Human*; Walcott, "Genres of Human"; Wynter, "Unsettling the Coloniality of Being/Power/Truth/Freedom"; Fanon, *Black Skin, White Masks*; Césaire, *Discourse on Colonialism*.

34 See Robinson, *Black Marxism*. I am also inspired by Latin American thought on coloniality, mostly notably Quijano, "Coloniality of Power"; Quijano, "Questioning 'Race'"; Zapata Olivella, *Por los senderos de sus ancestros*.

logistics, supply chain security (figure I.6).[35] Building on the work of scholars who highlight the centrality of logistics to capitalism, I approach logistics as a world-making project with profound social, political, and ecological implications—in other words, I attend to processes of "logistification" and their effects.[36] Among these processes, I focus specifically on the securitization of the Magdalena River and on the rationalities and technologies through which circulation along the waterway is enabled and sustained.[37] Based on ethnographic fieldwork in port terminals, on commercial vessels, and in riverside towns, I examine the logics and optics that underpin the work of securing the logistics corridor against disruption. However, the smooth operation of logistics is not always opposed to the resistant sociality and unruly materiality of the world it seeks to remake. Instead, logistics is a contingent and contested field in which a range of actors work to protect continuous circulation, but not always in the most predictable or compatible ways.[38] Yet despite these inconsistencies and incongruities, the logistics industry still manages to reap rewards from racialized inequality and resource extraction.[39]

While there are good reasons to distrust the project to remake the Magdalena River, I engage in a mode of analysis that is critical but not denunciatory. Many studies conflate these two, so that a critique of something becomes tantamount to its repudiation. Inspired by Stuart Hall, the distinction this book makes between these modes of analysis is at the level of contingency; that is, the possibility that history may not play out exactly as our analytical and political commitments would predict.[40] This does not mean ignoring per-

35 Cowen, *The Deadly Life of Logistics*, 8.
36 Cowen, "A Geography of Logistics"; Tsing, *The Mushroom at the End of the World*; Easterling, *Extrastatecraft*; Guyer, *Legacies, Logics, Logistics*; Cross, "Detachment as a Corporate Ethic"; Hepworth, "Enacting Logistical Geographies"; Easterling, "The New Orgman"; Graham, "FlowCity"; Rothenberg, "Ports Matter"; Khalili, *Sinews of War and Trade*. For the concept of "logistification," see LeCavalier, *The Rule of Logistics*, 6.
37 Lobo-Guerrero, "Los seguros marítimos."
38 An inspiration here is Kiran Asher's work on the politics of development in the Colombian Pacific. See Asher, *Black and Green*; Asher, "Fragmented Forests, Fractured Lives."
39 Appel, *The Licit Life of Capitalism.*
40 Hall's concept of "articulation" and his emphasis on the conjunctural method both inspire my interest in the limits of economic determinism and the possibilities of historical rupture. Hall does not, however, claim that everything is contingent: "Contingency . . . does play a role in the unfolding of history, and we must allow for it." See Hall et al., *Policing the Crisis*, 6. Yet in that same study, Hall and his collaborators emphasize that the "moral panic" of 1970s Britain, like earlier paranoias about crime, was "both less contingent and more significant" than was commonly assumed at the time.

FIGURE I.6. Port terminal and logistics hub, Barrancabermeja, Santander.
Source: photograph by author.

nicious, persistent forms of injustice and oppression, but that their relentless exposure and excoriation, as Katherine McKittrick cautions, reifies abjection and inhibits curiosity.[41] The denunciatory mode also has the unfortunate effect of obscuring unexpected positions, unconventional alliances, unpredictable events, and uncommon projects, as well as the unintended complicity of the analyst in what is being denounced.[42] While this book embraces the ethical horizons of antiracism and environmental justice, and aspires to push, however incrementally, in the direction of both, it also checks, indeed relinquishes, any pretense of certainty. If the coordinates of race, nature, and capital are shifting alongside transformations of planetary proportions, our critical standpoints must adjust to the radical uncertainty the world is facing.

This imperative is as much analytical as personal, which means that attention to positionality and self-reflexivity is essential. Alongside efforts to grapple with the social and environmental orders of the Magdalena basin, then,

41 McKittrick, *Dear Science and Other Stories*, 46.
42 I'm thinking here of the kinds of encounters and connections that have been at the heart of Anna Lowenhaupt Tsing's work. See Tsing, *Friction*; Tsing, *The Mushroom at the End of the World*.

are attempts to account for my own racial and epistemological formations and their implications for what it is possible to think, know, say, do, and be. Following W. E. B. Du Bois's proposition that the "race problem" in his native United States might be understood better in relation to the Warsaw ghetto—an idea that resonates with me for biographical reasons—I scrutinize my formation as a racial subject as necessary for coming to terms with racialized hierarchies in a social world other than my own.[43] If knowledge systems always bear traces of the embodied emplacement of the knower, as feminist science studies has shown, then the intellectual traditions and academic disciplines to which I belong deserve similar scrutiny.[44] Anthropology, geography, perhaps the social and human sciences in toto, have enduring alliances with colonial and neocolonial relations of power and knowledge and their constitutive logics of patriarchy and white supremacy—this much we know.[45] But even as decolonizing initiatives become more prevalent, the dominant gesture remains one of undoing, of deconstruction.[46] How to respond to this predicament from a reconstructionist standpoint—that is, to ask what can be done in addition to what must be undone?[47]

My critical and analytical engagement with racial and environmental orders, in the past and the present, also has a stylistic correlate. Many scholarly communities are presently reckoning with the question of how to write about the worlds we now inhabit, and various proposals have been put forth. Here I seek a prose whose theoretical baggage is light, empirical details are privileged, disciplinary jargon is minimal, and contextual specificity is paramount.

---

43 Du Bois, "The Negro and the Warsaw Ghetto." There is a long tradition of antiracist and anticolonial thought and practice that finds common ground and forges alliances across different experiences of racism. For example, see West, *Race Matters*. See also discussions of Nazi anti-Semitism and European imperialism in Césaire, *Discourse on Colonialism*; Arendt, *The Origins of Totalitarianism*.

44 Haraway, "Situated Knowledges"; Harding, *Whose Science? Whose Knowledge?*

45 Mignolo and Walsh, *On Decoloniality*.

46 See Bonilla, "Unsettling Sovereignty." Bonilla prefers "the term *unsettling* to *decolonizing* not only because it privileges the perspective of settler colonialism (which has often held a backseat within postcolonial studies) but also because I remain skeptical as to whether one could truly decolonize either sovereignty or anthropology, given that there is no precolonial status to which either could return. *Unsettling* avoids the telos of decolonization. What is unsettled is not necessarily removed, toppled, or returned to a previous order but is fundamentally brought into question" (335).

47 See Jesse McCarthy's comments on "reconstruction" in McCarthy and Shatz, "Blind Spots."

This does not mean that conceptual concerns are elided, disciplinary debates ignored, or intellectual debts forgotten. Rather these are presented in clear language, limited to brief discussions, and placed in footnotes when further exposition is warranted. Moreover, in an attempt to minimize the divide between theory and data, the book's theoretical commitments are implicit in the description and analysis. Ethnographic and historical details are foregrounded and presented in the form of stories that convey both their particularity and their wider relevance.[48] These stories are meant to be immersive and evocative and ultimately to provoke thought rather than provide closure: as McKittrick puts it, the "story opens the door to curiosity."[49]

* * *

THE RIVERBOAT JOURNEY with which I began came to an end when, after seven days on the water, we arrived at our destination—the river port of Barrancabermeja, approximately 630 kilometers inland from our point of embarkation. Still weak and weary, I decided to seek medical attention at a local clinic. Not surprisingly, tests revealed the presence of waterborne parasites, and the doctor on call prescribed a potent antibiotic cocktail. Physical recovery was nearly instantaneous, but cognitive unease lingered. Although my illness had been given an identifiable cause, I was left wondering about the racial schema used onboard to explain it, especially given the organism—a parasite—found responsible. After all, parasites were not only integral to the scientific racism underpinning Nazi anti-Semitism and the Holocaust; their place in the history of raciological knowledge stretches back to Charles Darwin's legendary 1871 treatise *The Descent of Man*, in which he extended to humans his earlier arguments about evolution and natural selection from *On the Origin of Species*.[50] In the later book, the puzzle of whether "the races themselves ought to be classed as distinct species" hinged on reports of parasites reacting differently to differently racialized bodies.[51] Darwin's case against polygenesis, or the theory that different races descended from different ancestors, grappled with many such reports: "The surgeon of a whaling ship in the Pacific assured me that when the Pediculi [lice], with which some Sandwich Islanders on board swarmed, strayed on to the bodies of the English sailors, they died

---

48 In *Dear Science and Other Stories*, McKittrick "understands theory as a form of storytelling," which could also include storytelling as a form of theorizing (7).

49 McKittrick, *Dear Science and Other Stories*, 7.

50 Raffles, *Insectopedia*; Darwin, *The Descent of Man*.

51 Darwin, *The Descent of Man*, 220.

in the course of three or four days."[52] This inaugural instance of what Sylvia Wynter calls the "biocentric version of humanness" is also staged over water, and with reference to the bodies of crew members laboring on a cargo vessel.[53] It is the still unfolding and unfinished history of such entanglements of race and nature that this book aims to examine and, if not undo, at least unsettle.[54]

* * *

CHAPTER 1, "ARTERIAL CURRENTS," introduces the concept of *geo-racial regimes*: hierarchical orderings of society and space organized primarily along racial lines. The chapter highlights the importance of infrastructural environments, like the Magdalena River, to the historical emergence of the modern/colonial world. The regimes of racial and spatial difference structuring social and environmental orders in Colombia have had a constitutive relationship with the Magdalena River. During the periods of Spanish colonial rule and postcolonial nation building, the river has been central to these regimes. And it continues to be in the ongoing project to create a logistics corridor along the artery.

The most recent scheme to boost commercial shipping on the river is the subject of chapter 2, "Dredging Up the Future." It focuses on the sociotechnical imaginaries and interventions attending this megaproject, and in particular their relationship to entrenched racial taxonomies and regional hierarchies. This chapter examines the practices and performances of both fixing and destabilizing ontological divides (land/water, being/nonbeing, subject/object, human/nonhuman, person/thing) and considers their consequences for who and what either flourishes or perishes. How do racial formations work with and through infrastructural environments? Which entities, living and nonliving, are relegated to the past, and which are afforded a future?

Chapter 3, "Securing Flow," takes on the fluvial transport and logistics industry and its governing rationality: supply chain security. It examines the forms of expertise deployed to secure the smooth and uninterrupted flow of cargo, paying close attention to the categories, calculations, and probabilities used to manage the multiple factors threatening to disrupt circulation: from droughts and pandemics to strikes and accidents. Underpinning the logics and optics of supply chain security are hierarchical orders of value. Attending

52 Darwin, *The Descent of Man*, 219.
53 Wynter and McKittrick, "Unparalleled Catastrophe," 16.
54 Meehan et al., "Unsettling Race."

to both the value gradations specific to Colombia and those endemic to the logistics industry worldwide, this chapter demonstrates how logistics renders some people and things security threats, while caring for and protecting others.

Chapter 4, "In the Wake of Logistics," foregrounds the workforces powering the movement of goods along the waterway from the colonial period to the present. It argues that the labor power required by the fluvial transport and logistics industry depends on regimes of difference-making whose racial underpinnings have both persisted and changed over time. Alert to continuities and divergences, this chapter engages with the afterlives of colonization and enslavement as well as with their geographically situated manifestations and historically specific transformations. The focus on articulations of race and labor in the domain of logistics reveals the persistence of racial hierarchies and their perpetual instability, which in turn enables the links between past, present, and future to be analyzed without teleological assumptions.

Gendered idioms and practices circulating along the river are the subject of chapter 5, "Madre Magdalena." This chapter considers the relationship between masculinity and bestiality presumed endemic to the region in the national imaginary as well as the attribution of femininity to the water body itself. It then considers the gendering of human-environment relations, which traditionally associate women with care work and men with productive labor. Although stereotypical gender roles are reflected in the fluvial transport and logistics industry, an intersectional analysis attuned to interlocking hierarchies of gender, sexuality, race, class, and region reveals heterogenous forms of gendered personhood that defy binary, essentialized logics of logistical capitalism.

Chapter 6, "Navigating Racial Ecologies," foregrounds the navigation techniques of river captains and pilots, and their entanglement with the pervasive inequalities of Colombian society and the logistics industry. As in other vocations, intuitive knowledge and embodied skill are relied upon to maneuver ships and boats in challenging and changeable environments. However, in a world structured by interlocking hierarchies, and along a waterway central to formations of colonial and racial capitalism, these techniques are more than just practical solutions for getting from port to port. How do those occupying an indispensable yet disregarded vocation use navigational expertise to ensure their survival, defend their autonomy, and assert their humanity?

Two parallel movements toward social and environmental futures are considered in the afterword: confronting racial injustice and redressing environmental injury. In Colombia, both movements are taking shape in the cultural sphere as well as in legal and institutional reforms, and efforts are being made to link them together in pursuit of a wider progressive agenda. While these initiatives are timely and significant, the analysis put forth in *Artery* suggests that more work is needed to overcome stubborn hierarchies and to disentangle race and nature.

Arterial Currents

In 1923, the *Journal of Geography* published an article by a promising young faculty member at the University of Michigan titled "The Transportation Problem of Highland Colombia."[1] Its author, Preston Everett James, would go on to enjoy a distinguished academic career, publishing influential texts, supervising countless students, chairing a major department, serving as president of the American Association of Geographers, and receiving prestigious awards. Like those of other geographers of his generation, James's scholarly triumphs were paralleled by four decades of decorated military service.[2] He initially volunteered during World War I and would later serve as chief of the Latin American Division of the Office of Strategic Services (the predecessor to the Central Intelligence Agency), where he eventually expanded his remit to Europe and

---

1 James, "The Transportation Problem."
2 For a wider examination of the role of US geographers in Latin America, with emphasis on Isaiah Bowman, see Salvatore, *Disciplinary Conquest*; Smith, *American Empire*.

Africa and ascended to the rank of colonel.[3] In his 1923 article, the first of many publications on Latin American geography, James sought to answer the question of how Colombia might overcome its status as an "undeveloped country."[4]

The crux of the problem, James reasoned, was a stubborn misalignment of race, geography, and infrastructure: "The white people in Colombia have always sought the elevated plateaus where there are cooler temperatures. . . . These elevated plateaus of the interior are . . . the regions best suited to white habitation, and are the seats of Colombia's largest groups of white population. Bogotá, the capital, is located on one of the largest of these, at an elevation of 8659 feet (2640 meters). Consequently, one of the most important of Colombia's transportation problems is the connection of Bogotá with tide water."[5] Following this matter-of-fact statement of the problem, James's article evaluated two possible infrastructural solutions: one route following the Magdalena River to the Caribbean Sea, another traversing overland to the Pacific Ocean. While James saw promise in the latter, he concluded by endorsing the former: "Those who believe in the intensive development of tropical lands in the future will regard construction on the Magdalena route as the only course leading to the development of Colombia's potentially richest territory."[6]

Published a century ago, James's article contains elements likely to rankle contemporary sensibilities. Although he eventually came to question strict environmental determinism, adopting a more moderate understanding of geography's effects on human development, James's early work was steeped in the racialism endemic to the German tradition of biogeography, which was propagated in the United States by figures like Ellen Churchill Semple.[7] Semple, who served on James's doctoral committee, was herself a student of Friedrich Ratzel, whose notorious concept of Lebensraum provided a "legitimizing spatial logic to the Third Reich."[8] While biogeographical thought was more complex than its blending with Nazi ideology would suggest, James's analysis of the impediments to development in Colombia rested on racial logics that were axiomatic within the discipline of geography at the time. A telling example is the passage quoted above, for it suggests James's reasoning was a matter of common sense: if white people are inherently suited to the temperate zone, and

3 Jensen, "Memorial."
4 "Preston E. James Receives."
5 James, "The Transportation Problem," 347.
6 James, "The Transportation Problem," 354.
7 Peet, "The Social Origins."
8 Ratzel, "Lebensraum"; Keighren, "History and Philosophy of Geography III."

this area is disconnected from overseas trade routes, Colombia's hopes of progress naturally hinged on forging links between the highlands and the coast. The burning question was not why or how this correlation between whiteness, geography, and development came to be, but rather which infrastructural intervention was most likely to correct its unfortunate asymmetry in this case.

This was not the first time the Magdalena River appeared to provide the answer to Colombia's conundrums, nor would it be the last. James's article joined a long line of arguments for harnessing the waterway's potential to contribute to the national good, which stretched as far back as the nation itself. His intervention also adhered to the established tradition of mapping racial hierarchies onto geographical space that flourished in Colombia during the century after independence. These two lines of thinking often converged, as they did for James, on the river's ability to connect people and places positioned at different civilizational or developmental stages; they also united in heralding the Magdalena as the remedy for a modernization process impeded by the supposed incongruity between geography, infrastructure, and race. A study like this is noteworthy not for its novelty but rather for affirming the Magdalena's centrality to the interlocking hierarchies structuring Colombian society and space. Since its early role as a conduit for colonization, the artery has been constitutive of these hierarchies, which in turn have shaped how the waterway would be understood and managed.

When I first came across James's article, its unambiguous racialism felt dated, but many of its presuppositions and propositions struck me as familiar. Its assessment of impediments to progress in Colombia, for example, is echoed by contemporary demands for investment in transport infrastructure between the cities of the interior and port terminals and logistics hubs on the coasts. Moreover, James's optimism for the Magdalena route as the solution to underdevelopment is mirrored by recent boosterism surrounding the waterway's vital importance for the future of Colombia. While explicitly racial logics are mostly taboo in public and political forums, they nevertheless continue to impact matters of development, environment, and infrastructure through related idioms of difference (like region), which are no less hierarchical in structure or unequal in effect. The problematic James described in the 1920s—organized around the correlation between whiteness, geography, and development—is discernable a century later in laments over the infrastructural disconnect between implicitly racialized spaces: the Andean interior and the Caribbean and Pacific coasts. James did not inaugurate this way of thinking about social and geographical hierarchy, nor was he solely responsible for its propagation, but he did present it in especially clear terms. In meetings with government officials and business leaders, I often found myself thinking back to James's article as we discussed interventions along the waterway that my interlocutors said were a century overdue.

The interdependence of racial and spatial orders, far from unique to Colombia, has also been a recurrent feature of modern geographical thought.[9] Inspired by Enlightenment philosophers, Immanuel Kant foremost among them, early geographers in Europe and the Americas focused on the relationship between environment and race as their central problematic.[10] Establishing a science of geography, according to Audrey Kobayashi's appraisal of the discipline, involved "both mapping the world according to race and developing an understanding of the factors, climate in particular, that determined racial characteristics."[11] Heterodox understandings of human-environment relations notwithstanding, the race-based doctrine of "environmentalism," which prevailed until the postwar period, reached its apex in the figure of Yale University professor Ellsworth Huntington, who served as president of the American Association of Geographers and later of the American Eugenics Society.[12] Huntington first published the influential *Civilization and Climate* in 1915, followed by his infamous eugenicist tract, *The Character of Races*, in 1924.[13] Such was the intellectual milieu from which Preston James set out to assess trade routes along the Magdalena River, and the resulting study represents one of many points of convergence between geo-racial regimes in Colombia and geographical thought at large.

Geo-racial regimes are symbolic and material systems of hierarchically valued difference (and difference-making, to state things more processually) that organize society and space primarily, though not exclusively, along racial lines.[14] This concept is germane not only to the Magdalena, but to river systems

---

9 Livingstone, "Race, Space and Moral Climatology."

10 Kobayashi, "The Dialectic of Race," 1103.

11 David Livingstone, cited in Kobayashi, "The Dialectic of Race," 1104.

12 In his 1924 presidential address to the American Association of Geographers, Huntington declared, "The pinnacle of geography is reached when we are able to explain why certain types of human character, certain manifestations of genius, and hence certain lines of progress and stages of civilization are localized in various parts of the world." Huntington, "Geography and Natural Selection," 1. Cited in Kobayashi, "The Dialectic of Race," 1104.

13 Huntington, *Civilization and Climate*; Huntington, *The Character of Races*.

14 I use the term *geo-racial* as shorthand to refer to the coproduction of racial and geographical difference-making in Colombia and the enduring yet unstable articulation of racial and regional hierarchies. Many scholars have documented this phenomenon in both his-

throughout the Atlantic world. Rivers as far-flung as the Mississippi, the Thames, the Orinoco, and the Congo have all been integral to the coemergence of modernity and coloniality and to the racial taxonomies and geographical disparities underpinning this world-historical phenomenon. The remainder of this chapter advances the analytic of geo-racial regimes by examining the hierarchical systems of racial and spatial difference structuring social and environmental orders in Colombia and their constitutive relationship with the Magdalena River. The following account is divided into three sections, each highlighting how the river has been not simply subjected to geo-racial regimes but essential to their formation: (1) the centrality of the artery to Spanish colonial rule; (2) the importance of fluvial transport to postcolonial nation-building; and (3) recent efforts to revive commercial shipping along the waterway. This account focuses both on the endurance of race and nature as articulating principles and on their shifting manifestations at different points in time. The central question is: When, why, and how does a river become a racial formation?[15]

* * *

THE ARTICULATION OF race and nature, such as that found along the Magdalena River, has been fundamental to the emergence of the modern/colonial world.[16] Beginning in the Caribbean archipelago and spreading throughout

---

torical and contemporary contexts. For an overview, see Leal, "Usos del concepto 'raza' en Colombia." For the historical process through which regional typologies began supplanting racial taxonomies after Independence, see Appelbaum, *Mapping the Country*; Arias Vanegas, *Nación y diferencia*. For contemporary iterations of this dynamic, see Wade, "Espacio, región y racialización"; Koopman, "Mona, Mona, Mona!" By referring to geo-racial regimes, I am also drawing loosely on Cedric Robinson's notion of "racial regimes," which he defines as "constructed social systems in which race is proposed as a justification for the relations of power." Robinson, *Forgeries of Memory*, xii. I reference class, gender, sexuality, region, and other categories to account for the articulation of race with intersecting regimes of difference-making, which in Colombia often substitute for explicitly racial idioms of justification. Stuart Hall is another inspiration for analyzing race as an articulating principle of social (and spatial) formations that rarely, if ever, act alone. See Hall, "Race, Articulation and Societies."

15 Inspiration for thinking about the river as a racial formation comes from an anonymous reviewer of the manuscript. Another inspiration is Hardy, Milligan, and Heynen, "Racial Coastal Formation."

16 In referring to the modern/colonial world, I am building on one of the key insights of the modernity/coloniality/decoloniality (M/C/D) research program, which is that coloniality and modernity are mutually constitutive. See Escobar, "Worlds and Knowledges Otherwise."

the mainland Americas, what Aníbal Quijano calls the "coloniality of power" has been organized around civilizational hierarchies among different categories of humans as well as the superiority of humans over all other living and nonliving beings.[17] These are two sides of the same coin. On one side, swaths of humanity initially deemed less than human on cultural grounds became classified as "naturally dysselected," which is Sylvia Wynter's term for how racialization has operated through an evolutionary schema defining certain people (non-European) as intrinsically (or by nature) inferior.[18] On the other side of the coin, the idea of nature as an extractable resource legitimated the exploitation of lands, waters, plants, animals, and minerals located in places designated by racialized cartographies as different from (and subordinate to) the West.[19] The naturalization of race and the racialization of nature have been entwined processes essential to the coemergence of coloniality and modernity.

The social and environmental orders of the modern/colonial world have been governed by the logic of mastery. These are orders in which certain people and things, categorized as inherently lesser, could be subjugated for the purpose of harnessing their accumulative potential. But as Wynter points out, mastery has involved a dialectical struggle as much material as philosophical, whereby one "conception of human freedom," based on the "natural-scientifically enabled *technological* mastery over nature, as well as other peoples," would be countered by another that would eventually provide "a new answer to the question of who we are as *humans*."[20] This latter conception of freedom,

---

17 Quijano, "Coloniality and Modernity/Rationality." See also Wynter, "Unsettling the Coloniality of Being/Power/Truth/Freedom"; Escobar, *Pluriversal Politics*.

18 This schema is what Wynter calls the "biocentric perspective of the human as a natural organism." Wynter and McKittrick, "Unparalleled Catastrophe," 63. Historians translate the early modern category of *naturaleza* in Spain and Spanish America as "nativeness" and position it in opposition to "race." See Herzog, "Beyond Race." My interest is in how to account for the intertwined relationship between these categories—race and nature—without analytically collapsing them.

19 Arnold, *The Problem of Nature*; Escobar, *Pluriversal Politics*; Alimonda, "La colonialidad de la naturaleza."

20 Wynter here uses the example of the slave ship to reflect on the constitutive relationship between "mastery over nature, and correlated conception of human freedom, as actualized in the increasing size and power of the Negro/Negra slave-trading ships." Wynter and McKittrick, "Unparalleled Catastrophe," 62. In conversation with Katherine McKittrick, Wynter is responding to McKittrick's writing on transportation technologies, such as the slave ship, as key sites for what she calls the "meaningful struggle for freedom *in place*." See McKittrick, *Demonic Grounds*, x–xi.

linked to a radical reconfiguration of the exclusionary order of liberal human-ism, remains as yet unrealized.[21] Nevertheless, the logic of mastery has proven neither fixed nor unidirectional: the social and environmental orders governed by it have been dynamic and mutable, and the subjects-cum-objects of domina-tion have played a major role in defining and creating their own place in the world.[22]

Like other water bodies, such as the Atlantic Ocean and the Caribbean Sea, the Magdalena River was more than a mere backdrop for these world-historical developments: indeed, the artery has been constitutive of them.[23] When Rodrigo de Bastidas and the first wave of Spanish colonizers arrived at the mouth of the estuary in 1501, the basin had been home for over two thousand years to Indigenous societies who depended on the river for rit-ual, transport, trade, irrigation, and food.[24] The waterway already had many names (Yuma, Guacahayo, Arlí), but the Spaniards' first deed was to baptize it with a Christian one—Río Grande de la Magdalena in honor of Mary Magda-lene.[25] This symbolic act of domination was followed by another in the form of a *cédula real* (royal decree) asserting control over the river and authorizing further exploration.[26] Despite initial setbacks, the Magdalena would soon be-come the primary medium of transport for the movement of people, goods, and information between Spain's mainland possessions and maritime routes throughout the Caribbean and across the Atlantic.[27] Early maps highlight the artery's outsize importance, even relative to terrestrial settlements (figures 1.1

21 Wynter indicates that this conception of human freedom was "only potentially realizable over many centuries." Wynter and McKittrick, "Unparalleled Catastrophe," 62.
22 The work of artist Kerry James Marshall has been an inspiration for thinking about the complex contours of "mastery," which he subversively recasts as "mastry" to invoke the dualistic (or dialectical) relationship between histories of anti-Blackness and the struggle for freedom expressed through control over one's own aesthetic and embodied practice. See Molesworth, *Kerry James Marshall*. Marshall's painting titled *Gulf Stream* is an example of this dualism that, not incidentally, invokes the history of water (and navigation) as a medium of oppression and liberation, trauma and pleasure, terror and joy; see Kerry James Marshall, *Gulf Stream*, 2003, acrylic and glitter on canvas, 108 × 156 in, Walker Art Center. https://walkerart.org/collections/artworks/gulf-stream. See also Frantz Fanon's discussion of mastery, language, and the racial ontology of being in *Black Skin, White Masks*, 17–18.
23 The same could be said about the Mississippi River. See Johnson, *River of Dark Dreams*.
24 Ferro Medina, "El río Magdalena," 34.
25 Ferro Medina, "El río Magdalena," 34; Alvear Sanín, *Manual del Río Magdalena*, 14.
26 Silva Fajardo, *Champanes, vapores y remolcadores*, 20.
27 Serrano López and Hernández Chitiva, *Del Río Grande de la Magdalena*, 15.

and 1.2). During the colonial period, the power to govern territory, appropriate land, exploit labor, and extract riches depended heavily on the artery's circulatory capacity.

Making the Magdalena into a conduit for colonization required the mastery of nature, and doing so depended on mastering supposedly inferior categories of humans. However, the estuary's swift currents and strong winds initially thwarted navigation, and irregular rainfall and heavy sedimentation made upstream travel treacherous for Spanish vessels.[28] The introduction of watercraft better suited to local conditions was followed by efforts to transform the hydrological system itself, which began in the 1580s with the opening of the Canal del Dique, a canal connecting the river to the seaport of Cartagena.[29] This was the first of many attempts to tame the Magdalena's unruly course in order to facilitate navigation—a major preoccupation for colonial authorities who recognized their dependence on the waterway—but the river would remain, in the words of historian Gustavo Bell Lemus, "capricious and indomitable."[30] These efforts would require vast amounts of labor, as would the operation of vessels and the transport of goods—objectives that depended on the indenture and enslavement of Indigenous and African workers deemed by Europeans to be intrinsically suited to grueling physical tasks. Yet like the river's hydrogeomorphic dynamics (rainfall patterns, sediment loads, channel depths), the people pressed into service (canal diggers, dock workers, riverboat crews) were active in the dialectical struggle between mastery and freedom. As a result, the domination of the artery and its human and nonhuman constituents, while integral to the creation of the modern/colonial world, never fully succeeded or went unchallenged.

The Magdalena's role as a strategic corridor for colonial expansion involved not only the domination of nature, but also, following Ashley Carse, "the notion that nature is—or might become—infrastructure."[31] The infrastructural mediation of coloniality, in turn, depended on a related process by which the colonized subject was made into "an instrument of production," or what Aimé Césaire called "thingification."[32] In *Discourse on Colonialism*, Césaire introduces this concept by way of a staged debate with a generic group of col-

28 Arango Echeverri, "Los conocimientos de embarque," 74.
29 Bell Lemus, "El Canal del Dique."
30 Bell Lemus, "El Canal del Dique," 15.
31 Carse, "Nature as Infrastructure," 540.
32 Césaire, *Discourse on Colonialism*, 42. For more recent discussions of the coloniality of infrastructure, see Davies, "The Coloniality of Infrastructure."

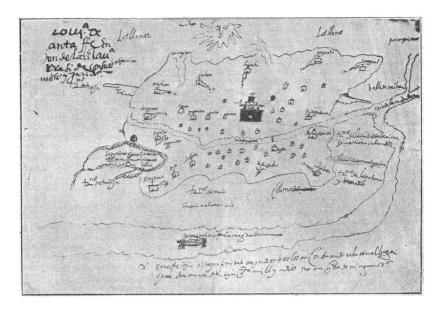

FIGURE 1.1. Anonymous, map of the province of Santafé, its towns and districts, 1584. A note at the bottom reports, "In this river there were infinity of rivers, all of them have been consumed by the cruel *boga*, and of more than fifty thousand Indians not one has remained." Source: Banco de la República, Biblioteca Virtual.

onizers: "They talk to me about progress, about 'achievements,' diseases cured, improved standards of living. . . . They throw facts at my head, statistics, mileages of roads, canals, and railroad tracks."[33] To this barrage of justifications, Césaire replies, "I am talking about societies drained of their essence, cultures trampled underfoot, institutions undermined, lands confiscated, religions smashed, magnificent artistic creations destroyed, extraordinary possibilities wiped out. . . . I am talking about thousands of men sacrificed to the Congo-Océan [railway line]. I am talking about those who, as I write this, are digging the harbor of Abidjan by hand."[34] Césaire's emphasis on infrastructure, although somewhat fleeting, seems neither incidental nor inconsequential. After all, the word *infrastructure* itself was a French colonial invention.[35] For its role in mediating

33 Césaire, *Discourse on Colonialism*, 43.
34 Césaire, *Discourse on Colonialism*, 43. See also Rodney, *A History of the Guyanese Working People*.
35 Carse, "Keyword."

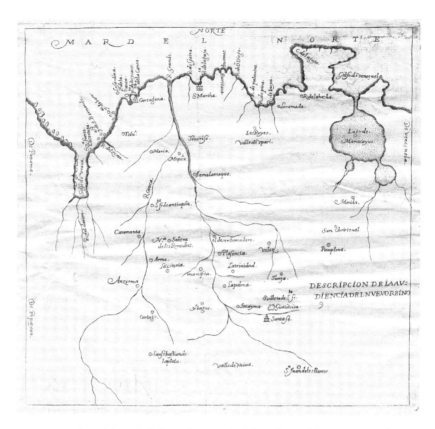

FIGURE 1.2. Juan López de Velasco, *Descripción de la Audiencia del Nuevo Reino*, 1601. Source: Banco de la República, Biblioteca Virtual.

the mastery of colonized peoples and places, the Magdalena was nature-as-infrastructure avant la lettre.

Like other Black radical intellectuals, Césaire sought to revise historical materialism to foreground the anticolonial struggle and to center race within the dialectical antagonisms animating history. Robin Kelley notes that, for Césaire, "the coming revolution was not posed in terms of capitalism versus socialism . . . but in terms of the complete and total overthrow of a racist, colonialist system that would open the way to imagine a whole new world."[36] The process of thingification, which Césaire introduced with infrastructural allusions, was endemic to that "racist, colonialist system," which was simultaneously an economic system (of accumulation), a political system (of domina-

36 Kelley, "A Poetics of Anticolonialism," 10.

tion), and an ontological system (of subjectification/objectification). Césaire's mention of roads, canals, ports, and railways speaks to infrastructure's material and ideological role in upholding that system. Meanwhile, his references to the bodies sacrificed to build its infrastructural foundations point to what we might call, following Jonathan Rosa and Vanessa Díaz, the "raciontological" violence of blurring the boundaries between people and things, subjects and objects, humans and nonhumans, and to the centrality of that violence to the creation of the modern/colonial world.[37] Forcing unfree labor to perform infrastructural work on the Magdalena while transforming the river itself into an infrastructural system were both constitutive of the racialized domination of human and more-than-human nature.

The mediation of coloniality through the Magdalena River lives on in the geo-racial regimes structuring social and environmental orders in Colombia. The artery has been central to the hierarchical systems of difference that organize society and space along racial lines, and these regimes continue to influence how the waterway is imagined and governed. However, the logics of civilizational hierarchy and human superiority dominant in the colonial period have neither been static nor exclusively defined by race. In her historical

---

37 Rosa and Díaz, "Raciontologies." Rosa and Díaz draw inspiration from Frantz Fanon, whose work also sheds light on the infrastructural dimensions of colonial modernity and, conversely, the raciontological makings and workings of infrastructure. For example, the famous opening from "On Violence" in *The Wretched of the Earth*, in which Fanon juxtaposes the spatial and material conditions of the "compartmentalized world" of colonial society, makes explicit and recurring references to buildings and building materials (stone and steel), to electricity, transport, and sanitation systems (paving, lighting, garbage), to the planned divisions in education and health care, and to the spatial technologies of military occupation and policing (borders and barracks). Fanon, *The Wretched of the Earth*, 4–5. This reference point has occasionally been invoked in infrastructure studies. The introduction to an oft-cited volume opens with an epigraph from that same section of "On Violence" (though ellipses remove the racist invectives in the original) and then moves on to consider what the editors call the "black cities" of Detroit and Flint, Michigan, in order to argue that here we see how "water infrastructure is a sociomaterial terrain for the reproduction of racism" and that "infrastructures have been technologies that modern states use not only to demonstrate development, progress, and modernity . . . but also to differentiate populations and subject some to premature death." Appel, Anand, and Gupta, "Introduction," 1–5. The rest of the volume, however, does not engage with questions of race, aside from a chapter by Antina von Schnitzler that shows how racialized rule in apartheid and postapartheid South Africa worked on and through infrastructure, and how infrastructures (even mundane ones, like water meters and toilets) became terrains of political claim-making for oppositional struggles.

overview of racial classification in Colombia, Joanne Rappaport argues that racial terminologies (for example, *mestizo*, *negro*, and *blanco*) "have been in circulation for almost five centuries, but their meanings have changed over time and space."[38] Moreover, according to Rappaport, colonial regimes of difference "were not exclusively racial, in the sense of being determined by phenotype, but instead involved a complex combination of genealogy, skin color, occupation, place of origin and of residence, and condition as free or slave."[39] Things got more complicated with the break from Spain and the establishment of an independent republic in the first half of the nineteenth century. At this critical conjuncture, influential politicians and intellectuals heralded *mestizaje* (or racial mixing) as "the unifying thread of Colombian nationality" while establishing a racial cartography in which places, rather than people, were ranked along "an evolutionary continuum marked by disparate levels of civilization."[40] If racial hierarchies in the colonial period were far from a "coherent system," following Rappaport, and have mutated over time, a more complex picture emerges of the colonial-racial underpinnings of social and environmental orders in Colombia, past and present.[41]

The same is true for dominant ideas of nature, which have also multiplied and diversified. Early encounters with the majesty of Spanish American environments inspired colonial scholars to consider the territory "a providentially designed space."[42] One magistrate asserted "that Peru was so bountiful and temperate that it was home to the Garden of Eden and that the Amazon, Mag-

38 Rappaport, "Colombia and the Legal-Cultural Negotiation," 1. In a more theoretical register, Julio Arias and Eduardo Restrepo offer an approach to "historicizing race" that "goes beyond the frequent enunciation that race is a historical construction in order to suggest how it could be concretely understood as a singularity that allows, at the same time, the multiplicity of racial articulations." Arias and Restrepo, "Historizando raza," 48.

39 Rappaport, "Colombia and the Legal-Cultural Negotiation," 3. For an effort to further historicize colonial racialization strategies by examining their emergence out of Iberian anti-Judaism, see Hering Torres, "Purity of Blood." Hering Torres "questions the idea of racism as a linear process . . . without historical differentiations" (34).

40 Rappaport, "Colombia and the Legal-Cultural Negotiation," 9. Rappaport summarizes this racial-cum-regional hierarchy: "Politicians and writers understood climate to be a major determining factor of the nature of the population of a region and saw the highlands—where they themselves lived—as the civilizing center located in the midst of a barbarous periphery. They associated whiteness with the center and Blackness (and to a lesser degree, Indianness) with the periphery." See also Appelbaum, *Mapping the Country*; Arias Vanegas, *Nación y diferencia*.

41 Rappaport, "Colombia and the Legal-Cultural Negotiation," 6–7.

42 Cañizares-Esguerra, "How Derivative Was Humboldt?," 152.

dalena, La Plata, and Orinoco were the four rivers of Paradise mentioned in Genesis."[43] Praising the paradisaical qualities of the so-called New World did not, however, imply that its nature was benign—the climate as well as the flora and fauna were often depicted as threatening and unhealthy—or that it was safe from plunder.[44] The imperative to convert tropical biodiversity into imperial wealth motivated the accumulation of knowledge, and countless expeditions were dispatched to survey, map, collect, categorize, and order the natural world for the purpose of appropriation.[45] But when political currents moved in the direction of independence, tirades against the rapaciousness of Spanish rule positioned nature as a resource to be protected against foreign exploitation and as a cornucopia that could nurture national sovereignty.[46] Advances in scientific knowledge and technical expertise eventually fostered the notion that nature could be managed, controlled, even improved for specific ends.[47] And this included human nature, with the notion of an immutable body competing with debates about factors that could strengthen or weaken the biological fitness of the population.[48] While the concept of coloniality suggests a singular logic persisting for over five centuries, in practice social and environmental orders are varied and shifting. As central as the Magdalena River has been to these orders, and for all the influence they have had over the management of the waterway, articulations of race and nature defy the simple binary of domination and freedom.

* * *

43 Cañizares-Esguerra, "New World, New Stars," 34. Cañizares-Esguerra argues that the identification of Spanish American nature with Paradise was in tension with the classification of its peoples as intrinsically inferior.

44 Alimonda, "La colonialidad de la naturaleza"; Coronil, *The Magical State*; Pérez Morales, *La obra de Dios*.

45 Historians have referred to the eighteenth century in the Viceroyalty of New Granada as the "century of classification." Díaz Ángel, Muñoz Arbeláez, and Nieto Olarte, *Ensamblando la nación*, 28. See also Nieto Olarte, *Orden natural*.

46 For early republican environmentalism, see Davis, *Magdalena*. For the depiction of the nation as a cornucopia, see Afanador-Llach, "Una república colosal." For divergent valuations of natural resources in a proximate river system in northern Colombia during the twentieth century, see Camargo, "Una tierra bondadosa."

47 On the expertise behind the "political economy of circulation" in mid-nineteenth-century Colombia, see Castillo, *Crafting a Republic*.

48 Leal, "Usos del concepto 'raza'"; Restrepo Forero, "Trópicos, mestizaje y aclimatación."

IN THE FIRST half of the nineteenth century, *mestizaje* came to be seen as "constituting the essence of the nation" across much of Latin America.[49] Colombia was no exception. If racial hierarchy had been intrinsic to centuries of colonial rule, an independent republic would have to establish a social and political order in which all citizens were equal, at least in the eyes of the law and the state. In opposition to the notion of *limpieza de sangre* (purity of blood), which had animated Spanish colonial ideas of differential belonging and entitlement, biological mixing became valorized by republican elites hell-bent on constructing a model of popular sovereignty around a unified and homogenous national identity. The presumed affinity between *mestizaje* and democracy was so strong that liberal ideals, such as equality and freedom, seemed to depend on it. However, these progressive hopes had to contend with a paradox: a social order that valued racial mixing could accommodate and reproduce the very same hierarchies *mestizaje* was expected to dismantle. This was because, as Peter Wade argues, the "glorification of the mestizo rarely divested itself completely of the superior value attached to whiteness."[50]

The Magdalena River figured prominently in nineteenth-century debates over the democratizing potential of racial mixing. Advocates of *mestizaje*, such as Simón Bolívar himself, believed the waterway was a unifying force that could advance the goal of democratic nation-building by integrating geographically fragmented territories and intermingling racially differentiated populations.[51] By midcentury, liberal conceptions of freedom also hinged on the river, with advocates of free labor and free markets both seeing riverboat workers (*bogas*) and fluvial transport as fundamental to their cause.[52] Many elites who endorsed race mixture on political grounds fixated on inhabitants of the river basin, particularly *bogas*, who were often categorized as mixed race (*zambos* or *mulatos*) (figure 1.3). However, their depictions of riverine populations reflected the tension between racial hierarchy and democratic equality. A stark example comes from liberal politician and intellectual José María Samper, who espoused the link between *mestizaje* and democracy and yet depicted *bogas* as subhuman: despite being "fruit of the crossing of two or three different races," Samper argued, they "had of humanity almost only the external form

---

49 Peter Wade argues that *mestizaje* was never only about biology or genetics, but rather "entangled with ideas about difference and sameness, hierarchy and democracy, and equality and inequality." Wade, *Degrees of Mixture*, 1–2.

50 Wade, *Degrees of Mixture*, 8.

51 Davis, *Magdalena*.

52 McGraw, *The Work of Recognition*.

and the primitive needs and forces."[53] The ascendance of *mestizaje* as an ideology that espoused equality while permitting discrimination, that disavowed racial difference without challenging racial hierarchy, was deeply entangled with the Magdalena River.

The waterway's relationship to the politics of racial mixing shifted with the rise of eugenics—the science of racial improvement. This intellectual movement spread throughout Latin America in the early twentieth century, as it did in many parts of the world, and in Colombia foregrounded the influence of environmental factors (such as climate and diet) on the moral, intellectual, and biological fitness of the population.[54] This strain of eugenicist thought was neo-Lamarckian in its adherence to a theory of genetics that posited the hereditary nature of acquired traits. The implication was that the nation's genetic stock was susceptible to degeneration, but degeneration could be slowed, even reversed, by strategic interventions, which in Colombia targeted health and hygiene. At the turn of the century, the national government began introducing a series of policies and programs that sought to combat disease and promote sanitation, focusing particularly on the working classes of the Caribbean coast and the lower Magdalena valley.[55] According to Jason McGraw, public officials from the interior saw these "as regions full of tropical diseases and inferior people of mixed race who were not apt for modern industry."[56] And the environments of northern Colombia's tropical lowlands had long been understood, by European travelers and criollo intellectuals alike, as insalubrious.[57] However, as McGraw notes, "the problem went beyond the region itself."[58]

Home to the country's main commercial ports and largest foreign-born population, the Caribbean coast was seen as especially vulnerable to cultural and biological contamination from the outside world. And as the primary axis of travel and trade between the coast and the interior, the Magdalena River was thought to spread disease and disorder into the heart of the nation.[59] Concerns about the contamination of upstream society, however, were not just about protecting health or promoting hygiene. Eugenicists like the congressman

---

53 Samper, *Ensayo sobre las revoluciones políticas*; cited in Wade, *Degrees of Mixture*, 8.
54 Stepan, *"The Hour of Eugenics"*; McGraw, "Purificar la nación," 314.
55 McGraw, "Purificar la nación," 315.
56 McGraw, "Purificar la nación," 322.
57 Villegas, "El valle del río Magdalena," 153; Villegas Vélez and Castrillón Gallego, "Territorio, enfermedad y población."
58 McGraw, "Purificar la nación," 322.
59 McGraw, "Purificar la nación," 317, 332.

FIGURE 1.3. Edward Walhouse Mark, *Bongo del Magdalena*, 1845.
Source: Wikimedia Commons.

Luis López de Mesa raised the alarm that the Magdalena also "channeled 'African blood' toward the interior of Colombia," thus encouraging miscegenation and threatening the purity of populations and territories invested with whiteness.[60] Racial intermixing and regional integration, which the Magdalena was once celebrated for facilitating, became anathema to leading proponents of eugenics. As both strategic transport corridor and conduit for genetic circulation, the river was now an artery in more ways than one.

The national project of hygiene and its concerns about contamination paid special attention to fluvial navigation. River ports, boats, and crews were increasingly subjected to extensive regulations and strict protocols—some mandated by law, others instituted by employers—that saw them as vectors for the transmission of infectious diseases.[61] Sanitation committees and inspectors were granted jurisdiction over everything from operational logistics, such as the time vessels could spend in port, to intimate aspects of riverboat life, such as food, clothing, and accommodation. Even the comportment of crews

---

60 López de Mesa put it this way: "today the African blood rises, slowly and unstoppably, through the veins of our rivers towards the veins of our race." Cited in McGraw, "Purificar la nación," 321.

61 McGraw, "Purificar la nación," 332–33.

became a hygienic matter, leading to prohibitions against intoxication and obscenity.[62] This regulatory expansion had multiple motivations—imposing workforce discipline, bolstering state power, protecting private enterprise, facilitating free trade—but it also reflected the association of fluvial navigation with Black and mixed-race workers from the lower Magdalena valley.[63] In the name of combating racial deterioration and moral decline, eugenics reinforced long-standing patterns of anti-Blackness, class inequality, and regional hierarchy even as it unsettled the dominance of *mestizaje* as national ideology. The Magdalena River again played a constitutive role in the making and remaking of Colombia's geo-racial regimes.

The eugenics movement in Colombia was somewhat unusual in that whitening the population was not actively pursued through immigration. Compared to Argentina and Brazil, Colombia received relatively few European immigrants in the nineteenth and early twentieth centuries, for it had neither attractive political and economic conditions nor a coherent recruitment policy.[64] Migration significantly shaped Colombian society, however, especially along the Caribbean coast, only not in the most predictable ways. This was because the largest groups of immigrants—Jews and Arabs—conformed neither to the tripartite structure of Black/white/Indigenous presumed to constitute the nation's racial composition nor to the pure/mixed binary central to the ideologies of *mestizaje* and eugenics. The first wave of immigrants were Sephardic Jews from Curaçao and other islands in the Dutch West Indies, the majority of whom arrived in the early to mid-nineteenth century.[65] They were followed by Syrian, Lebanese, and Palestinian Christians who migrated steadily to the Colombian Caribbean between 1880 and 1930, and another influx of Jews in the 1920s and 1930s, first from Eastern Europe and the Levant and later from Germany and Austria.[66] These populations occasionally faced discriminatory and exclusionary treatment, but their history in Colombia was mostly one of acceptance and integration, especially relative to the Afro-Antillean migrants from places like Haiti, Jamaica, and Barbados who

---

62 McGraw, "Purificar la nación," 334.
63 McGraw points to the limited long-term consequences of these policies and programs, especially given the strength of the organized labor movement representing many of the workers targeted by them.
64 Fawcett and Posada-Carbo, "Arabs and Jews."
65 Sourdis Nájera, "Los judíos sefardíes," 31; Fawcett and Posada-Carbo, "Arabs and Jews," 60–61.
66 Fawcett and Posada-Carbo, "Arabs and Jews," 58, 64.

also settled on the Caribbean coast around the same time, or the proposed recruitment of Japanese workers to the *llanos orientales* (eastern plains).[67] Racially marked as other (*judíos* and *turcos* were the broad and inexact categories applied to them), Jews and Arabs were nevertheless seen as contributing to progress—not quite white yet still good for the country.

This assessment was based on racial stereotypes that depicted these groups as shrewd merchants intrinsically skilled at moneymaking. However, these assumptions would soon converge with reality as both communities established themselves quickly in local commercial, social, and political life. The Curaçao Jews arrived with experience, contacts, and capital, which they leveraged to remarkable success, first in commerce and later in industry, real estate, and banking.[68] Subsequent Jewish and Arab immigrants came with less, starting off as peddlers, but also thrived across a range of pursuits, from trade to agriculture to politics. Despite their relatively small numbers, both groups had an outsize influence on economic growth and development throughout the Caribbean coast region. Nowhere was this more pronounced than in the city at the mouth of the Magdalena River. Barranquilla's "spectacular transformation" from "insignificant village" to "Colombia's principal commercial entrepôt" in less than fifty years was due in no small part to the contributions of its immigrant community.[69] In addition, the city's meteoric rise was enabled by the Magdalena River estuary, since Barranquilla's geographical advantage stemmed from its location at the interface of maritime and inland shipping routes. Together these factors point to the social and environmental order organized around articulations of race, nature, and capital, and the waterway's infrastructural mediation of that order. While river trade and travel were powered by mixed-race wage laborers from the lower Magdalena valley, vessel owners occupied their place within the geo-racial regimes structuring Colombian society and space.

---

67 For the acceptance of Jewish and Arab immigrants, especially in Barranquilla, see Fawcett and Posada-Carbo, "Arabs and Jews," 72–73. For the dual case of Syro-Lebanese and Afro-Antillean migrants to the Caribbean coast, which tracks the shift from considering both groups racially inferior and socially undesirable to only the latter, see Rhenals Doria and Flórez Bolívar, "Escogiendo entre los extranjeros 'indeseables.'" For debates surrounding Japanese immigration to Colombia in the 1920s, see Martínez Martín, "Trópico y raza."

68 Fawcett and Posada-Carbo, "Arabs and Jews," 61–62.

69 Nichols, "The Rise of Barranquilla," 158; Fawcett and Posada-Carbo, "Arabs and Jews," 61.

During the colonial period, fluvial transport was dominated by wooden rafts and barges (*bongos* and *champanes*) owned by propertied men of Spanish descent.[70] However, the introduction of steamboats (*vapores*) in the 1820s brought about changes in the social complexion of vessel ownership. Shortly after independence, a Jewish businessman of German extraction, Juan Bernardo Elbers, was granted exclusive control over the waterway on the expectation that he would establish steam-powered transport.[71] Elbers was ultimately unsuccessful, and his concession was revoked, but by midcentury American, German, British, and other overseas investors had founded companies and imported vessels to move cargo between the Caribbean coast and upriver ports. Although ownership was no longer an exclusive privilege of the Spanish elite, the association between property and whiteness remained intact. However, the geo-racial regimes organized around the artery diversified when firms owned by Jewish and Arab businessmen entered the fluvial transport sector.[72] They were racialized minorities from the Caribbean coast, but their proximity to whiteness and their access to capital afforded them opportunities for advancement—opportunities mediated infrastructurally by the river.

The more well-resourced members of Barranquilla's Jewish community also undertook efforts to improve navigation along the waterway. In 1904, the Colombian government signed a contract with the industrialist Jacob Cortissoz for canalization and maintenance on a stretch of river near the estuary.[73] The descendent of Curaçao Jews, Cortissoz was involved in a range of commercial, financial, and industrial concerns and had acquired knowledge about fluvial transport through his close relationships with other Jewish-owned shipping companies.[74] Leveraging these connections and skills, Cortissoz was appointed director of the Compañía Colombiana de Transportes in 1905 as steamboats were becoming increasingly important to the export of coffee, indigo, and tobacco and the import of textiles, beer, and other merchandise.[75] The Magdalena's hydrological conditions remained an obstacle to stable and profitable circulation, however, and the imbalance between economic growth and unreliable shipments created demand for state-backed projects to improve

70 Solano, *Puertos, sociedad y conflictos*; Posada-Carbó, "Bongos, champanes y vapores."
71 Viloria De la Hoz, *Empresarios del Caribe colombiano.*
72 Sourdis Nájera, "Los judíos sefardíes"; Repetto et al., *Los árabes en Colombia*; Fawcett and Posada-Carbo, "Arabs and Jews."
73 Mora Angueira, "Compendio histórico," 2.
74 Sourdis Nájera, "Los judíos sefardíes."
75 Sourdis Nájera, "Los judíos sefardíes."

navigability.[76] Another large contract was awarded in 1920 to a German engineering company, Julius Berger Konsortium, to carry out studies of flow and sediment, to install equipment for fluviometric monitoring, and to assess the potential for hydraulic works.[77] Although the results published by the company were considered "the first report . . . to perform a complete analysis of the hydraulic characteristics of the river," a series of breaches led to the cancellation of the contract in 1928.[78] Shortly thereafter the German-Jewish director of the company, Julius Berger, was forced by the National Socialists to abandon his post. He was then deported to the Theresienstadt concentration camp, where he died in 1943.[79]

Jacob Cortissoz's interest in fluvial transport led him to venture into the lumber industry, and he set up a sawmill on the banks of the Magdalena River to supply ships and shipyards with wood.[80] This location attracted other businesses and grew into an industrial complex, which proved strategic when Jacob's son, Ernesto, partnered with Colombian and German investors to found the Sociedad Colombo Alemana de Transporte Aéreo (SCADTA), South America's first airline.[81] Using the complex's docks as an aquatic airfield, SCADTA imported seaplanes from Germany and recruited pilots who relied on the river for takeoff and landing and to chart their course (figure 1.4). The company flew regular routes, serving river towns as far as Neiva, nearly 1,000 kilometers from the coast, until Hitler's rise to power sparked concerns about the airline's German and Austrian shareholders and about its possible acquisition by the Nazi regime.[82] When World War II broke out, SCADTA was forced to suspend operations and merge with a state-owned airline, forming what would eventually become Avianca, Colombia's flagship carrier.

This marked the end not only of aviation along the river, but also of the steady influx of Jewish and Arab immigrants to the Caribbean coast. Barranquilla was awash in Nazi propaganda at the time, especially among citizens of German origin, and severe restrictions barring the entry of Jews and Arabs were imposed by the minister of foreign relations—the same Luis López de

---

76 Posada-Carbó, *The Colombian Caribbean*.
77 Posada-Carbó, *The Colombian Caribbean*.
78 Silva Fajardo, *Champanes, vapores y remolcadores*, 84; Posada-Carbó, *The Colombian Caribbean*.
79 "Julius Berger."
80 Sourdis Nájera, "Los judíos sefardíes," 43.
81 Meisel Roca, "Volando sobre la ruta."
82 Meisel Roca, "Volando sobre la ruta."

FIGURE 1.4. SCADTA seaplane on the Magdalena River, ca. 1920.
Source: Wikimedia Commons.

Mesa who had feared the river's potential to dilute the racial purity of the white populations of the interior.[83] This coincided with the deterioration of conditions for navigation along the waterway, which increased the risk of shipwrecks, and before long major shipping companies began suspending operations, bringing the heyday of fluvial transport to a close.[84] This was another moment in which transnational circuits of race and racism shaped Colombia's social and environmental orders, and in which the Magdalena River played a constitutive role.

* * *

IN 2014, THE Colombian government initiated the process of reactivating commercial shipping on the Magdalena River. In 2016, the same administration signed a peace accord with the largest and most active guerrilla group, the Revolutionary Armed Forces of Colombia (FARC). These were separate phenomena, at least on paper, but the navigability project soon became integral to

---

83 For the spread of Nazi propaganda and support for National Socialism in the Colombian Caribbean in the 1930s, see Lázaro, "Los medios impresos." For the ban against Jewish refugees from Germany and Austria, see Fawcett and Posada-Carbo, "Arabs and Jews," 65. For government restrictions barring the entry of immigrants from the Arab world, see Fawcett and Posada-Carbo, "Arabs and Jews," 73.
84 Márquez Calle, "Un río difícil."

the government's plan "to construct a durable and lasting peace." The historic 2016 agreement with the FARC was followed by an ambitious program of infrastructure building, which dovetailed with the goal of reactivating fluvial transport through engineering works along the river. This convergence of priorities emerged out of a paradigm of peace building that sought to address the underlying causes of the armed conflict through regional integration and economic development.[85] Alongside other large-scale infrastructure projects, transforming the waterway into a logistics corridor was invested with the potential to advance Colombia further along the path to peace and prosperity. Both the navigability project and the peace process have been deeply fraught, but they continue to be seen by many politicians and policymakers as mutually reinforcing and equally vital to Colombia's future.

In its 2014 version, the navigability project allocated approximately $1 billion for removing barriers to commercial shipping along 900 kilometers of river. A public-private partnership was formed and tasked with the challenge of establishing and maintaining a navigable channel through which commercial vessels could reliably transport cargo between the coast and the interior at all times of year. A contract was awarded to a consortium named Navelena to dredge sediment from the river bottom at strategic locations and to install levees to contain water within the shipping lane. According to the plan, towboat-and-barge convoys would eventually be able to navigate all the way from Cartagena and Barranquilla on the Caribbean coast to the interior river port of Puerto Salgar, roughly equidistant from Colombia's two largest cities, Bogotá and Medellín. New port terminals and logistics hubs would be licensed and built along the waterway to facilitate connection with other modes of transport. The goal was to turn the river into an *autopista fluvial* (fluvial expressway) that could overcome some of the challenges stemming from the country's notoriously rugged topography and shift away from road transport. After years of delays and setbacks, however, Navelena collapsed in 2017 under the weight of a gargantuan corruption scandal. Efforts to restructure the project ensued and the expectations surrounding it remain as great as ever.

A year before Navelena's collapse, I set off for the Middle Magdalena river town of Puerto Wilches, where dredging operations were underway. I had been doing fieldwork in nearby Barrancabermeja and had decided to take a short trip downriver to see what townspeople were thinking about the prospect of a consistently navigable waterway. Puerto Wilches had once been an important

---

85 Zeiderman, "Concrete Peace."

trading post for the department of Santander: a railway connected the river port to the industrious city of Bucaramanga, and roads led onward to the hinterlands of northeastern Colombia and the Venezuelan border beyond. The town's fortunes plummeted in the second half of the twentieth century, however, as sedimentation clogged the navigable channel, and commerce along the waterway declined. The armed conflict eventually arrived, trapping residents between opposing forces intent on capitalizing on the town's strategic position. Given this history, I was prepared to find expectations that a transformation in hydrological conditions would bring about an economic revival, perhaps even social stability. I was less prepared for the geo-racial logic embedded within hopes for the future.

Approaching the town by boat, I caught a glimpse of rudimentary dredge rigs excavating sand from the riverbed and depositing it on islands dotted throughout the channel. A few of these islands showed signs of habitation—stalks of corn, a thatched hut—and our pilot cut a curvilinear route around them to reach the docks. Despite its flat bottom and shallow draft, the boat was forced to veer sharply to avoid sandbanks and shoals, which indicated that larger cargo vessels would struggle to navigate these waters. Most watercraft moored here were smaller and more agile still—mainly canoes, some equipped with outboard motors, others simply oars. I disembarked quickly and ducked into a shady park. As I swiveled around to catch my bearings, it struck me that I had lost sight of the river due to a head-high embankment running the length of the town center. I continued walking away from the water to the main commercial street located at the park's far end. The town seemed to face inland, as though appealing to the terrestrial interior for validation, but my interest in its relationship to the river led me back to a dockside café.

I was sipping coffee and pondering my next move when my concentration was broken by an elderly man tapping the pavement with a white cane. Turning into the café, he began feeling his way around, eventually gravitating to the table where I was sitting. He expressed surprise when his hand found my arm (clearly this was his customary seat), so I guided him into my chair and relocated myself to one directly opposite. Realizing he still had company, the man pulled a bag of coins from his pocket and asked for help counting them (he had 4,100 pesos in total, which he would exchange for bills). I offered him a drink, but he declined, since providing the cashier with small change entitled him to complimentary coffee.

I explained that I was writing a book about the river and visiting the town to hear how people felt about its past and future. This account, however brief, was enough to trigger a flood of memories from his days supplying goods to riverside villages and farms. Born in 1940, Ernesto left his hometown of Bucaramanga at fourteen for Puerto Wilches, which was known then as a place for commerce. "I was a *gamín* (street urchin) when I arrived," he recalled. "I was homeless and completely alone." But the town was awash in money, since it was an important stopover for riverboats transporting cargo between the interior and the coast. "I started small," he said, "traveling back to the city to buy goods—just two boxes per trip—and selling them up and down the river for double or triple their cost." Though he now seemed to live a humbler existence, Ernesto reported that he eventually expanded his operations by purchasing in larger quantities, renting a warehouse, hiring employees, and acquiring his own boat.

Ernesto hastened to add that the wholesalers he bought from in those days were *antioqueños* (people from the neighboring department of Antioquia), and being himself *santandereano* (from Santander, to which his birthplace and adoptive hometown both belong), he declared that they "saw eye to eye." With a glint of admiration, Ernesto summarized the affinity between the two regional types: "The *antioqueño* never gets bogged down—he always moves forward. We're the same [referring collectively to *santandereanos*]." He then asked whether I was familiar with Santander. I responded affirmatively, as I had friends and family from the area, including in the city of his birth, and I smugly rattled off a list of smaller towns in the department's heartland I had recently visited. "So, you know the people from Santander are good people [*gente de bien*]," he asserted. To emphasize that he was talking about more than their can-do attitude, Ernesto gave a concrete example: "You can leave your door open, and nothing will happen. We are civilized people." He then put his moral judgment in geographical perspective: "Downriver from here to the coast, there is no civilization."

Like Antioquia, Santander has long been ranked favorably within Colombia's racialized hierarchies of regional identity. Although the department encompasses a diversity of elevations, climates, and peoples, it is commonly associated with the temperate highlands and with whiteness. The region boasts of its predominantly European ancestry—initially Catalonians and Aragonese from northern Spain, later Germans—as well as its supposed lack of people of Indigenous and African descent.[86] The typical *santandereano* is

---

86 Lamus Canavate, "'Aquí no hay negros,'" 116; Arias Vanegas, *Nación y diferencia*, 114. Racial mixing, or *mestizaje*, in Santander has been understood as a process of whitening (*blanqueamiento*) whereby European stock successfully incorporated other influences while remaining dominant.

presumed to have blue or green eyes, fair hair, and light skin and is stereotypically law-abiding, hardworking, and forthright (figure 1.5).[87] This typology dates from the 1850s, when the nation's preeminent geographical survey, the Chorographic Commission led by Italian-born military engineer Agustín Codazzi, mapped the territory and population according to racialized regional hierarchies. Inspired by their expeditions to the northern Andean provinces (later Santander and Antioquia), the commissioners constructed a prototype of the model citizen based on their depictions of the white inhabitants of the highland interior.[88] The state-sanctioned geography texts that emerged from these expeditions, which synthesized the Chorographic Commission's findings, consistently counterposed the *santandereano* and the *costeño* racial-regional "types."[89] These texts circulated widely, not only in Colombia but also among leading geographers overseas, such as Élisée Reclus in France and Alfred Hettner in Germany, contributing to debates about the environmental determinants of human variation.[90] The geo-racial regime that emerged in the nineteenth century was not unique to Colombia, nor was it bound to this moment in time. The same typology of race and region continues to inform popular understandings of diversity and difference today, even among those who consciously oppose racial thinking.[91]

Despite its association with the highlands, the department of Santander descends to the Magdalena River valley at its western border. Nevertheless, according to another geographical classification with similar racial connotations, river towns like Puerto Wilches are grouped within the Magdalena

---

87 Arias Vanegas, *Nación y diferencia*, 113–16.

88 Appelbaum, *Mapping the Country of Regions*, 54–80.

89 For example, Felipe Pérez's *General Geography* (1865) "argued that the robust highland inhabitant of Antioquia or Santander was as different from the 'apathetic' inhabitant of the river valleys or the 'verbose' *costeño* (Caribbean coastal resident) as was a Spaniard from a Frenchman." Likewise, Francisco Javier Vergara y Velasco's *The New Geography of Colombia Organized by Natural Regions* (1901) said that the *costeño*, "commonly of color, is talkative, petulant, active, boastful," while "in the heart of Santander . . . is the true Santandereano, pallid, robust, genteel, polite, hard working, intelligent." Cited in Appelbaum, *Mapping the Country of Regions*, 191, 210.

90 For the back-and-forth relationship with European geographical thought, see Appelbaum, *Mapping the Country of Regions*, 203–4. Appelbaum concludes that the "theorization of region [and race] that was going on in Colombia thus paralleled and was informed by—and perhaps in turn informed—theories that were being elaborated and debated in Europe and North America" (210).

91 Schwartz-Marín and Wade, "Explaining the Visible."

FIGURE 1.5. Carmelo Fernández, *White Ranchers Near Vélez, Province of Vélez*, 1850. Source: Library of Congress.

Medio (Middle Magdalena) rather than the Bajo Magdalena (Lower Magdalena), the former commonly associated with the Andean interior, the latter
with the Caribbean coast. Parallels in elevation and climate aside, and despite
their location within the same watershed, the division between the Middle
and Lower Magdalena enables towns like Puerto Wilches to claim superiority over their riverside counterparts in departments (such as Bolívar, Cesar,
Magdalena, and Atlántico) nearer to the sea. Ernesto's assertion that "there is
no civilization" downstream demonstrates how the river itself functions as a
racialized measure of value, with the watershed gradient of high-middle-low
corresponding to moral hierarchies between people and places. The artery is
not simply inserted with the geo-racial regimes governing social and environmental orders in Colombia; it is constitutive of them.

Ernesto was a self-made man, at least in his telling, though he admitted to
being dependent on the river. "Puerto Wilches stopped being a port around

1985," he recalled, "when they did away with the riverboats [*cuando se acabaron con los barcos*]." Sensing ambiguity in his account, I asked whether he held the government responsible. "No," he replied, "it wasn't the state's decision, it was the river's decision. The water stopped being navigable [*El agua dejó de ser navegable*]." This shift hurt Ernesto's business, but its significance was greater: "Now the closer you get to the coast," Ernesto lamented, "the better the conditions are for navigation." Returning to the racialized hierarchy he had previously used to characterize the civilizational gradient between the Middle and Lower Magdalena, Ernesto gave it hydrological specificity: "Up here we have good people but bad water. Downriver they have good water but bad people." This incongruity between race and nature, he hoped, was what the government's plan to improve navigability would ultimately resolve. If stretches of river belonging to the Magdalena Medio received the appropriate sort of management, they would resume their rightful place within the social and environmental order. "Good people" and "good water" would be realigned, and the Bajo Magdalena would serve merely as a passageway between the interior and the sea.

This hydro-social imaginary has not gone uncontested, however. Moving closer to the Caribbean coast, the civilizational hierarchies present in Ernesto's vision are often called into question. For example, people from riverside cities and towns in the Lower Magdalena lay claim to the river as "their river" against claims asserted by people from elsewhere that the waterway belongs to Colombia at large and therefore equally to them. This challenges the assumption—one with racial and regional overtones—that the management of the waterway should reside in the hands of those who know best, namely the political and economic elite from Bogotá and other cities of the Andean interior. It also casts the navigability project in a different light, as business interests and political leaders from Barranquilla and Cartagena see it as a means by which to rebalance the hierarchies structuring Colombian society and space. Indeed, the collapse of the Navelena consortium created an opening for regional representatives from the Caribbean coast to intervene in the restructuring of the project. Once appointed to the advisory committee, they began pushing for more money to be allocated to dredging at the river's mouth in Barranquilla as well as in the Canal del Dique connecting to the seaport of Cartagena. This contrasts sharply with earlier iterations of the navigability project, which leaned heavily toward reestablishing navigation upstream of Barrancabermeja in the Middle Magdalena, where the itineraries of commercial vessels currently end. The regions stereotypically associated with whiteness—Antioquia and Santander—initially stood to benefit most from the large investment of public funds in engineering the river, whereas one of the regions associated with Blackness—the Caribbean coast—is now making a bid to shift the management of the river in their direction. This is less a matter of mastery versus freedom, but rather competing versions of mastery over the more-than-human world in the service of recalibrating relations of mastery between different categories of humans.

Dredging Up the Future

The quayside in Barrancabermeja is an eventful place. The city's center of gravity is the Ecopetrol oil refinery, which abuts the Magdalena River but is generally inaccessible. The public waterfront, in contrast, constantly buzzes with life. On a visit in late 2017, I strolled down to the river just after daybreak. Vendors had already set up their stands and were busy hawking cassavas, limes, yams, and coconuts. A plantain seller rolled by with a pushcart painted vibrant green to match his merchandise. Fishermen were lining up their dugout canoes along the embankment and broadcasting news of their morning haul to a crowd eager to bag fresh *bagre* and *bocachico* (figure 2.1). Perched a good three meters above the waterline, the expectant customers gazed down at the fishermen's catch laid out in orderly rows. The physical gap between buyers and sellers was so great that each canoe had dispatched a representative to street level. These brokers also mediated across another gap—one with geographical, racial, and class connotations—separating river people (*ribereños*) from their land-bound patrons.

FIGURE 2.1. Fishermen selling catch at quayside, Barrancabermeja, Santander. Source: photograph by author.

I remarked to one fish seller that the river seemed unusually low. "Sí, pero se está echando agüita," he responded, indicating that the water level had indeed dropped but was starting to rise. Difficult to translate, his phrase conveyed optimism tinged with ambiguity: the cause of the shift was unspecified; in fact, the reflexive pronoun (*se*) made the river both subject and object. I pressed further for an explanation, knowing that the Magdalena River basin is a vast, complex hydrological system prone to dramatic and frequent fluctuations for any number of reasons: a burst of rainfall near the headwaters; a release from an upstream hydroelectric dam; a seasonal shift in channel morphology.[1] Instead, I got variations on the same autogenic diagnosis whereby changes in the conditions of the river arise from within. After all, for those whose daily existence is deeply entangled with the waterway, the Magdalena is often concep-

---

1 The Magdalena River has a length of 1,540 kilometers and a catchment basin of over 250,000 square kilometers, which is equivalent to a quarter of the total surface area of Colombia. See Alvear Sanín, *Manual del Río Magdalena*.

tualized as a powerful force with a life of its own.[2] When water levels ascend, the river is replenishing itself, and they must learn to read and respond to its fickle nature.

This scene, seemingly insignificant, reflects everyday encounters with a social and environmental order that assigns different entities their respective ontological status, delimiting the boundaries separating subject from object, human from nonhuman, person from thing. The gap negotiated by fishers and their customers stems from long-standing racial taxonomies and regional hierarchies, according to which people throughout the tropical lowlands of northern Colombia have often been equated with nature, likened to nonhuman animals, and had their subjecthood (indeed, their humanity) called into question on account of their proximity to Blackness.[3] And questions about the river's agency are not limited to bankside banter; they reach back to the Magdalena's historical vocation as political unifier and economic catalyst as well as to its more recent investment with legal personhood and, consequently, rights.[4] This milieu, in which ontologies are in flux, may resonate with posthumanist imperatives: to blur the boundaries between natural and social orders; to celebrate the entanglement of humans and other beings; and to appreciate nonanthropocentric forms of agency. However, rather than embracing these principles as analytical foundations or ethical horizons, I am guided by scholars of race, who have long grappled with the often deadly consequences of ontological fluidity.[5] Adopting what Jonathan Rosa and Vanessa Díaz call a "raciontological perspective that attends to the central role that race plays in constituting modern subjects and objects," I focus on the practices and performances of both fixing and undermining ontological divides and their

2 For the entanglements (*enmarañamientos*) linking river dwellers to the water body, see Bocarejo Suescún, "Gobernanza del agua." For numerous accounts of people attributing agency to the waterway, including the author himself, see Davis, *Magdalena*.

3 Múnera, *Fronteras imaginadas*.

4 One of the most iconic endowments of agency and personhood to the river is Gómez Picón, *Magdalena, río de Colombia*. For analyses of the river as political actor, see Bocarejo Suescún, "Lo público de la Historia pública"; Serrano López and Hernández Chitiva, *Del Río Grande de la Magdalena*. For the recent recognition of the Magdalena River's legal personhood, see *Semana*, "Fallo de tutela reconoce."

5 Malini Ranganathan points to ontological ambivalence as "a necessary (and not accidental) political rationale for the production of racial ecologies" ("The Racial Ecologies of Urban Wetlands," 722). Some scholars in the environmental humanities and social sciences have made similar points, though not necessarily in relation to race. See Roberts, "What Gets Inside."

consequences for who and what either flourishes or perishes.[6] If modern civil society, legal frameworks, knowledge systems, and governance institutions are organized around anti-Blackness, then endowing something or someone with ontological certainty is equivalent to investing it with whiteness.[7]

I was in Barrancabermeja to visit to the headquarters of Navelena—the consortium resulting from a public-private partnership between the Colombian government, the Brazilian engineering firm Odebrecht, and the local construction company Valorcon, which in 2014 had won the tender to restore commercial navigation to the Magdalena River over a thirteen-year period (figure 2.2).[8] Nearly $1 billion had been earmarked for the navigability plan (as it was called), which aimed to resuscitate shipping traffic along the waterway. The plan mandated a permanently navigable channel with a consistent depth of seven feet (2.13 m) and a minimum width of 150 feet (46 m) along a 900-kilometer stretch of river between the Andean interior and the Caribbean coast. This would require dredging operations, which would excavate massive volumes of sediment from the river bottom at critical choke points, as well as channeling works, which would create a system of levees to prevent the lateral spreading of water outside the shipping lane. According to the plan, these interventions would ultimately enable convoys of commercial barges powered by pusher towboats to ply the river nonstop with cargo loads upward of 7,000

6 Rosa and Díaz, "Raciontologies," 125. There are connections with Arturo Escobar's interest in ontological politics and his commitment to pluriversality, and especially his engagement with race and anti-Blackness in the preface to the English edition of *Otro posible es posible.* See Escobar, *Pluriversal Politics.* Another inspiration is the large body of work on what Annemarie Mol calls "ontological politics." See Mol, "Ontological Politics."

7 I'm referring here to Afro-pessimist thought and its emphasis on an ontological and institutional order organized around the relegation of Blackness to what Frantz Fanon called the "zone of nonbeing." See Wilderson, *Afropessimism.* However, I also heed the warnings of Katherine McKittrick and Deborah Thomas, both building on the insights of Sylvia Wynter, who foreground what McKittrick calls an "analytics of invention" that "necessarily dislodges the naturalization of dysselection." See McKittrick, *Dear Science,* 2; McKittrick, *Sylvia Wynter,* 7. Thomas argues, "Like all logics, Afro-pessimism is (as Claude Lévi-Strauss would have said) 'good to think with,' but, of course, logics must be understood as contingent. They can exist in the world only as engagements, always in motion, always entertaining the possibility of human action." In a world organized around anti-Blackness, Thomas asks what it means to "be a human capable of acting politically in and on the world" and how we might "bear witness to these enactments" by attending ethnographically to the dynamic practices and embodied performances of sovereignty. See Thomas, *Political Life,* 4–5.

8 Estrada, *Análisis del Proyecto.*

FIGURE 2.2. Offices of Navelena and Cormagdalena, Barrancabermeja, Santander.
Source: photograph by author.

tons. The building of new port terminals was not mandated by the plan, but
it was stipulated that Cormagdalena, the environmental authority with jurisdiction over the river, would expedite the granting of concessions. The result
of the contract awarded to Navelena would be an *autopista fluvial* (fluvial expressway) with the capacity to move 10 million tons of freight per year. The
river's ontological indeterminacy would be stabilized, and progress and prosperity would follow.

Dredging and channeling are sociotechnical interventions that simultaneously reconfigure the physical conditions of a hydrological system as well as
the semiotic order that gives it meaning. Dredging removes matter from the
bed of a water body while bringing up forgotten, perhaps unwelcome aspects
of the past. Likewise, channeling transforms the width and straightness of a
waterway at the same time that it gives purpose and direction to a potentially
unwieldy force or idea.[9] However, dredging and channeling are also practices

9 It is worth noting that, in Spanish, *canalización* signifies both the physical work of canalizing as well as the conceptual work often associated with the word *channeling* in English.
   To retain the simultaneously material and symbolic dimensions of the Spanish term,

and performances that enact ontological work.[10] They do not simply intervene in material and symbolic realms—they actively constitute the divides separating land from water, past from present, nature from culture, being from nonbeing. As technical operations belonging to an infrastructure megaproject with the ambition to transform the social and environmental order of the Magdalena River basin, dredging and channeling recalibrate metrics of viability and disposability, potentiality and obsolescence. At the heart of this process are geo-racial divides, such as the ones separating *ribereños* from their land-bound customers, which ultimately determine which entities, living and nonliving, are relegated to the past and which are deemed to have a future.

* * *

ON AN EARLIER visit to Barrancabermeja, in 2016, I interviewed Antonio, Navelena's social and environmental manager—a rotund man from Medellín who embodied the self-assured whiteness characteristic of *paisas*, especially when stationed far from home. Urban elites from the department of Antioquia have often wielded political influence, economic power, and technical prowess over lowland Colombia's less-white inhabitants, from the colonization of neighboring territories in the nineteenth century to the projected Highway to the Sea, which would grant Medellín direct maritime access.[11] And my conversation with Antonio made it abundantly clear that the popular myth casting *antioqueños* as "intrepid white pioneers who civilized a wild frontier and integrated Colombia into the international market economy," as Nancy Appelbaum puts it, remains alive and well among technicians dispatched to manage infrastruc-

---

I use *channeling* even when referring to the more technical process. It is also worth noting that, in Spanish, *dragar* does not have the dual meaning associated with the verb "to dredge (up)" in English. Respecting the difference between words and concepts, I refrain from allowing either linguistic context to determine analytical possibilities.

10 Here I am building on the insights of Andrea Ballestero, who offers a "way of thinking about water that does not take for granted its materiality or the political valence of particular water forms." Ballestero argues that attending to an "extended materiality reveals how water can never be separated from the ideal forms that we use to describe it and prevents us from extending into the twenty-first century a naturalism that takes for granted the materiality of the world as a stable object." Ballestero, *A Future History of Water*, 191. For an approach to holding in question the ontological status of hydrological forms, especially rivers, see Da Cunha, *The Invention of Rivers*.

11 Roldán, *Blood and Fire*; Appelbaum, *Muddied Waters*; Ballvé, *The Frontier Effect*; Steiner, *Imaginación y poder*.

FIGURE 2.3. Navelena motorboats docked at fluvial transport terminal, Barrancabermeja, Santander. Source: photograph by author.

ture megaprojects like this one (figure 2.3).[12] But the case of Antioquia is only the most cited example of a more general pattern, whereby such projects rely on and reinforce entrenched geographical hierarchies of many kinds—between the interior and the coasts, between the cities and the countryside, between the highlands and the lowlands, between the capital and the provinces—all of which intersect with structures of institutional racism and white supremacy that privilege lighter-skinned Colombians with real or imagined proximity to Europe and North America above those of darker complexion with ties, whether cultural or biological, to African and Indigenous ancestry.[13] Despite promises to increase equality through connectivity, the Magdalena River project remains entangled with enduring geo-racial divides.

At that meeting, Antonio told me that the project was slow to get started, but that we'd soon see dramatic results. Invoking the terrestrial ontology

12 Appelbaum, "Whitening the Region," 622.
13 Viveros Vigoya, "Social Mobility, Whiteness, and Whitening."

implicit in the notion of a fluvial expressway, which implies the primacy of land over water, he said, "The river is like a barrio with unpaved streets. Once you pave the roads, people start to see opportunities. The dynamics of the barrio change completely, and not just in terms of transport but everything." Reflected in this vision is the technological determinism of Medellín's famed model of social urbanism, here applied to an entire river system, as well as a temporal framework that positions the Lower Magdalena and its people in the past, waiting patiently for benevolent patrons from the highland regions with technical expertise to bring them into the future.[14] Antonio continued, "The navigation project is about turning our attention back to the river after many years of neglect. Every river municipality already wants to have a port. Of course, they can't all be Puerto Salgar [a town less than 200 kilometers from Bogotá, which would be the inland head of commercial navigation, according to the plan]. But everyone from Puerto Salgar to Barranquilla [where the river meets the sea] knows this is going to be a major game changer." The confidence animating his forecast was not only a case of stereotypical *paisa* hubris, for he was echoing the sociotechnical imaginaries animating the navigability plan since its unveiling in 2012.

In multiple public forums, the plan's virtues had been enumerated by smartly dressed, well-spoken, expensively educated experts—most of them white men from Bogotá. With the help of impressive statistics and sleek infographics, they had summoned a vision of the virtuous cycle that would ensue once the project was completed and 900 kilometers of river had become navigable twenty-four hours a day, seven days a week, 365 days a year. Transport costs would drop, and delays would be reduced; productivity would rise; jobs would be created; the gap between rural and urban areas would be bridged; socioeconomic inequality would be cut; greenhouse gas emissions would decrease; river towns would come back to life; national firms would be internationally competitive; overseas investors would flock to the country; new markets would emerge; tourism would return to the river; a fragmented nation would be finally united; and much more.[15]

---

14 My understanding of this dynamic is indebted to Teo Ballvé and his analysis of state-building projects in the northern Colombian region of Urabá.

15 This summary of the promises attached to the navigability plan is based on an analysis of media articles, online forums, and government reports between the plan's initial release in 2012 and its collapse in 2017. For the promise of infrastructure, see Hetherington, "Surveying the Future Perfect," 40–50; Appel, Anand, and Gupta, "Introduction." For a related case in Colombia, see Camargo and Uribe, "Infraestructuras."

These sociotechnical imaginaries, though future oriented, did not presume a clean break with the past. Indeed, they were infused with myths of the river's illustrious history. With frequent use of terms like *recuperación* (rehabilitation), the navigability plan aimed to resuscitate cargo transport between the Andean interior and the Caribbean coast and to return the inland head of commercial shipping closer to its former location. Not only would this restore the prosperity of communities lining the riverbanks; it would also make the river once again the backbone of Colombia's aspirations for progress and development. On the political front, the river would be reinvested with the promise of national unification at another watershed moment. However, only certain aspects of the river's past were seen to belong to its future, while others were rendered anachronistic and anatopistic—out of time and out of place. For example, the historical pattern of failed attempts at technological improvement would be undone and perennial impediments to navigation finally removed. And the disastrous environmental impacts once associated with fluvial navigation (mass deforestation for wood-burning engines) would be transcended, and extractive accumulation (fossil fuel production) would be replaced by sustainable development, at least on paper. These undesirable legacies of the river's past would supposedly be rendered safely historical and comfortably distant.

Meanwhile, the future visions animating the navigability plan relegated certain aspects of the river's present to the status of historical artifact or geographical outlier. This would be achieved discursively by the plan and by the fanfare surrounding it, but it would also be accomplished materially by the engineering works designed to guarantee a permanent shipping lane.[16] For example, dredging and channeling would undoubtedly have major impacts on local fisheries and their habitat, which would threaten to make *pescadores* untimely relics.[17] The watercraft currently predominating along the river—canoes, *moto-canoas*, and *chalupas*—and the forms of mobility they enable were also in danger of becoming vestiges of the past. So, too, were the older shipping lines, which were predicted to have trouble competing once the river was overhauled; their vessels, crews, and navigation techniques all classified as remnants of a bygone era. Smallholders farming the riverbanks or islands in the channel were also confronting their planned obsolescence, as their plots would be either expropriated or inundated. And the amphibious habitats and species of all kinds

---

16 Carse and Lewis, "Toward a Political Ecology."
17 Boelens et al., "River Lives, River Movements."

that depend on the floodplain's complex ecology were similarly in danger of being outdated or displaced.[18]

There is a paradox at the heart of these sociotechnical imaginaries: one of the primary rationales underpinning the navigability plan is the imperative to tackle climate change, and yet the vast majority of goods transported along the waterway are fossil fuels. Here climate change is problematized as a question of mitigation that pertains primarily to the inland transport sector, which in Colombia is dominated by roads. This sector is predicted to grow along with Colombia's increased connectivity to global markets, but cutting greenhouse gas emissions requires a shift from road to other, more environmentally sound modes of cargo transport. Due to the poor state of rail infrastructure, fluvial navigation is positioned as the most viable alternative.[19] However, at present, the transport of goods by river is dominated by the oil industry; the state-owned oil company, Ecopetrol, is the primary client of shipping companies. Despite occasional political proclamations against natural resource extraction, a significant economic transition is far from reality. According to this logic, climate mitigation does not imply a reduction of the fossil fuel economy, only moving its products more efficiently and sustainably. And doing so requires significant interventions in the Magdalena basin.

Within prevailing social and environmental orders and their geo-racial hierarchy of being and belonging, the river and its living and nonliving constituents are malleable objects that can be rearranged or removed to facilitate flows of capital and cargo and to reduce CO_2 emissions.[20] Unless strategically aligned with the river's reconfigured role as fluvial expressway, many people and things would be rendered, materially and symbolically, out of place and out of time. However, while the river can be reconfigured to facilitate commercial shipping from the interior to the sea, the precise way in which its past, present, and future intermingle cannot be engineered. That which is being made anachronistic and anatopistic is not so quick to disappear.

* * *

---

18 The mitigation efforts that often accompany large-scale development projects have not played a major role in the planning process thus far. See Carse, "The Ecobiopolitics."

19 IDEAM et al., "Tercera comunicación nacional."

20 Alejandro Camargo shows how human and nonhuman entities depend on the slowing or stoppage of water flows, and how stagnation creates the material conditions for sociopolitical conflict. See Camargo, "Stagnation," 83.

AS THE NAVIGABILITY plan was gathering momentum, I made periodic visits to riverside towns and cities between Puerto Salgar, the projected inland head of navigation, and the Caribbean coast. I wanted to know how people—some directly involved with fluvial transport and the planning process, others less so—were understanding the sociotechnical imaginaries under consideration. Although I hesitated to explain my interest in precisely these terms, I wanted to see how actors differently positioned along racial, geographical, and class lines made sense of this megaproject and the social and environmental order it sought to instate. I hoped to assess how people were engaging with the primary interventions central to the project—dredging operations and channeling works—and their social and political implications.

In the main cities connected to fluvial transport—Barranquilla, where the river meets the sea; the nearby port of Cartagena, which connects to the Magdalena via canal; and Barrancabermeja, the main inland river port—I met with executives and managers from some of the shipping lines currently in operation, who were the navigability plan's primary beneficiaries. In air-conditioned offices and well-appointed conference rooms, I heard predictably positive outlooks from courteous, well-dressed, light-skinned businessmen. Many of them had personal and professional ties with Europe and North America and were enthusiastic to regale me with tales of recent visits to London, Paris, and New York. Some even had links to my employer, the London School of Economics and Political Science, which was not surprising given the university's reputation as a finishing school for the developing world's political and economic elite. A condo in Miami, a degree (especially in business or economics) from the LSE: in Colombia, as elsewhere, these are assets that advantageously position those who possess them within a social order that privileges proximity to whiteness. A river that functions as a true conduit of commerce is the environmental and infrastructural equivalent.

Many in the fluvial transport business in Colombia spoke enviously of major inland waterways elsewhere in the world. The Mississippi was the most frequently cited, but the Rhine, the Danube, and the Thames also came up periodically. Other commercially important river systems in Asia or even South America did not figure. And the fact that hardly any cargo still moves up the Thames and its vast canal network seemed immaterial. The point was that, if the Magdalena River were to carry Colombia forward to a future of progress, development, and modernity, it would have to become more like its North American and European counterparts. In other words, to realize its true and full potential as a historical subject, the river would have to undergo the hydro-infrastructural analog to racial whitening. The superintendent of a port terminal that handles large volumes of riverboat cargo underlined the Mississippi's role as the normative standard, though with a patriotic twist: "The Mississippi is what a river should be as a logistical artery. If well managed, the Magdalena will be like the Mississippi, only prettier!" Reflecting on this later, I couldn't help but draw parallels with eugenicists who saw racially "improved" postcolonial populations as superior to the "pure" stock of the imperial metropole.

A partner in one of the larger companies invested in fluvial transport—I'll call him Jonathan—commented on the unusually favorable hydrological conditions at the time of our meeting: "At the moment, there's lots of water after a long period of drought. The river is flowing beautifully. It's showing everyone it can be a disciplined river. And when there's a disciplined river—a river that's navigable 24/7, 365 days a year—disciplined business follows." Jonathan attributed subjectivity to the river, endowing it with agency and human characteristics, but he also recognized the need for disciplinary technologies to "keep the water where it should be" (in the navigable channel). "A common misconception," he said, "is that dredging is what we need. Dredging should really only be about 10 percent of the project, whereas 90 percent should be diking and canalizing. Dredging is a temporary solution—sediment always returns. The problem here is that water is not being channeled into the right places. We need seven to eight feet of water year-round, and if water overflows the channel, flooding adjacent fields, tributaries, or swamps, we cannot achieve that." The infrastructural work of channeling was tied to the ontological work of separating land from water in an amphibious world that rarely respects this distinction.[21]

In other conversations, I found this was not the only categorical divide that needed buttressing: many industry representatives I spoke with referenced the importance of separating "us" from "them." Though not always uttered explicitly, these pronouns indexed an underlying social order divided between the fluvial transport companies and riverside communities. One security expert described this as an operational matter of risk management: "The more contact our equipment and personnel have with *pueblos ribereños*, the more exposed we are to theft, vandalism, extortion—basically to losses of all kinds. If we could eliminate the need for stopovers, I would sleep much better." A human resources officer saw the problem in more social terms: "Although

---

21 Gutiérrez Campo and Escobar Jiménez, "Territorio anfibio y despojo"; Camargo, "Land Born of Water"; Fals Borda, *Historia doble de la Costa*.

our guys come from those towns and villages [of the Lower Magdalena], they have been carefully selected and thoroughly trained. They're different from the general population," he said, implying a taxonomic hierarchy with quality gradations. "But when our vessels stop along the way, even though disembarking is prohibited without the captain's permission, the temptation is still there." These situations were common, since adverse hydrological conditions often forced towboat-and-barge convoys to moor for extended periods of time (sometimes overnight) along a stretch of riverbank. The ultimate solution, invariably, was channeling—an intervention that, once implemented, would eliminate the need for stoppages by establishing a permanently navigable shipping lane. Enforcing one divide (between land and water) would simultaneously reinforce the other (between fluvial transport companies and riverside communities). Ontological mixing—or miscegenation, in racial terms—was a threat the navigability plan promised to neutralize by enabling continuous navigation throughout the entire journey from port to port.

* * *

CAPTAINS AND CREW members saw things differently. At first, I naively broached the subject with them in binary terms: Did they endorse or oppose the sociotechnical imaginaries manifested in the navigability plan? This question rarely elicited a straightforward answer. They were not against the idea of improving navigation, for many agreed that the river had been ignored for too long by the government's transport and infrastructure agencies, especially relative to roads. But they were not exactly in favor of the project either, and for various reasons. Its success, some feared, would lead to labor restructuring by rendering their experience and expertise, perhaps their jobs, superfluous. Many more doubted the project would ever come to fruition given the history of similar attempts that ultimately amounted to nothing. Some worried the expectations generated by the plan would magnify the pressure to work faster, harder, and longer—and since improvements were unlikely to materialize, this would only make their jobs more difficult and dangerous. A few referenced the inevitability of climate change: heightened seasonal volatility, worsening droughts, increased sedimentation—all of which seemed to portend more, not fewer, navigational challenges, which would again fall on their shoulders. Still others, despite their profession, disliked the technocratic hubris of notions like "fluvial expressway," which (in the words of one seasoned pilot) "sought to make this river what it was not meant to be."

A common thread running through these conversations with riverboat workers was that the navigability plan could never contend with larger and more powerful forces. One crew member explained that the river's fickle nature ensured that interventions would always fail: "These projects will not work, nor will they ever work. I say that because all this money is being spent on dredging over here, and then the river decides to change course." A telling expression I learned from them suggested that everyone's fate is in the river's hands: *el río le pone, el río le quita*, or "the river gives, the river takes away."[22] The tacit reference, of course, is biblical (from Job 1:21), drawing a not-so-subtle comparison between the river and the Lord. In this and other discussions of the river's future, God and nature, though not one and the same, would ultimately determine whether the waterway would become more or less navigable. Irrespective of the immense financial resources and impressive technical expertise behind it, the capacity of a public-private partnership to transform the Magdalena River basin paled in comparison to natural and supernatural forces. "God is almighty, the river does what it wants, and we humans are relatively powerless," a young helmsman told me.[23] Such statements, not uncommon, always caught my attention for their clear-cut distinctions between categories, especially when they emphasized the human and made sure to identify the speaker as belonging to it. In contrast to posthumanist commitments to ontological fluidity, riverboat workers upheld distinctions between the human, the natural, and the supernatural as fundamental to their livelihoods, indeed to their survival.[24] For a racialized workforce, positioned somewhere between the realms of subject/object and nature/culture, ontological certainty is part of the process of asserting humanity that has been historically denied.

---

22 Alluding to the interplay of fortune and misfortune, people apply this expression to all sorts of situations concerning their relationship with the waterway: fisherfolk whose livelihood depended on the river until their boat was swept away by the current; townspeople who lost their advantageous position when the channel suddenly changed course; farmers who irrigated their bankside fields only to find them later eroded by excess flow.

23 For a characteristic account of divine intervention determining hydrological conditions, see Davis, *Magdalena*, 269–70.

24 Examining experiments in sculpting waves to hide landforms, like islands, Stefan Helmreich offers a useful discussion of the difference between "environmental infrastructures," in the work of someone like Casper Bruun Jensen, and "infranature," which "keeps analytically audible the continued durability of the concept of nature." Helmreich makes another helpful contrast: "If the supernatural is that which is transcendent—above nature, outside of history—then the infranatural names that which becomes immanent—inside the putatively natural order of things." Helmreich, "How to Hide an Island," 84. See also Carse, "Nature as Infrastructure."

FIGURE 2.4. *Chalupa* loaded with passengers and cargo, Las Cruces, Santander.
Source: photograph by author.

My visits to riverside towns usually involved exhilarating but painful rides on rickety speedboats, or *chalupas*, that serve as the primary mode of transport for passengers traveling upriver and down (figure 2.4). Flat-bottom, fiberglass vessels without a keel, *chalupas* are designed to skim the surface of the water, the propeller on the outboard motor requiring minimal depth. However, to compensate for the high cost of fuel and the rate at which their motors consume it, *chalupas* frequently operate at full capacity, even squeezing in an extra passenger or two when demand is high. And once packed to the gills with passengers and loaded with their possessions and some additional cargo, their draft increases substantially relative to their small size, and their freeboard, or the distance between the waterline and the upper edge of the hull, sinks to nearly zero. This makes these vessels surprisingly susceptible to running aground in shallow water and to taking on water. Indeed, it is not uncommon for *chalupas* to capsize, occasionally losing cargo, even passengers, to the river's deceptively swift current. The Magdalena is a wide and shallow river with one of the highest sediment loads in the world, and sandbanks (as well as *islitas*, the "little islands" that appear in the channel) are constant concerns for *chaluperos*.[25] Accumulated sediment in critical locations can cause delays, accidents, even casualties.[26]

When *chalupas* are in motion, it is practically impossible to have a conversation with the skipper or his lone crewman. On land, however, *chaluperos* are usually game for a chat. My assumption was that the navigability plan would make their difficult jobs easier—after all, the objectives of reducing sedimentation and ensuring a navigable channel seemed tailored to their needs—and some did welcome attention to fluvial transport after years of neglect. Those more informed about the plan, however, depicted it as a threat. They reminded me that small watercraft like theirs must give way to the massive towboat-and-barge convoys, which have limited maneuverability, are slow to stop, and generate a substantial wake. Increased commercial traffic on the river would, therefore, force *chaluperos* to avoid the main channel and to explore unfamiliar branches that could present unknown hazards. When I would point out that the river's current conditions are not exactly easy to navigate, the response I got was usually some variation of the popular phrase: *Más vale malo conocido que bueno por conocer* (Better the devil you know than the one you don't). "This is our river; we know its true nature," an experienced pilot told me in the town of Puerto Wilches. "Once the government and their engineers get their hands on it, who knows what will happen, what it will become." This uncertainly is magnified by the fact that *chaluperos* have had little, if any, input into the planning process. Relative to the value of the cargo and capital prioritized by the navigability plan, their concerns, and therefore the lives and livelihoods of their passengers, are inconsequential.

* * *

ON A VISIT to the town of Puerto Berrío, I was fortunate to get invited to a meeting of the local fishermen's association. On the agenda that day was the navigability plan, which (in its current iteration) was promising to return commercial shipping to this stretch of river. Towboat-and-barge convoys from the coast currently stop 100 kilometers downstream in Barrancabermeja, and river traffic in these parts is limited to smaller watercraft, but the plan was prom-

---

25 Restrepo Ángel, *Los sedimentos del río Magdalena*; Hori and Saito, "Classification, Architecture, and Evolution."

26 For a series of interventions that place sediment at the center of the social and historical study of water and rivers, see Parrinello and Kondolf, "The Social Life of Sediment." For the political economy of sedimentation and its consequences for labor, see Bear, *Navigating Austerity*.

FIGURE 2.5. *Pescadores* in open water, Magdalena River. Source: photograph by author.

ising to move the inland head of navigation well upriver. The association's membership was meeting that day to discuss the opportunities and dangers presented by this prospect.

The meeting brought together leaders of Puerto Berrío's fishing community as well as other interested parties, such as representatives of local NGOs, and was moderated by an advisory consultant (*asesor*). The consultant, whom I will call Julio, presided from a desk in the front of the room, in suit and tie, while the more humbly dressed participants were assembled in a circle of plastic chairs. Introducing the gathering, Julio delivered a virtuoso performance of procedural propriety before inviting everyone to introduce themselves. After a few introductions, a prominent fisherman I'll call Enrique stood up, stated his name and profession, and proceeded to register his commentary on the navigability plan and its potential impacts on fishing (figure 2.5). "The government has big plans for the Magdalena River," he reminded the group, "and included within those big plans are lots of actors and institutions, both public and private. *El pescador* is not one of them. If the river is going to become more navigable, our back is against the wall." Enrique emphasized that he was not advocating an oppositional stance: "We're not in disagreement with the objective to turn the river into an expressway. What we're saying is that when the government decides to create a fluvial corridor, we don't want to be forced to move to Medellín or Bucaramanga [the closest major cities]." And he extended his plea to other livelihoods that depend equally on their access to the river: "This goes for us *pescadores* as well as the *cascajeros* and *areneros* (small-scale gravel and sand collectors): we want to be able to carry on with our ancestral activities right here in our territory, to continue to exist."

Enrique sustained his argument for another few minutes before the consultant, Julio, took it upon himself to intervene. Julio urged everyone to take a "panoramic view of the problematic" rather than getting bogged down in "complaints" (*quejas*). He criticized Enrique for "giving a speech" and, gesturing at me, for "protesting in front of a neutral observer." This irked me, since my sole reason for attending the meeting was to hear what Enrique and others had to say and because Julio was using me as a foil in his bid to regain control. However, upon reflection, I realized something deeper was unfolding. In Colombia, advisory consultants like Julio are frequently contracted by popular organizations, social movements, or other grassroots groups to help achieve their political objectives. These consultants may have some connection to the people they are hired to serve, but they are useful precisely because they belong to other, more valued categories of personhood. Being better educated, dressing in professional attire, speaking "without an accent" (that is, according to the linguistic norms of Bogotá or other parts of the highland interior), having lighter skin, being male: these are qualities that enable them to mediate successfully across the ontological divides separating those they represent from institutions of power. As I read through my field notes, I realized that in recognizing me as a "neutral observer," Julio was drawing affinities between the two of us to bolster his own position of superiority. I was reminded that, during my fieldwork, I often benefit from the very same forms of privilege and that the principles implied—objectivity, invisibility—underpin both ethnography and whiteness. During the meeting, however, not wanting to disrupt the conversation, I kept silent. It would not be unfair to call this complicity.

Later that day I met with a septuagenarian I will call Don Raúl, whose relationship to the river is indicative of the collective trauma felt by people from the region due to recurring cycles of violence centered on the waterway. As we walked and talked, he regaled me with stories from his days commanding commercial riverboats and working for the fluvial inspector's office. He recalled a time when Puerto Berrío was the region's commercial hub, and both barge convoys and passenger steamers would stop over on their way upriver. As the department of Antioquia's main riverport, Puerto Berrío handled all the goods coming from the coast or from overseas on their way to the industrious city of Medellín, and this brought wealth and status to the town. Those boom times eventually came to an end with the building of railways, roads, and bridges— all of which reduced the demand for fluvial transport and led the government to defer maintenance on the navigable channel. Don Raúl's recollections were infused with a sense of sadness, no doubt stemming from his nostalgia for Puerto Berrío's golden age. But Don Raúl also lived through the height of the armed conflict in Colombia, when Puerto Berrío was one of the epicenters of violence, the site of numerous massacres and countless disappearances, and the waters surrounding the town were overflowing with dead bodies.[27]

Puerto Berrío was once a stronghold of the National Liberation Army (ELN) and other leftist groups, which lasted until the right-wing United Self-Defense Forces of Colombia (AUC) and the Colombian military with support from the United States began their systematic annihilation of anything resembling insurgent activity. Another paramilitary group with a ruthlessly simple name, Death to Kidnappers (MAS), eventually launched its own counterinsurgency war, assassinating "subversives" to protect its wealthy patrons from abduction. When the paramilitaries officially demobilized, criminal organizations composed of their former members eventually infiltrated the port, capitalizing on its strategic location for the distribution of drugs, weapons, and other contraband, as they have done and continue to do throughout Colombia. For decades, fishermen and riverboat pilots would regularly find floating body parts from corpses that had been dumped upstream. When observers now comment on the Magdalena River as "Colombia's largest mass grave," they are often referring to the eddies and sandbars just downstream from Puerto Berrío. To this day, residents are said to avoid eating fish for fear that they may discover a severed finger or toe.

Compared to his somber reflections on the past, Don Raúl's projections for the future were bright. Being a former riverman himself, he fully endorsed the government's plan to improve navigability and revive commercial shipping in the Middle Magdalena. The reactivation of fluvial transport, for Don Raúl, might allow his town to leave behind the traumas of its past; restoring the river to its former state represented a way out of endless cycles of criminality, violence, and terror. However, Don Raúl and more than a few others worried that dredging sections of accumulated sediment from the bed of the river might surface unpleasant histories that are better left forgotten or submerged.

---

27 Nieto, *Los escogidos*.

Although "to dredge" in Spanish (*dragar*) does not have the dual meaning associated with the verb in English, the image of a machine scooping up organic matter in which the bodies of the disappeared have long been buried haunted what was otherwise a promising prospect. Upholding the separations between past, present, and future—all the while relying on paradoxical temporalities that reanimate certain histories while rendering others obsolete—is an ontological feat the project planners ultimately hoped to pull off.

* * *

THE STRATEGICALLY POSITIONED town of El Banco, some 215 kilometers downstream from Puerto Berrío, sits at the confluence of the Magdalena and Cesar rivers. Legend has it that, when Spanish explorers arrived in 1536 on their journey upriver in search of El Dorado, they named it Barbudo in reference to the bearded faces they encountered there. Attempts to establish a Spanish settlement on the site were repeatedly thwarted by the indigenous Chimilas, however, who waged a protracted war against the colonial state in defense of their territories, which ranged across the lower Magdalena valley and into the surrounding mountains. It began as a battle between imperial aggressors and rebellious natives, but Marta Herrera Ángel argues that, by the eighteenth century, the Manichean logic of Chimilas versus Españoles simplified a complex, ambiguous set of identities and interests—a simplification that was politically useful to both sides of the conflict.[28] This distinction, though rooted in the racial classification system used throughout the colonial period, had to be imposed on a heterogenous mixture of people with fluctuating political and territorial allegiances.

El Banco's origin story dates to 1680, when an emancipated Black man named José Domingo Ortiz, formerly enslaved in the nearby gold mines, led a group of freed men and women in search of refuge to settle at this auspicious river conflux. Ortiz named the settlement El Banco, either in reference to an especially pronounced riverbank or, according to some versions, after Benkos Biohó, the legendary leader of a maroon community in the hinterlands of Cartagena.[29] Ortiz and his followers occupied an ambiguous position—legally free but racially subordinated, which made their political and juridical status uncertain—even though they far outnumbered their enslaved counterparts in

---

28 Herrera Ángel, "'Chimilas' y 'Españoles.'"

29 Some sources date the foundation of El Banco to 1747, when José Fernando de Mier y Guerra was sent by the governor of Santa Marta to reclaim the town on behalf of the Spanish Crown. The town itself, however, recognizes the earlier date.

the lower Magdalena valley.[30] The location they chose, aside from giving them access to important waterways, was situated at the interstices of territory controlled by the Spanish colonial state and territory inhabited by Indigenous groups who maintained political, religious, and economic independence (the so-called Territorio Chimila).[31] From its inception, then, El Banco has been a liminal site, straddling the geographical and racial divides that define the social and environmental order of the Magdalena River basin and its constitutive taxonomies and hierarchies. In honor of the struggle for freedom exemplified by its founder and, possibly, its namesake, the town's official shield is bordered by a broken chain.

Today, El Banco is known far and wide as *la capital de la cumbia*, referencing its claim as the birthplace of the musical tradition renowned for fusing African, Indigenous, and European influences and the yearly festival celebrating its contemporary incarnations. In *cumbia*, some have seen the musical equivalent to *mestizaje*, a postracial unifier of the national imaginary; others have emphasized *cumbia*'s struggle for recognition within a social order that provincializes the cultural production of Black and mixed-race artists hailing from the coastal regions.[32] Not incidentally, El Banco also symbolizes the transition between the Middle and Lower Magdalena, and by some accounts serves as the gateway to *el Caribe colombiano*, despite the 200-odd kilometers separating it from the sea. Again, El Banco becomes significant to the social and environmental order of the Magdalena River basin, for it marks the boundary between *el interior* and *la costa*—ostensibly geographic designations that contain a raft of cultural, moral, and racial connotations. The ontological divides that govern gradations of value in Colombia depend, at least to some degree, on El Banco, and yet the town has long enabled people to mediate across these divides and to maneuver within the gaps between them.

On an average day, the town's residential areas may feel lethargic, but the commercial center pulses with energy. Thanks to its strategic location, El Banco serves as a marketplace for a range of goods—from agricultural products

---

30 Bonil-Gómez, "Free People of African Descent." According to the 1778–80 general census, "free people of all colors" (*libres de todos los colores*) accounted for 62 percent of the total population in the Caribbean coastal region, which in the Magdalena River valley would have referred mainly to people of African descent, whereas only 9 percent were registered as slaves. See Múnera, *El Fracaso de la nación*, 62.

31 For a map of the spatial organization of these territories, see Herrera Ángel, "'Chimilas' y 'Españoles,'" 9.

32 Flórez Bolívar, "Celebrando y redefiniendo"; Wade, *Music, Race, and Nation*.

FIGURE 2.6. Horse cart moving cargo between river and town, El Banco, Magdalena. Source: photograph by author.

to building materials to shipments of beer—which pass through on their way elsewhere, with local businesses taking a cut (figure 2.6). *Los banqueños* depend heavily on their ability to capitalize on connectivity, but that ability is not geographically guaranteed. The owner of one of the more successful businesses in town—a hardware store in operation for over sixty years—told me that the very thing that gave life to El Banco is also the bane of its existence. Sitting in the back office of his shop, with a window peering onto the river, I asked for his opinion of the navigability plan, expecting to hear optimism for potential commercial opportunities. Instead, the shop owner recounted a vivid history, illustrated by images stored on his mobile phone, of regular floods in which his property—indeed, much of the town center—was inundated by a river unconstrained by its banks. The more we spoke about flooding, the more I realized that, for this merchant and many of his neighbors, the navigability plan seemed to promise protection more than connection. When I pressed him about the commercial implications of an upsurge in fluvial shipping, he took me to the rear of the shop floor, where a loading dock that once enabled direct trade with riverboats had since been sealed off. "Our business no longer depends all that much on the river. Plus, the boats they're talking about [in the navigability plan] would float right past El Banco without batting an eye."

Other *banqueños*, merchants and residents alike, shared the view that they had little reason to expect prosperity from a fluvial expressway, were it eventually to materialize. For what had once been their town's distinguishing feature—its liminal position between the interior and the coast, its ability to straddle racial, geographical, even ontological divides—is now under threat. The ability of *banqueños* to capitalize on these divides depends on the continuous flow of people, vehicles, goods, and money through their town. As the navigability plan aspires to make that unnecessary—after all, the selling point of expressways is no stopping—the agency of *banqueños* to position themselves favorably within the social and environmental order of the Magdalena basin would be negated. And if El Banco, like all intermediary places, had once enabled the artificiality of categorical, territorial, or political divides to be revealed, the town now finds itself confronted with their hardening as valuable circulations increasingly bypass it altogether. It is no wonder, then, that protection rather than connection has become the topic of the day. Whereas proximity to the river once promised livelihoods, *banqueños* are increasingly concerned about simply staying above water.

Of the various interventions proposed by the navigability plan, dredging was the one said to offer the most hope. I was even shown photographs of protests during a recent flood event in which demonstrators held up signs with a curious slogan (¡No más sacos, no más mercados, la solución es el dragado!) that rejected aid in the form of clothing and food in favor of dredging. It did not immediately make sense to me why deepening the navigable channel would be the best way to reduce the river's propensity to flood until a local government official mentioned an earlier precedent: "People see the dredging operations currently underway as *pañitos de agua tibia* [literally 'lukewarm towelettes'; figuratively a 'Band-Aid solution']. Maybe twenty-five, thirty years back," he explained, "the policy was to dredge and use the spoil as fill to raise up the low-lying settlements [*las poblaciónes bajas*]. There are settlements today that do not flood thanks to material extracted from the riverbed years ago." Jumping ahead to the present, he emphasized what had changed: "These days, they no longer remove material from the channel, but rather scoop it out and throw it back in somewhere else. The next day that material has shifted, maybe even back to its original location. People see that as doing nothing, as wasting resources." When *banqueños* plead for dredging to save them from flooding, they are appealing to a technical solution that, in ontological terms, works by reorganizing the boundaries between land and water to convert a source

FIGURE 2.7. Fluvial Inspectorate, El Banco, Magdalena. Source: photograph by author.

of threat into a form of protection. In doing so, they recognize that aligning themselves with the objectives of the navigability plan and laying claim to its material debris is the most strategic way to safeguard their homes, their businesses, perhaps even their lives.[33]

* * *

ACROSS FROM EL Banco's eighteenth-century cathedral, perched above a crumbling concrete embankment dating from the 1930s, is the office of the Fluvial Inspectorate (figure 2.7). In Colombia, the figure of the fluvial inspector was created by national decree in the 1880s to regulate steamboat companies operating along the river.[34] The spirit of the decree was evident in its antecedents from the 1840s and 1850s, when fluvial transport companies themselves demanded the government intervene to regulate *bogas* (boatmen)—a racialized

---

33 For a kindred analysis of small-scale gold miners and their productive engagement with leftovers, by-products, and waste as future-making practices on the "margins of capitalism," see Jaramillo, "Mining Leftovers."

34 Solano, *Puertos, sociedad y conflictos*, 48.

workforce long seen as unreliable, even ungovernable—and Congress complied by creating the Inspector de Bogas, based in Barranquilla.[35] This would later become one of the headquarters of fluvial inspection with a remit that expanded beyond labor discipline to include the mandate to keep detailed records on all vessels, cargo, captains, and crews. There are now thirty-three Fluvial Inspectorates across Colombia—in some cases, the only visible presence of the state for miles around—and they are responsible for enforcing the legal and regulatory apparatus that governs transport of all kinds along inland waterways. Nearly a third of them are sited on the Magdalena River, and though by no means the only governing body exercising authority over the basin, they help maintain its social and environmental order.

I arrived at the Fluvial Inspectorate in El Banco without an appointment. The security guard standing watch took my business card and within minutes the fluvial inspector himself was summoning me inside. Born in the nearby river port of La Gloria, Roberto studied transport engineering in the highland interior. Upon graduation in 1994, he applied for public service and was awarded the job of fluvial inspector. After a few short stints in other parts of the country, Roberto was assigned to El Banco. He had been stationed there ever since.

Our conversation about the river began, as many do, looking back to the "golden age of fluvial navigation in Colombia" when "the Magdalena River was the backbone [columna vertebral] of development." Roberto was referring to the 1940s when, he said, "everything revolved around the river." The period of decline that followed was no accident: "The government started to build railways, not to complement fluvial transport, but to replace it. Then they started building highways, which sank the railways." The culprit was politicking (politiquería) by big businessmen (grandes empresarios): vague but accurate descriptors for the political and economic interests that stood to gain from each successive wave of infrastructure building and from the shift from river to rail to road. The deterioration of navigability, however, was not simply due to willful neglect; in Roberto's account, it stemmed from the mismanagement of the entire hydrographic basin. "The policy had been to channel the current by blocking adjacent ciénagas [wetlands] and meandering branches," he recalled. "That was an error, since when the river would rise, it would overflow and flood riverside towns and villages, as there was nowhere to absorb

---

35 For the successive decrees instituted in the nineteenth and twentieth centuries to regulate fluvial navigation, see Solano, *Puertos, sociedad y conflictos*, 47–49.

the excess flow. This was compounded by the conversion of the riparian zone into oil palm plantations and cattle ranches. Big landholders took possession of these territories, dried up the wetlands, and cut down the trees, which also caused major sedimentation." In Roberto's political ecology of governmental negligence and rampant enclosure, the river emerged as victim and he as its defender.[36]

As Roberto described the injustices suffered by the waterway, he combined the technical mindset of the engineer with the moral indignation of the conservationist: "They abandoned the river, as much on the environmental side as on the navigation side. When I got here, the Ministry of Transport [his employer] had fluvial monitoring stations, they did research, they had agreements with universities abroad, they did simulations of water dynamics—all that is now gone." Rocking his head disapprovingly, Roberto expressed his concern for the river in terms of its function as a transport corridor: "They abandoned the fluvial mode, which once united the country from north to south." When our conversation turned to the current moment, in which attention seemed to be returning to the waterway, Roberto noted this shift with sarcasm: "After everything, they [the government] have just now discovered that the river is suffering [*el río está en agonía*]." I asked whether he felt policymakers might finally be acknowledging past mistakes and trying to correct them. "On paper, yes. In reality, no. They haven't even read everything that's been written. So many studies, so much analysis [*diagnóstico*]," he said, repeating the last word three times for emphasis. There is "no execution, no action. Whenever a new president takes office, they produce a new analysis and then comes another and another."

Roberto held more regard for the optimistic visions emerging from the fluvial transport industry, especially the multinational companies investing heavily in recent years. In the midst of our conversation, he cued up a promotional video made by one of these industrial heavyweights, which aligned with his argument about the abandonment of the river and the need to "reactivate Colombia's primary fluvial artery, which had been the country's most important economic resource fifty years ago." Roberto reclined in his chair as we watched over ten minutes of eye-popping visuals backed by a voice-over that promised to raise fluvial navigation on the Magdalena to international standards. Both of us were transfixed by the video's aesthetic quality, the scale of the technology on display, and the rhetorical power of the narrative. It felt

---

36 See Randle, "Missing Power."

somewhat uncomfortable to be admiring the prowess of the private sector in the office of a public servant, but when the spectacle ended, Roberto lit upon an unexpected detail: the satellite monitoring system the company was setting up, which would allow it to track the precise location of vessels on the river at all times, whom they belong to, where they are heading, what cargo they are transporting, and other useful information. Roberto added an important detail: the system would be shared with both the Ministry of Transport and the navy, which meant that he would have access to the data. "This would be a huge improvement on our current system," Roberto admitted, "since each inspection station currently has its own unique registry, its own database, which we send to headquarters in Bogotá." This act of corporate self-interest disguised as a commitment to the public good was met by Roberto with a sigh of relief: "Thanks to them, we will finally be able to have a national fluvial registry."

Roberto's enthusiasm for the satellite monitoring system was not altogether surprising, given the nature of his job. After all, his primary function was to uphold the legal and regulatory framework governing inland fluvial transport. And our long conversation did touch upon a number of such duties: checking vessel registrations and pilot licenses; registering statistics on passengers, crew, and cargo; coordinating with law enforcement agencies; devising navigation safety campaigns; and more. However, throughout our conversation it became clear that Roberto was much more than a transport cop, both in how he understood his position and in what he was dedicating his energy to achieving. Rather than simply enforcing the Magdalena basin's social and environmental order, Roberto was working hard to envision and create another order altogether in which the river would be properly cared for, both by the public authorities tasked with its management and by all other actors involved.

This was evident in a slideshow Roberto had presented to the mayor of El Banco and other local politicians, in which his ambitions had far exceeded his bailiwick. In the presentation, Roberto had proposed his original design and plan for the redevelopment of the town's waterfront, complete with diagrams of pedestrian walkways and renderings of flood control infrastructure. ("They didn't pay attention," he remarked.) He also gave me a copy of one of his self-published, quasi-official newsletters—nearly thirty elaborately illustrated pages packed with content, ranging from an analysis of the shrinking remit of fluvial inspectors and a detailed five-hundred-year history of the river to photographs of himself floating on a boat through the town's flooded streets and some of his son and dog promoting the use of life jackets. The majority of the newsletter, however, presented an impassioned case for restoring dignity both to the Fluvial

Inspectorate and to the river itself. Various pages were peppered with rhetorical questions and inspirational quotes, in yellow block lettering, suggesting that increased resources and greater autonomy would enable him to realize his commitments and aspirations. His vision for the future of fluvial navigation appeared in the form of a montage containing a mixture of vessels, some currently in operation (like the *chalupa* and the pusher tug), some artifacts of history (such as the steamboat and the *piragua*), and one (a hydrofoil) entirely unknown in these parts (at the center of this image, curiously, is a close-up of a baby's face). If one could deduce an alternative social and environmental order from Roberto's prolific output, it would be one in which the ontological framework that divides subjects from objects and assigns hierarchical gradations of value is flattened. All modes of fluvial transport and types of watercraft would be treated equally, regardless of whom they serve, and could safely and peacefully coexist. Meanwhile, river towns and their inhabitants would be shielded from the negative aspects of life along a major waterway while benefiting from the positive ones. Roberto's vision felt unrealistic, perhaps even utopian, but no more so than all the other projections being made for the river's future.

Leaving the Fluvial Inspectorate, I paused for lunch and then wandered down to the embankment to write additional notes while watching the boats float by. What I didn't expect to see was a full-blown towboat-and-barge convoy belonging to one of the fluvial transport companies I had just been discussing with Roberto. This felt like a stroke of serendipity, as if the universe were somehow catering to the concerns and curiosities animating my fieldwork, serving up my objects of inquiry on a platter. I knew such feelings were nefarious holdovers from an age in which researchers—especially male, white, European or North American—felt empowered to go anywhere and do anything and expected the world to comply. Yet I still felt giddy at the good fortune of catching a glimpse of this gigantic rig in action.

I watched as the convoy slid downstream, trying to discern what sort of cargo its barges were carrying (most were of the liquid cargo variety, which meant their tanks were probably full of crude oil). Just then a support launch carrying two men dropped into the water and zipped in my direction. After tying up at the base of the embankment, the more senior of the two walked quickly past, while his subordinate lingered behind. I learned that they had set off from Barrancabermeja two days earlier on their way to Cartagena, and they were stopping here to file paperwork with the fluvial inspector. Our chat was cut short by the speedy return of the captain, who paused for a few pleasantries. I managed to exchange phone numbers with both men, which felt like an accomplishment, but my excitement waned as they fired up their motor-

FIGURE 2.8. Idle equipment belonging to Navelena in Barrancabermeja, Santander. Source: photograph by author.

boat and quickly faded from sight. This brought me back to my conversations in El Banco that had cast doubt on the benefits that would accompany an increase in shipping traffic along the waterway. A brief chat with a captain or crew member might indeed be all they could reasonably hope for.

*　*　*

BACK IN BARRANCABERMEJA, on my 2017 visit to follow the progress of the navigability plan, I waited until well after 9 a.m. to make my way over to Navelena's office, but upon arrival found the front door locked—and not just locked as in closed, but with a chain and padlock. A sheet of paper taped to the inside of the window offered further instructions: "Navelena informs you that for the management of correspondence, documentation, deliveries, or to contact one of the members of our team, you must make your way to the security guard at the entrance to the parking lot who will attend to your request." Peering inside, I noticed that the reception desk where I announced my arrival on my last visit the year before had been removed. In its place was a pool of water that had accumulated on the floor after the previous night's heavy rains. The uniformed, sunglasses-wearing *guachimán* (as watchmen are sometimes called) deputized to speak on behalf of Navelena was of little help. We shared a laugh about the irony of a flooded office belonging to the company responsible for managing the river, but all he could do was register my name and telephone number.

The next day, while visiting a small riverside community on the outskirts of Barrancabermeja, I stumbled across a similar sight. A fleet of nearly a dozen motorboats emblazoned with the Navelena logo lay dormant in an impromptu junkyard (figure 2.8). Resting alongside them was a trio of hydraulic tracked excavators, now retired. In its early days of operation, Navelena had put these machines to work as makeshift dredge rigs by mounting them on flat-top pontoon barges—four of which had also been left here to rust in the humid tropical air. Protected by the river on one side and a razor wire fence on the other, located in a shaded muddy lot along a secluded country road, this cemetery of decommissioned equipment remained concealed from the casual passerby. Yet it was the physical remainder of a public fiasco that had already transpired in full view.

In March 2017, after years of delays and setbacks in which Navelena struggled constantly to secure financial backing and simultaneously comply with its contractual obligations, Cormagdalena, the agency with oversight of the public-private partnership set up to execute the navigability plan, declared that partnership void. This news did not come as a shock to many, since the firm with the majority stake (87 percent) in the partnership—the Brazilian construction and engineering giant Odebrecht—had been embroiled in high-profile corruption scandals since the arrest of its president, Marcelo Odebrecht, in 2015. Odebrecht was at the center of the Operation Car Wash investigation, in which former executives of the Brazilian state oil company, Petrobras, were found to have colluded with politicians and construction groups to extract billions of dollars in kickbacks in exchange for contracts. In December 2016, the US Department of Justice revealed that Odebrecht had paid $788 million in bribes across twelve Latin American countries, Colombia included, for lucrative infrastructure deals—the Magdalena River project foremost among them. Financiers quickly retracted their support, and after a few unsuccessful attempts to sell Odebrecht's stake and court other creditors, Navelena collapsed along with the project as a whole.

In the aftermath of this spectacular debacle, many casual observers I spoke with felt let down by the public and private actors implicated in the case, yet remained optimistic about the navigability plan even in its prolonged state of suspension.[37] Everyone connected even tangentially to fluvial transport demanded that someone take responsibility for maintaining a navigable channel by dredging problematic locations. Those in the fluvial transport industry tended to express critical views, but mainly about specific details of the former plan—how much emphasis had been given to dredging versus channeling or the amount of money allocated to engineering works upstream rather than in the estuary. For them, Navelena's disintegration was "for the best," in the words of one corporate executive—it was an opportunity to advocate for measures better serving their specific interests. Indeed, shortly after the initial fallout subsided, a committee was promptly assembled to form another public-private partnership to execute a bigger and better plan. When I pressed interlocutors about the lies, bribes, and cover-ups, these were quickly dismissed as individual transgressions, aberrant mischief. Since the illegal and unethical practices in question were associated with actors and institutions endowed with normative whiteness, they resisted categorization as systemic failures.[38] This allowed the project to emerge unscathed from the corruption scandal—if anything, its appeal and viability were thereafter enhanced.

---

37 Here I am thinking with work on suspension as inherent to infrastructure projects. See Uribe, "Suspensión."

38 Sarah Muir and Akhil Gupta remind us that "perceptions of corruption can map all too easily onto longstanding racialized sociogeographic distinctions of development and modernity." Muir and Gupta, "Rethinking the Anthropology of Corruption." See also Doshi and Ranganathan, "Towards a Critical Geography."

3

Securing Flow

On an ordinary Wednesday in the port of Cartagena, the workday started off with a bang—two, in fact. Workers in a naval shipyard were busy repairing a commercial river barge when an explosion went off, leaving five dead and seventeen injured. Half an hour later, the same fate befell a similar vessel in a neighboring shipyard just a few kilometers away, taking one more life and wounding an additional five. Raging fires ensued, sending two columns of black smoke billowing into the sky as rescue workers rushed victims to nearby hospitals. Media outlets speculated on possible perpetrators, but the bomb squad dispatched to investigate found no evidence of foul play. The simultaneity of the blasts was deemed coincidental, as were two other details: despite taking place in different shipyards, the explosions had struck barges owned by the same company, and the repairs on both were being performed by the same contractor. Ruling the event an uncanny accident, Cartagena's fire chief hypothesized that flammable gases accumulating in the tanks of the barges had been ignited by sparks. While victims' families would mourn the tragedy a while longer, the normal operation of the port was only temporarily disrupted.

Around the same time, another disruption stalled the nearby port of Barranquilla. A crew from the port authority, during routine measurements of the harbor's access channel, found its depth alarmingly low. The harbor master issued an alert and restricted entry to vessels with under 8.3 meters draft, citing unusually high sedimentation in the estuary where the Magdalena River meets the Caribbean Sea. For four days, larger ships either had to drop anchor and wait or reroute to a nearby port. The mayor of Barranquilla urgently summoned his risk management committee to evaluate the potential costs of a prolonged slowdown in port operations. The following day, he joined the governor of Atlántico (the surrounding department) in declaring a public emergency, thus activating a legal mechanism that would permit the national government to expedite the contracting of a dredging company. Within a week, the Belgian firm Jan de Nul had signed a contract worth 6 billion pesos (about $2 million), and the *Pedro Álvares Cabral*, a high-powered dredger, was sailing toward Barranquilla. Working tirelessly for ten days, the twenty-two-person crew removed over 340,000 cubic meters of sediment, deepening the access channel to approximately 12 meters (or 39.5 feet, the Panamax standard). The end of the emergency was promptly declared, and port operations resumed.

When I first heard about the shipyard explosions in Cartagena, guerrilla insurgency came immediately to mind. After all, attacks on strategically important infrastructures, as well as efforts to protect them, have been a recurring feature of Colombia's long-running armed conflict.[1] The most frequent targets have been things like electricity networks, oil pipelines, and transport corridors, while port facilities have faced their fair share of threats. But following on the heels of a historic peace accord that was being promoted as an economic opportunity, this case seemed to point in another direction: promptly declared an industrial accident, blame was assigned to volatile materials, not rebellious militants. The same could be said of the disruption to port operations in Barranquilla: the culprit was accumulated sediment, not entrenched ideology. But the underlying problem was the same: as with previous attacks attributed to the FARC or ELN, these incidents threatened the infrastructural networks undergirding the Colombian economy and linking it to international markets. Even as guerrilla insurgents were losing potency, protecting

---

1 Parish, "Burning and Rebuilding Bridges." See also Zeiderman, "Concrete Peace." The role of infrastructure in the armed conflict is not confined to the binary logic that positions the state as builder and the guerrilla as threat. See Uribe, Otero-Bahamón, and Peñaranda, "Hacer el estado."

valuable circulation remained a key priority for the state and for companies doing business in the country.

Supply chain security is the name given to this increasingly important yet relatively unexamined dimension of global capitalism, in which spaces of economic connectivity—such as docks, shipyards, vessels, vehicles, parking lots, offices, databases, and warehouses—are governed by a range of techniques designed to minimize threats to the smooth and seamless circulation of cargo (figure 3.1).[2] This is the domain of logistics—indeed, it has been said that supply chain security is the logistics industry's governing rationality. And like other security paradigms, supply chain security organizes the world according to certain categories (who or what is to be protected and from who or what), calculations (how valuable are the goods in question and what are the costs of protecting them), and probabilities (how likely are threats to materialize and how effective are the techniques used to manage them).[3] These organizing logics and optics allow the logistics industry to bring a wide range of actors, objects, and events into a single framework by rendering them commensurable as factors that either facilitate or threaten circulation.[4] This is what linked the emergencies that unfolded in Cartagena and Barranquilla, besides being located along the same stretch of Caribbean coastline. Regardless of whether combustible chemicals, submerged sandbanks, or armed insurgents were to blame, what mattered was how quickly and economically the normal operation of the transport network could be restored.[5]

2　In her wide-ranging analysis of logistics, Deborah Cowen argues, "The threat of disruption to the circulation of stuff has become such a profound concern to governments and corporations in recent years that it has prompted the creation of an entire architecture of security that aims to govern global spaces of flow." Cowen, *The Deadly Life of Logistics*, 2. For other work on the securitization of global supply chains, see Chalfin, "Recasting Maritime Governance in Ghana"; Eski, *Policing, Port Security and Crime Control*; Senu, "Stowaways, Seafarers and Ship Security." For a perspective from urban studies, see Silver, "Corridor Urbanism."

3　See Rushton, Croucher, and Baker, *The Handbook of Logistics*.

4　My analysis of supply chain security builds on studies of commensuration and value, especially Ashley Carse's thorough examination of environmental mitigation, which foregrounds the value-laden processes and hierarchical frameworks that determine what survives, what dies, and what flourishes. See Carse, "The Ecobiopolitics of Environmental Mitigation." I am also indebted to Pablo Jaramillo's examination of exchange and commensurability in clean energy and carbon markets. See Jaramillo, "Sites, Funds and Spheres."

5　This resonates with Foucault's genealogy of security as a mode of power distinct from discipline. For security, an event's cause or culprit is less important than maintaining circulation at an optimal level, and security mechanisms seek to return circulation to that

FIGURE 3.1. Perimeter fencing surrounding logistics hub, Magdalena River. Source: photograph by author.

When I interviewed logistics managers about these distinct yet related events, one thing stood out: the recurring focus on quantifying factors impeding circulation in monetary terms. Vessels damaged in the blasts, operational delays from idling ships, manual laborers killed or injured by the explosions, cubic meters of sediment dredged from the harbor: all were accounted for by a financial logic that made equipment, time, lives, and silt comparable. Insurance policies were a key part of the equation: payouts to the shipyards and their clients would have mitigated the financial burden caused by the explosions, while the injured workers and the families of the deceased also received compensation. And although the emergency dredging of Barranquilla's harbor was the national government's responsibility, it was also a financial calculation. I was not privy to exact figures, apart from the cost of the dredging contract, but it was evident that all threats to circulation were measured against the same metric, and that different values were assigned to each one.

level without undue attention given to any single disruption. See Foucault, *Security, Territory, Population*.

These differences reflect the fact that logistics works with and through hierarchical gradations of value—some industry-wide, others context-specific.[6] An example of the former is the separate pay scales for differently racialized workers onboard container ships and the unequal values assigned to their lives by both hijackers and maritime insurance companies.[7] Another is the patriarchal norms found throughout the logistics industry and the masculinist ideals permeating both boardrooms and dockyards.[8] These racial and gender hierarchies are endemic to logistics, irrespective of context. However, security protocols, despite their promise of universal applicability, also work with, on, and through situated social and spatial orders.[9] In Colombia, techniques of suspicion, surveillance, and protection both draw upon and recalibrate contextually specific valuations that rank subjects and objects alike. This is exemplified by the geo-racial distinction between Colombia's Andean interior and Caribbean coast, which was reflected in the value of the lives and limbs lost in the Cartagena shipyard explosions—miniscule in comparison to the value of the cargo bound for the highland cities of Bogotá and Medellín.

In the stories that follow, I pay close attention to the discursive and material work of securing smooth and uninterrupted flow along the Magdalena River. Drawing on ethnographic fieldwork among fluvial transport and logistics companies and interviews with their management teams, I examine the techniques deployed to protect their operations from interruption. Of primary interest are the categories, calculations, and probabilities through which these companies manage the many factors threatening to disrupt unencumbered circulation: from droughts, attacks, and pandemics to strikes, theft, and accidents.[10]

---

6 As Charmaine Chua, Martin Danyluk, Deborah Cowen, and Laleh Khalili put it, logistics "contributes to the material conditions through which the security and well-being of human and nonhuman lives are rendered subordinate to the imperative of smooth, efficient circulation." See Chua et al., "Introduction," 622.

7 Dua, *Captured at Sea*, 138–39. For the racial orders governing the global logistics industry and its constitutive components, see also Khalili, *Sinews of War and Trade*; Cowen, "Following the Infrastructures"; Lara, *Inland Shift*; Alimahomed-Wilson, "Unfree Shipping." For a parallel discussion of racialized logics underpinning security and surveillance, see Kahn, *Islands of Sovereignty*; Browne, *Dark Matters*; Benjamin, *Captivating Technology*. For an effort to think across these discussions, see Brooks and Best, "Prison Fixes and Flows."

8 Peano, "Gendering Logistics"; Chua, "Indurable Monstrosities"; Leivestad and Markkula, "Inside Container Economies."

9 Rothenberg, "Ports Matter"; Gambino, "The Georgian Logistics Revolution."

10 Achille Mbembe asks questions about the global condition that resonate with my analysis of logistics and supply chain capitalism: "As multiple wave fronts of calculation expand

But underpinning the logics and optics—the ways of thinking and seeing—proper to supply chain security are hierarchical orders that rank both human subjects and nonhuman objects according to their relative value. These value gradations are sometimes expressed in quantitative (or monetary) terms, while just as often they are based on qualitative rankings. With one eye trained on hierarchies specific to Colombia and the other focused on those endemic to the logistics industry worldwide, my aim is to show how logistics both depends upon and recalibrates the differential valuations that render some people and things security threats, while others are to be cared for and protected.

* * *

EARLY ON IN my research, I struggled to figure out how to approach the shipping and logistics companies operating along the river. In the past, my research had involved studying up, but mainly with municipal government agencies and their employees. Although states are institutional manifestations of the politically and economically powerful, the rank-and-file officials I came to know had class positions not dissimilar to my own. Moreover, the public nature of their jobs made them accustomed, even receptive, to inquiries from interested parties, ethnographers included (indeed, some of them were also trained anthropologists). I was now entering uncharted territory: large industrial firms, some with annual revenues in the billions (or hundreds of billions) of dollars, with no mandate for accountability or transparency, aside from their calculated strategies of public relations, marketing and communications, and corporate social responsibility.

As a shot in the dark, I wrote to a generic email address listed on the website of one such company explaining who I was and that I was interested to learn more about their operations. Within minutes I received a short yet positive response from the director of corporate affairs for the Latin America region, and less than an hour later another email arrived from someone even higher up suggesting we speak by phone. This took me by surprise, partly because I expected my inquiry to be ignored and partly because it seemed the com-

---

across the planet, incorporating more and more life and matter into systems of abstraction and 'machine reasoning,' it becomes urgent to resist an epistemic hegemony that reduces the earth to a financial problem and a problem of financial value. . . . Who will define the threshold or set the boundary that distinguishes between the calculable and the incalculable, between that which is deemed worthy and that which is deemed worthless, and therefore dispensable, or between what can and cannot be insured, what can and cannot be made to or allowed to circulate?" See Mbembe, "Futures of Life," 27–28.

pany had also taken an interest in me—not always a good thing for researchers studying powerful actors in Colombia. But this opportunity felt too good to pass up.

The following day I received a call from a mobile phone with a European country code. The high-level executive on the other end, whom I will call Henry, must have sensed astonishment in my voice, since he began by explaining why he was amenable to my initial message. "When your email came through," Henry said, "I was sitting next to our director of corporate affairs. She showed me your message and I thought, 'Wow, here's an email in Spanish from a researcher in London who appears to have a long-standing interest in Colombia. I grew up in London and my parents still live there, and I've been working in Colombia for decades.'" What really piqued Henry's interest, he allowed, was my name: "Austin Zeiderman," he stated didactically, pronouncing the surname as my family had always done; "such a curious combination. It's like oil and water!" I chuckled nervously, not yet sure what he meant, so Henry elaborated: "Zeiderman is a Jewish name, no? So what made your parents call you Austin?" This threw me for a loop: not only was this caliber of meeting unfamiliar, but my personal history was now the primary focus. I rattled off an awkward answer about my parents both admiring the writing of Saint Augustine but preferring the abbreviated version since neither was religious. I also explained that my paternal grandmother rejected my first name, insisting on calling me by my middle name, Gabriel, in honor of her long-deceased husband, as tradition dictated. This explanation must have been satisfactory, as our conversation then turned to the ins and outs of the logistics industry and the pleasures and challenges of working in Colombia.

Our phone call lasted for nearly an hour, and I came away startled at how fluid and productive it had been. I had been expecting tension, given that ethnographers are known to be critical of powerful figures, especially those possessing major wealth, as well as staunch defenders of the common people. And yet Henry seemed to treat me as a confidant—as someone with whom he shared a natural affinity—and despite my epistemological formation and ethical orientation, I had to admit I felt similarly. This would be the first of various exchanges we would have over the next few years—by phone, over email, and eventually in person—and it led to meetings with many of his colleagues as well as visits to his company's installations in Colombia. Each time we spoke, additional details of our family histories seemed to solidify our connection—most of them stemming from our respective relationship to diasporic Jewishness—and I sensed that this heightened Henry's interest in my research and willingness to support it. Although doors had previously opened on account of my whiteness, never before had this facet of my background been an asset. Though not entirely reducible to this single detail—I'm sure my educational pedigree also helped—my interpellation seemed to facilitate access to the restricted world of logistics. Acknowledging this feels dangerously close to endorsing the racist tropes that fuel global conspiracy theories; ignoring it would conceal the privileges and serendipities saturating the ethnographic endeavor.

* * *

THE LOGICS GOVERNING supply chain security came into greater focus during visits to fluvial transport and logistics companies. Some of the companies moving cargo along the river during the time of my research were relatively small and operated solely in Colombia, while others were subsidiaries of multinational firms that specialized in sourcing and transporting commodities for industrial clients worldwide. Many had been doing business in the country for decades, whereas others had recently taken a significantly more active role, investing in the creation of new multimodal supply chains centered on the Magdalena River with the aim of "reinventing logistics" in Colombia, as one promotional brochure promised. This investment was concentrated in and around the oil industry, whose nucleus is the riverfront city of Barrancabermeja, which is also the inland head of commercial navigation (figure 3.2). Large sums of money were being spent acquiring land, building infrastructure, and installing equipment at strategic locations along the 630-kilometer stretch between Barrancabermeja and the Caribbean coastal ports of Cartagena and Barranquilla, while fleets of towboats and barges were being expanded to move greater volumes of cargo—primarily crude oil and other petroleum products—downriver for export.

On the few occasions I was allowed inside logistics hubs, my visits inevitably began with security protocols. On one visit, I had flown in from Bogotá the day before, and upon arrival received a string of text messages with precise instructions. I was to appear at 8 a.m. the next morning at the company's office, where I would meet a member of the corporate social responsibility team in charge of my visit, whom I will call Lucia. I was also given a list of necessary items: jeans, long sleeve shirt, and safety work boots. I followed instructions and arrived a few minutes early to find Lucia waiting. She and the receptionist confirmed that my identification and insurance documents had already been verified and that all security checks had been completed. They outfitted me with safety equipment—high-visibility vest, hard hat, and protective glasses—and, noticing my boots were inadequate, attempted to find a pair that would fit (this was prior to the pandemic, so biosecurity protocols were less preva-

FIGURE 3.2. Ecopetrol oil refinery, Barrancabermeja, Santander. Source: photograph by author.

lent). Although I was not particularly concerned about my personal safety, providing my body with an adequate level of protection seemed to be a high priority for my hosts.

Once I had been properly equipped, Lucia ran through the stipulations of my visit. I would be taken to see the main functions of the installation, but I would be accompanied at all times and would have to ask permission before taking photographs. (Both precautions, incidentally, were for my own safety, as we would be around dangerous equipment and materials, and electronic devices could cause an explosion.) Meetings with various members of the management team had been arranged, and I would be allowed to take notes during these meetings, even record them, but I would not be permitted to use any specific information about the company or any direct quotations. The company had one official spokesperson, whom I was not scheduled to meet, so everything said during my interviews would have to be treated as background. Although moments before I had received considerate attention to my personal safety, I now started to feel like a security threat. Regardless, I agreed to the terms presented, as I would with other companies, since my access to their operations was predicated on them.

As a result, the following accounts have had to undergo adaptations beyond the standard conventions of ethnographic writing. Some details have been left out while others have been changed, but always with the intention of retaining their original significance. Pseudonyms are used to maintain anonymity without sacrificing narrative flow, and job titles are given to provide context. Although descriptions of specific sites and individuals sometimes appear, these are often based on visits to different locations or conversations with various people, and occasional direct quotations are composites of statements made by multiple sources. Though bordering in some cases on fictionalization, these adaptations adhere strictly to standards of rigor and authenticity and are necessary compromises between, on the one hand, my intention to foreground empirical details and contextual specificity and, on the other hand, my desire to comply with legal and ethical protocols. I mention these adaptations here, rather than in a footnote, since they are intrinsic to the security logics governing the logistics industry—indeed, they are the epistemological and representational manifestation of those logics.

Once I had agreed to Lucia's stipulations, she issued me a visitor badge and proposed we head straight to the river without delay. "You'll see we do things differently here," she quipped, referring to the punctuality of their operations. With over a decade of fieldwork experience in Colombia, where hour-long waits for meetings are not uncommon, I was already struck by the company's efficiency. We then loaded into one of their standard-issue pickup trucks fitted with a roll bar, fire extinguisher, and other protective features. While navigating confidently through frenzied motorcycle traffic, Lucia went into greater detail about her job as the corporate social responsibility team's on-site point person. Shortly after the team was formed, they created a map of everyone who could potentially impact, or be impacted by, the company's operations. The objective was to identify and mitigate risks, Lucia's boss had explained when we met a few days before. Although Lucia highlighted her efforts to establish good relations with adjacent communities, the range of potential issues extended much further. "Anything that could possibly interrupt our current and future operations along the river," she added, "is of concern to us."

One of the main ways Lucia's team managed potential disruptions was through a system they referred to with an acronym that translates roughly to "questions, complaints, petitions, and suggestions."[11] Others I met in fluvial

---

11 This type of system, frequently called PQRS (*peticiones, quejas, reclamos, y sugerencias*) or some variation thereof, is common among both private companies and public agencies in Colombia.

FIGURE 3.3. Embankment allegedly damaged by riverboat traffic, Pinillos, Bolívar.
Source: photograph by author.

transport and logistics had similar procedures, whereby anyone could register concerns at public information points, by email, or through toll-free hotlines. When I asked for examples of typical cases, I often heard about a company's vessel damaging a fisherman's net, its wake flooding riverfront land, or its ropes uprooting a bankside tree (figure 3.3). When a petition is registered, companies then investigate, and if they can verify its legitimacy, they offer the petitioner compensation. Often closed-circuit television (CCTV) footage from a towboat helps to determine whether there are signs of an incident; a vessel's location history can also be tracked to prove whether it was near the location at the time in question. Whether or not incidents are deemed legitimate, however, these systems alert companies to potentially disruptive activities along the river, especially in key areas. If people are calling from a specific town, one manager explained, that's a clue something may be brewing there. It might be an indication that resentment is beginning to develop, or perhaps people are starting to mobilize collectively around shared concerns. Soliciting, interpreting, and reacting to this information allows fluvial transport and logistics companies to classify riverside towns and villages according to their disruptive potential. Decisions can then be made about where and how to intervene.

For those on the other end of the hotline, claiming damages and request-ing compensation are demands for economic inclusion. These demands mir-ror the promises made and expectations generated by representatives from the Colombian government and from the logistics industry itself, who are often quoted in the media extolling the virtues of fluvial transport and trade—in particular, its potential to bring economic opportunities to riverside commu-nities. In reality, these opportunities are scarce: those living near land-based installations might find temporary work directing traffic or performing other menial tasks, but the vast majority of river towns and villages sit and watch as vessels laden with cargo float by. Towboat-and-barge convoys aim to stop as infrequently as possible during their journey from port to port, and when they find it necessary to stop, interactions with locals are kept to a minimum. In most cases, all someone along the riverbank can hope to receive is a hand-out for permission to tie up overnight on the trunk of a large tree. Social and economic exchanges between riverboats and riverside communities were once more commonplace. Many riverboat workers recalled a bygone era in which they would moor frequently, and each time they did, they would trade with locals: a few jerrycans of diesel for the mooring or even for some fish, soft drinks, or newspapers. As these practices have been ended by stricter regula-tions governing fuel supplies onboard and limitations on stoppages during journeys, requesting compensation for damages caused by commercial river-boat traffic is the only remaining hope for receiving economic benefits from fluvial transport. The logic of supply chain security is not only essential to the logistics industry's ability to extract value from circulation along the waterway—it also becomes the primary, sometimes only, way riverside popu-lations can hope to do the same.

* * *

THE DRIVE TO one port terminal took me down dusty, unpaved roads since the installation had been sited some distance from the city center and was still under construction. The employee giving me a lift, whom I will call Julián, ex-plained that this location was strategic, since it reduced the number of possi-ble incidents that might arise. Nearing the terminal, we crossed an unfinished highway that would eventually cut transport times between the terminal and other urban areas. Julián also pointed out that his employer would soon be lay-ing its own paved access road. "These are important projects," he said, "as they will enable us to avoid routing heavy traffic through the city. Currently trucks must go past neighborhoods, schools, and everything. That slows things down, but more importantly it increases the likelihood of accidents." Julián then described a hypothetical situation: "If a truck coming from our terminal kills a *mototaxista* in a residential area, obviously it wouldn't be our fault, but it could interrupt our operations for who knows how long. And interruptions like that can be very expensive."

This comment stuck with me, partly because it revealed how the spatial and material properties of logistics—where a terminal is built, whether a road is paved—can embody security logics. It also lingered in my mind because, as with the tragic events in the Cartagena shipyards, the loss of life had been reduced to a financial calculation, and accountability again seemed less important than the restoration of business as usual. But there was something different about this case, which took me time to identify. Those who reflected on the shipyard casualties as operational calculations were light-skinned, highly paid managers, whereas those killed or injured, like most of the workforce powering the logistics industry, were darker-skinned, low-paid manual laborers. In contrast, Julián shared characteristics with the hypothetical victim— both were humble vehicle operators from the same city positioned unfavorably within the geo-racial regimes structuring Colombian society and space. Regardless, in Julián's estimation, a truck serving his employer's port terminal could conceivably take the life of someone just like him without being held accountable. The hierarchical gradations underpinning supply chain security, which render subjects and objects differentially valuable or dispensable, can become naturalized as common sense.

Arriving at another logistics site, the employee accompanying me, whom I will call Mariana, informed me that a permanent entrance had not yet been built, so we would have to enter through an opening in the chain link fence. Recognizing Mariana, the security guard monitoring the site's perimeter quickly checked my credentials and waved us through. Mariana then parked in a gravel lot and took me to visit the temporary headquarters, which were housed in modified shipping containers. After a short visit with the construction company working on the site, we dropped in on Pedro, a lawyer who worked for a firm specializing in outsourcing. "We take care of everything," he said, "from work contracts to employment laws to social security, so the operator doesn't have to. There are thousands of subcontracted workers on site now, and their contracts could be as short as a week or even a day, depending on the job they're hired to do." Mariana and Pedro together recounted the story of a strike that froze construction for an entire month, until the company managed to negotiate an agreement with its workers. Since then, Pedro assured me, everything had run smoothly: "We work in a preventative manner to resolve disputes before they escalate." This was my first indication that the ability to protect supply chains from stoppages and slowdowns also depends on specific regimes of labor.

Discussions with logistics managers frequently referenced the contentious history of labor relations in the oil industry and adjacent sectors. After all, Colombia's primary inland riverport, Barrancabermeja, is also the country's oil capital, where the first wells were drilled and the first refineries built. Ever since, fluvial transport on the Magdalena River has functioned essentially as an oil pipeline. Despite plans to serve multiple industries and diversify their shipments, companies moving cargo along the waterway continue to cater to Ecopetrol, the state oil company, which has long been embroiled in disputes with the powerful oil workers union (La Unión Sindical Obrera de la Industria del Petróleo, known as USO). In the darkest years of Colombia's armed conflict, these disputes involved leftist guerrillas, like the ELN, who supported organized labor and frequently targeted oil infrastructure, as well as right-wing paramilitaries and state security forces, who joined forces in massacring union organizers, human rights defenders, and anyone suspected of collaborating with them.[12] Today, fluvial transport and logistics companies distance themselves from that history. "People think we are part of Ecopetrol," a human relations officer told me, "and that we have to follow the same hiring procedures and pay the same wages as the oil industry. We had to tell them, 'Look, we're owned by 100 percent private capital; we're not an oil company, and we have no such obligations.' That comes as a big shock!"

Given that workforce management and paramilitary violence have long gone hand in hand in Colombia, it is noteworthy that companies now seek to reduce the power of organized labor through other, more subtle means. In another conversation, an executive mentioned that his company had "effectively neutralized the unions," in his words, through first-rate legal expertise. "Our approach has been respectful and always according to the letter of the law. That kills them," he said, drawing an unfortunate parallel with the murderous tactics used not so long ago to stop workers from disrupting operations. Relying now on legal counsel with extensive experience in labor relations, companies emphasized that following laws was more effective in preventing stoppages than bending or breaking them.

In a similar vein, one veteran of the logistics industry boasted that his firm had lobbied the government for stronger, not weaker, regulations governing

---

12 Gill, *A Century of Violence*.

fluvial transport. "Everyone on the river used to use single-hulled barges to transport oil. Those boats were time bombs. Even small driftwood could puncture their hulls and cause an oil spill. If there's a serious accident, it's game over for everyone [in the shipping business]. Heavy crude oil sinks, and there's not much you can do. We pushed for a change to the law, and now everyone must phase out the old, dangerous equipment." Others in the logistics industry referred to their hope that the Colombian state and environmental NGOs would pay closer attention to sectors, like agriculture and mining, whose unregulated toxic runoffs and forest clearances severely threatened the river's ecological health. Contrary to the assumption that violating laws and weakening regulations are always aligned with corporate interests, here the opposite was true. Like subcontracting and union busting, respecting legal and regulatory frameworks could help safeguard valuable circulation. But while the former devalued the human bodies powering the logistics industry by framing organized labor as a threat, the latter exalted the water bodies on which the industry depends as something to be cared for and protected.

* * *

ON ANOTHER PORT terminal visit, entering was a much more serious affair. The corporate offices of the company's management were not located offsite but rather were ensconced inside the terminal's fortified perimeter (figure 3.4). I was dropped off at a checkpoint where I would have to request clearance, since the employee driving me was prohibited from passing through the vehicle entrance with a visitor in the truck. Feeling apprehensive, I approached a long bank of reinforced windows shielding security personnel. I gave my name to the receptionist and, upon request, handed over my *cédula de extranjería*—the national identification card issued to noncitizens—which she passed directly to her supervisor. With an air of authority, the supervisor scanned my ID card and immediately rejected it on account of its 2010 expiration date. I was surprised, since I was accustomed to presenting my expired *cédula* in various public and private settings, and no one had ever seemed to care. The supervisor then asked for my passport and insurance certificate, which I had left behind at my hotel, thinking the scanned copies I sent by email would be sufficient. She then rebuked me for failing to include a scan of the page on which my passport was stamped by an immigration official and directed me to take a seat while she investigated further.

Meanwhile, another security guard escorted me to a classroom where I was made to watch an eight-minute safety video. The high-quality production sped through a litany of health, safety, and environmental concerns, covering

FIGURE 3.4. Tanker truck approaching security checkpoint. Source: photograph by author.

everything from hazardous waste disposal to emergency response protocols. Once the video ended, I was asked to sign a form declaring that I had viewed it and then was taken back to the waiting area, where I sat nervously next to subcontracted workers also awaiting entry clearance. After nearly thirty minutes, the supervisor called me back to the window and granted me entrance, though her facial expression and tone of voice both signaled her continued misgivings. She issued me an access card for the metal turnstile gates, but it took me a few tries before I could get the locking mechanism to release. My initial foray into the world of logistics had gone smoothly, but I now found myself struggling just to get a foot in the door, even though I possessed nearly all the embodied characteristics that regularly facilitate access to exclusive spaces in Colombia. Unlike those subjects and objects that are unambiguously categorized as worthy of either suspicion or protection, my presence as a visiting researcher seemed to hover between the two.

Once inside, the indeterminate waiting I had experienced at the checkpoint gave way to a precisely orchestrated schedule of meetings. Like a visiting dignitary, I was ushered into a glass-walled and heavily air-conditioned conference room where I was offered coffee and snacks. The person organizing my visit had sent me an ambitious agenda the day before, and I expected the usual contingencies to intervene. Instead, I spent the day interviewing the company's full management team, one after another at half-hour intervals. My minder remained present during all of my meetings, quietly typing on her laptop or sending text messages, while each of the managers I met—all of them well-spoken, carefully groomed men from Colombia or other Latin American countries—gave detailed descriptions of the area of the business they knew best.[13] Although they relied upon different forms of expertise, their common denominator was the objective of securing uninterrupted circulation, which depended upon a hierarchical framework that sorted people and things according to their relative value.

At the end of the day, I was directed to exit the terminal on foot through the security checkpoint. The minders accompanying me could drive through the perimeter, so they gave me a head start. Thankfully, exiting was quicker than entering, which allowed time for casual conversations with a few subcontracted laborers finishing their workday. All men whose complexion was noticeably darker than those I had met on the inside, these workers were clustered in groups, each with matching coveralls corresponding to their employer and the service it provided. I sat down next to three electricians who were resting on the pavement while they awaited their transport back to the city. Having observed this company's manual workforce throughout the day without managing more than a mere hello, I had many questions.

The men I spoke with told me that their contracts were usually short-term, sometimes just for a day, and that their foreman would confirm later that evening whether they would be working tomorrow. Often, they said, they would wait days, even weeks, to get tapped for a shift. They reported that there was no waiting around once they were on the job, however. Inside, things moved quickly and happened on time, and delays and breaks were kept to a minimum. But once they left the worksite, or their contract ended, they entered a different temporal order: the smooth, predictable, and uninterrupted operation of the port terminal was tied, not coincidentally, to the punctuated, uncertain, and fragmented timescape of labor.[14] For those hired to maintain

---

13 To comply with the terms of use imposed by my hosts, my account of the forms of expertise deployed to manage threats to circulation is based on interviews conducted at different companies, and some direct quotations are composites of statements made by multiple sources.

14 Bear, "For Labour."

the terminal's infrastructure—to keep its basic systems functioning without fail—flexibility was the norm.

* * *

INTERVIEWS I CONDUCTED with logistics managers in charge of the volume and profitability of trade often revolved around a single metric: time. "Speed of movement," one port superintendent said, "may be our greatest source of pride, but things also must arrive when they're meant to arrive. That's what we offer, and if we can't deliver that, we get a bad reputation." The superintendent underscored this point with reference to delayed shipments and missed connections: "Many of our dry bulk clients are shipping internationally, and if we don't deliver while the ship is docked, we've lost." The consequences of temporal disjuncture were, of course, financial: "If that happens, then their cargo must wait around until another departure, and our client ends up paying high storage costs. And it's not going to be the same week, more like the next one or the one after that." This results in losses not only for the client but also for the company itself. The example given involved container shipments (figure 3.5): "Containers are simply borrowed boxes. Shipping companies rent you a container; you put your cargo in and move it. When you arrive in port, you return the container to them. And since shipping lines have set itineraries, you have to get the container back to them on time." This is enforced by lease agreements with penalties for noncompliance. As it was explained to me: "The daily penalty for one container, on the very low end, is $120. A barge can carry forty containers, and let's say we're moving eight barges in one convoy. For each day that convoy is held up, that's a lot of money we end up losing." I did some basic calculations and, in this scenario, a one-day delay could cost the company a minimum of $38,400.

During these conversations, I was aware that I was speaking with people who specialized in the cargo side of the fluvial transport and logistics business. For them, time and money were conjoined by an organizing logic that rendered commensurable all factors potentially threatening their ability to move things quickly and efficiently. When I pressed them to list the key factors, most mentioned things beyond their control. Foremost among them were the environmental conditions along the river—rainfall patterns, water levels, channel depth, sediment load, and so on. "At the end of the day," one manager told me, "each product we move has its own characteristics, but they all move along the same river. And it's a highly variable river, very unstable, especially these days [referring to climate change]. It has its bad days and good days—and seasons, I should add." His colleague, who specialized in liquid cargo, also discussed the

FIGURE 3.5. Shipping containers parked at fluvial port terminal. Source: photograph by author.

importance of time with reference to keeping the port open around the clock, so that a shipment (of naphtha, for example, a liquid hydrocarbon mixture) could arrive at any hour of the day or night. However, again the river was the wild card. "Even if a terminal is open twenty-four hours a day," he explained, "barges are often forced to wait for water levels to rise. It's difficult to establish parameters for something you cannot control. The river is a bottleneck and always will be because it's a force of nature."

Fluctuations are essential to hydrological cycles, but from the perspective of the logistics industry, regularizing them is the state's responsibility. "The river doesn't maintain itself," as another interviewee put it. "The government is supposed to guarantee a permanently navigable channel. At present that's not happening, and this is creating stoppages. We lose a lot of money during stoppages." The short-term solution, I was told, was to shift business in the direction of less time-sensitive cargo. Another solution mentioned was to stock-pile reserves: "This only works for certain products, obviously, but if a drought causes delays, and a shipment needs to be loaded onto tanker trucks, we can tap into our reserves and deliver on time. The same thing applies if there's a trucker's strike, as there was in 2016. It lasted for a few months, but luckily, we had reserves of crude [oil] in our tanks, so exports were not affected." According to this logic, time had value and was therefore to be protected, while nature and politics were threats, although ones that were hard to control. For these managers, cargo was the variable that could be manipulated to neutralize the impacts of climate change, industrial action, government ineptitude, and all other factors threatening to disrupt the temporal order of circulation.

This came into play during the two events described at the outset, both of which disrupted the logistics network connecting Colombia to overseas markets and triggered responses from public and private actors seeking to keep circulation flowing. Although operations were quickly restored, in neither case did the problem go away: the depth of Barranquilla's access channel hit a record low a month later, and another explosion, this time of a tanker truck carrying oil in Barrancabermeja, occurred the following week. These incidents again delayed operations indefinitely, and managers specializing in cargo recognized them as problems, but also as opportunities. If such disruptions could not be prevented, they could still be managed (by tapping into reserves or shifting to other products and transport modes), and if done more quickly or efficiently than the competition, could lead to significant profit. Even with the logistics industry's technical prowess, economic means, and political might, the objective of supply chain security is not always to prevent all forms of disruption. If managed correctly, disruptions can be moments of unexpected profit.[15]

Unlike with other logics of supply chain security, these cargo specialists did not have much to say about the human actors who people the world of logistics—neither managers, nor workers, nor those outside the industry who could conceivably impact its operations. I found this curious, especially since some of the same people who approached their business through the metric of time referenced their own personal experience. "I don't get much sleep, and I rarely spend time with my family," one mentioned in passing. Others concurred that the logistics industry required demanding chronotypes, but they always deferred to the temporal order of operations—that was ultimately what mattered most. I often heard similar comments from crew members on commercial riverboats, but with the critical implication that their biological and social rhythms were valued less than the temporal exigencies of the cargo they

---

15 On "capital's structural need for an 'outside' for its operations," see Mezzadra and Neilson, *The Politics of Operations*, 7. Mezzadra and Neilson see these outsides as "new spaces and temporalities for valorization and accumulation."

were transporting. In contrast, managers' time was valued highly, so temporal irregularities seemed an acceptable compromise.

I also found it surprising not to hear more about the political side of supply chain security, since I knew some also had personal experiences in this domain. A few had faced death threats, extortion, even kidnapping, and these dangers continued to hover on the horizon, even if materializing less frequently these days. Again, I had often discussed this concern with riverboat workers, many of whom reported run-ins with armed groups looking to use intimidation and violence to extract value from a world that otherwise excluded them. But the high value placed on the time, bodies, and lives of managers and executives made them more likely targets, while simultaneously granting them enhanced protection by state security forces and by private security agencies bankrolled by their employers. Like the cargo they were paid handsomely to manage, the levels of compensation and protection offered to them far surpassed what was given to the workers powering the riverboats, manning the shipyards, and handling the cargo—a workforce positioned lower within the geo-racial regimes that structure Colombian society and the logistics industry alike.

* * *

IN THE DOMAIN of logistics, the prevention of disruption falls mostly on the shoulders of two very different types of people. The first are managers of what is often called some variation of "health, safety, and environment." Incidentally, people I interviewed from this line of work usually referred to their area of specialization using its English-language name or acronym (HSE), with some preferring to converse in English. This seemed to lend their domain of expertise an air of authority and universality, as though discussing it in Spanish would have made it somehow less authoritative, more context-bound. The logic through which they approached their job also seemed universally applicable: in the words of one HSE manager, a slight man in glasses whom I will call Roberto, "My mission is to reduce the likelihood of business interruptions by minimizing risk." Roberto cited the adage that "accidents happen," acknowledging that preventing them was impossible, and then proceeded to list a range of events (oil spills and gas explosions, for a start) that could disrupt operations for significant time. There were "subtle differences" (*matices*, he called them) between these incidents, since they varied in terms of probability of occurrence and severity of impact. For example, those inside the port terminal were low probability, since the variables were limited, and low impact, since the accident could be contained (figure 3.6). On the river, however, the probability of occurrence and the severity of impact both increased, since variables

FIGURE 3.6. "Danger." Source: photograph by author.

multiplied and containment was more difficult. With this actuarial framework, HSE managers were able to prioritize the risk factors most deserving close attention.

This strategy included insurance policies covering the company's liability in a range of unfortunate events, such as accidents resulting in harm to workers or the environment. For an employee injured on the job, Colombian law establishes levels of compensation, depending on the type and severity of injury.[16] These sums are set by something called the table of valuation of disabilities resulting from workplace accidents (*tabla de valuación de incapacidades resultantes de accidentes de trabajo*), which assigns values to each body part and function.[17] Running athwart the hierarchical orders ranking workers along lines of race, gender, class, or region, this schema standardizes the value of the human body according to a universalist logic based on the body's capac-

16 Presidencia de la República, Decreto 1295 de 1994.
17 Presidencia de la República, Decreto 776 de 1987.

ity to perform remunerative work.[18] The table contains percentage ranges that correspond to amounts of time (number of months) and money (the worker's monthly salary); the loss of an eye, for example, is set at 35–60 percent reduced work capacity, which is equivalent to eight to thirteen months' full pay.[19] Employers are legally required to hold insurance policies covering their liabilities for these indemnifications, as well as others specific to the fluvial transport industry. In the case of an accidental death while transporting cargo along the river, Colombian law mandates a minimum coverage of $47,000 to compensate the victim's family.[20] Fluvial transport companies must also be indemnified against damages to the environment; for example, coverage in excess of $120,000 is required to compensate for a shipyard accident that contaminates the waterway.[21] According to this metric, workers and waterways are rendered commensurate, which allows different monetary values to be assigned to each one.

These legal obligations, and the insurance policies that indemnify companies against them, do not prevent disruptions from happening, though they do minimize their impact.[22] When legal codes mandate compensation levels in the event of an accident, and insurance companies are on hand to help companies fulfill their obligations, business as usual can resume quickly. Moreover, insurance shapes the logics of supply chain security by mediating the decisions companies make about what to protect themselves against. If compensation can be counted on to cover costs resulting from certain kinds of events, these events become less concerning; conversely, that which lies outside the terms of the policy merits greater attention. Actuarial frameworks also contribute to the hierarchical orders that rank subjects and objects according to their relative

18 The ableist implications of this false universalism have been highlighted by numerous scholars in the field of disability studies. See for example Puar, *The Right to Maim*.

19 Presidencia de la República, Decreto 776 de 1987.

20 Ministerio de Transporte, Resolución 3666 de 1998. Amounts are calculated according to *salarios mínimos legales* (monthly minimum wage), which at the time of writing was set at 908,526 Colombian pesos.

21 Ministerio de Transporte, Resolución 3666 de 1998. In cases of planned projects or economic activities that result in environmental impacts, the Ministry of the Environment establishes compensation levels for damages in its "Manual of Compensations," according to a calculation called the "compensation factor" *(factor de compensación)*, which assigns different values to different environments according to various criteria.

22 Here I am building on insights of critical insurance studies. See Lobo-Guerrero, "Lloyd's and the Moral Economy"; Lobo-Guerrero, "Los seguros marítimos"; Dua, *Captured at Sea*; Booth, "Critical Insurance Studies."

FIGURE 3.7. Marine infantry patrol boat. Source: photograph by author.

value. Like the companies that push for weakening the bargaining power of unions while strengthening environmental protections, the calculative frameworks of insurance value the bodies of fluvial transport workers less than the bodies of water on which they work.

The second type of manager responsible for protecting fluvial transport and logistics networks from interruption is often identified by the self-evident title "head of security." Meetings with these figures tend to start right on time. During the interview I conducted with Julio, a serious man with penetrating eyes, two mobile phones always in view flashed constantly with notifications. Our conversation began with a brief history of the armed conflict in Colombia and its impact on fluvial transport. In the 1980s and 1990s, and even into the early 2000s, all vessels were accompanied by armed guards from the Colombian Navy. Shipping lines were constantly under siege, and shipments were frequently held for ransom or delayed by assaults. Julio assured me that those days were long gone: "Today, even though we're a large company, we've had no problems of that nature—no threats of terrorist attacks, no demands for extortion payments, nothing. This is a very secure operation." Support from the authorities was still crucial, he told me, and fortunately military battalions were now stationed along the river (figure 3.7). But the only incidents that had arisen were minor: people throwing stones at barge convoys or stealing small pieces of equipment at night. In these cases, his security team communicated directly with the police, and the company's operations remained unaffected.

Nevertheless, Julio emphasized that he oversaw a complex human and technological system dedicated to eliminating disruptions. Contrary to the actuarial frameworks of insurance and risk management, which seek to minimize the impact of unexpected but inevitable occurrences, the security team, I learned, was "in the business of prevention—of preventing bad things from happening." Whereas HSE managers operated in a world of uncertainty and probability, their colleagues in security were full of confidence and certitude. An expression of this aspiration of total control, Julio assured me that the port terminals and vessels under his watch were constantly monitored by CCTV and other forms of internal surveillance. He also alluded to the multiple sources of intelligence he relied on to keep him abreast of problems before they materialized. A colleague of his I met later asked whether I had seen Julio's command and control center—I had not, but I had every reason to suspect I would be impressed.

A possible weakness, Julio said, was in the area of personnel, "but we're always training [*sensibilizando*] our people to watch out for suspicious situations." More basic than training, however, were moral characteristics intrinsic to certain categories of people: "We have a very rigorous selection process. The people operating our fleet, these are people who have lived their whole lives working along the river and are extremely difficult to penetrate. It could happen, but they are *gente del río* [people from/of the river]. River people are different from *gente urbana* [city people]. They have other mentalities and aspirations." The inherent virtues of certain workers also informed his selection of security guards: "They all go through a robust training program, they are all from neighboring communities, and 97 percent of them are women." These comments did not surprise me, since many others in the fluvial transport industry had invoked similar taxonomies of honesty, diligence, and reliability.[23]

---

23 The expression *malicia indígena*, which in the popular imaginary refers to a type of cunning that gives people the ability to anticipate situations and take advantage of them, was occasionally used to make sense of moral strength or weakness. For background on this expression in Colombia, see Morales, "Mestizaje, malicia indígena y viveza." For the racialized implications of the expression and the different meanings it conveys when applied to Indigenous people, see Sabayu C. Gil, "¿Qué es malicia indígena?" Special thanks to Melissa Martínez for highlighting this.

And cultivating an ideal mix of personnel was a common strategy for ensuring uninterrupted operations. Hierarchies of race, class, gender, and region are flexible enough to accommodate the valorization of subordinated groups for certain types of work.

With strategies like these, it seemed that Julio's security team had the entire logistics corridor under control. However, he also cautioned that his reach was limited to the company's installations and vessels: "There are still 630 kilometers of navigable river between the interior and the coast where we are vulnerable. Anyone can throw an explosive device at one of our boats from a motorized canoe and then take off, or even from the riverbank and then disappear immediately into the bush." The spatial challenges of security, he told me, had their temporal analog in future changes within the supply chain: "Criminal elements are always mutating according to the opportunities available. At the moment, we mainly move liquid cargo, and it's very hard to smuggle drugs or weapons in that sort of equipment." Julio then looked ahead to a future in which his company could export shipping containers to international destinations: "If that happens, certain illegal activities will become more attractive. With containers, smuggling becomes much easier and a situation like that could shut us down for quite a while." Although Julio assured me that he and his team were well prepared for these eventualities, the notoriously cunning criminal networks operating in Colombia would continue to present a challenge, as would the vastness of the logistics corridor his industry had created.

* * *

THE DAYS I spent visiting fluvial transport and logistics companies were some of the most efficient and productive of my career, and yet one thing eluded me: the boats themselves. The people coordinating my visits knew I was keen to see the vessels firsthand, and they appeared to make various attempts to facilitate that. During a visit to one port terminal, I was told that only a single towboat was in operation that day, and that the captain would call once he completed his maneuvers and had docked. As I conducted interviews, all of which started and ended according to schedule, reports on the riverboat's progress were frequent but inconclusive. "Todavía no han llegado," I was told countless times: "They still haven't arrived." The ambiguous temporality of the vessel's schedule contrasted sharply with the precise coordination of operations on land, and as the day ended, my minders apologized for their inability to grant my wish. I would subsequently make multiple requests for permission, but they were repeatedly rebuffed. Each company I contacted said they would be delighted for me to see their impressive fleet and hardworking crew in action, but that security protocols prohibited it. Although I had managed to gain some access to certain areas of the restricted world of logistics, the movement of cargo clearly enjoyed a higher level of protection.

Eventually I succeeded at getting permission for a voyage between the coastal seaport of Cartagena and the inland head of commercial navigation in Barrancabermeja. The day before my scheduled departure, a phone call came with precise yet guarded instructions: take a taxi to a specific mileage marker on the road leading from the city to the port and arrive promptly at 8 a.m. Enthusiastic for this long-awaited opportunity, I left my hotel early, allowing an hour for what should have been a thirty-minute ride. Yet when the clock struck eight, I found myself still stuck in bumper-to-bumper traffic. Our surroundings indicated we weren't far from the destination: the familiar sights of the city had long given way to a logistical landscape of shipyards, port terminals, gantry cranes, customs offices, petrol stations, repair shops, truck stops, and storage facilities. But with traffic at a standstill, I could do nothing more than apologetically message my contact and hope the same delay was affecting everyone.

When we finally neared the specified location, the driver veered onto a gravel path branching off from the main road. His guess proved fortuitous, as we quickly spotted the shipping company's name emblazoned on a small cinderblock building surrounded by 2-meter chain link fencing. A security guard flanked by a hefty dog waved us through and directed me inside, which was a relief on multiple fronts: my contact, Yolanda, was herself delayed, and the air-conditioned office provided shelter from the blazing sun. I waited in one of the four cubicles partitioning a cramped open-plan workspace, and before long Yolanda arrived, though with unhappy news: a truck carrying goods along the roadway had swerved into a motorcycle, killing the driver. This was the cause of the horrendous traffic jam, which Yolanda had outwitted by ditching her taxi and walking the final stretch. But the accident's impact was far-reaching, occurring as it did on the one road serving the entire port zone—a critical choke point that makes this port especially vulnerable to disruptions like these.[24] "Anyone trying to move anything in or out of Cartagena today," Yolanda fretted, "is totally screwed. This will slow things down for hours, possibly days if you consider the backlog." A colleague replied somewhat reassuringly: "Luckily, at the moment we're not so reliant on road transport, but this will still cost us something."

---

24 Carse et al., "Chokepoints."

I thought back to my earlier discussion with Julián, the driver who depicted a hypothetical situation identical to the real one that had just transpired. As in Julián's account, an accident like this could disrupt operations indefinitely, and the costs could be extensive. Traffic fatalities were assessed by operational calculations in which the life of a motorcyclist was of limited value compared to the cargo circulating along the roadway and the time required to clear the scene. The key question, therefore, was not who or what was responsible, but how quickly and economically operations could be restored. Yolanda seemed to see things in comparable ways, except for one important difference: both parties involved in the accident were assumed to be men, and it was probably the aggressive driving of one or the other (or both) that was to blame. Echoing the gendered taxonomy of safety and security I had encountered elsewhere, Yolanda attributed the death to reckless masculinity.

Still harried from her long, hot walk, Yolanda began preparing me for my voyage. As health, safety, and environment officer, her first order of business was to confirm that I was fully insured. Once that was established, Yolanda began outfitting me with protective equipment: glasses, earplugs, and a helmet, which she carefully polished with a cloth. To reach the towboat, whose barges were currently being discharged at a nearby oil refinery, we would have to get permission from the oil company. "This might be difficult," cautioned Yolanda's colleague Emilio, who was the liaison between the two firms. "They are extremely strict about who can access their property." A few calls confirmed Emilio's suspicion, which meant Yolanda would have to find a workaround. She phoned the captain and hatched a plan to meet at a nearby shipyard whose security was relatively lax.

Yolanda informed me that she would also be boarding, though only temporarily to conduct a routine briefing with the crew. The objective of these briefings was to ensure health and safety protocols were being followed, which in theory would reduce the likelihood of workplace injuries, even deaths. The logic was one of supply chain security: protect the company's operations against costly interruptions arising in the event of a serious accident. Knowing this was a key part of her job, and that it required her to make regular visits to the male-dominated world of the boat, her earlier reflections on the traffic fatality took on new meaning. Yolanda mediated between the company's management and its workforce—both exclusively male yet located at opposite ends of the social order—and this exposed her to the gendered and racialized dynamics of her profession, especially around matters of health and safety. Being an HSE officer and a woman positioned her as an authority on these matters, though always subordinate to management. The light-skinned men back at headquarters expected her to minimize the financial risks of disruption by ensuring that the darker-skinned men onboard were protected from their own inherent carelessness.

During Yolanda's orientation, I noticed she was not the only woman in the office. Everyone else employed directly by the company was male, but a maid (*empleada de servicio*) worked alongside them, cleaning and distributing refreshments. Yolanda and this other woman were easily differentiated, however. First, they wore different uniforms, which signaled differences in education, occupation, and remuneration: Yolanda was dressed in company-issued work wear, the *empleada* in maid attire. Second, they were differentiated according to physical appearance: though both *costeñas*, Yolanda's light skin and dark hair would likely make her *morena*, whereas the cleaner would be classified as *negra*, or Black. These distinctions of color and class added another layer to the racialized and gendered hierarchies operative in the fluvial transport and logistics industry.

Once the traffic jam had cleared, Yolanda called the captain again. The boat had finished its final maneuver, but it was now low tide, which meant that the water level at the shipyard would be too shallow for the boat's draft. This implied an additional delay, but since the barges were being discharged and the towboat was idle, operations were not affected. Unlike the deadly accident that paralyzed the port zone's access road that morning, this delay would cost the company nothing. Tidal fluctuations and traffic fatalities were conjoined by an organizing logic that rendered them commensurable as factors that potentially threatened circulation, and were measurable in terms of time and money. In this case, waiting a few more hours for the tide to rise simply meant more waiting for the two of us.

* * *

I FINALLY DID board the vessel, and this gave me a wholly different perspective on fluvial transport and logistics—not from inside the land-based offices of port terminals and logistics hubs, but from the deck of a towboat-and-barge convoy as it moved slowly upriver (the next three chapters shift to this perspective). Following that trip, I kept in touch with crew members via WhatsApp and hoped to meet again. On my next visit to Colombia, I reached out to an engineer I will call Nelson, who had been especially charitable. It was the Christmas season, and he was visiting family in the riverside town where he was raised, so it was challenging to plan a rendezvous. By early January, Nelson had returned to Barranquilla. He had been temporarily assigned to one of the company's shipyards and was lodged in a downtown hotel frequented by riverboat workers. We arranged to meet early one Sunday, his only day off.

We walked to Barranquilla's central marketplace, where vendors line the streets and shaded kiosks offer everything from potatoes to pliers. An electronics repair shop run by friends from Nelson's hometown had a wobbly wooden bench where we could sit and talk. As we exchanged holiday anecdotes, Nelson ordered a round of beer from a neighboring kiosk. I sensed a somber tone as the conversation moved to his current assignment in the shipyard. "I prefer to be on the river even though the work onboard is more demanding," he said. A momentary smile crossed his face: "I'm a *navegante* at heart." Nelson then explained why he was currently stuck on land: "Unlike other crew members—deckhands, cooks, pilots, even captains—engineers are not interchangeable. We always stay with the same towboat. If it needs repairing, then we're off the river." I had come to know Nelson as a jovial, gregarious character, so his downbeat mood seemed unusual. I chalked it up to postholiday blues and an unwelcome assignment.

Bottles of beer were arriving faster than I could drink them, and I started to wonder whether this was a routine Sunday for Nelson. I had only known him previously onboard the boat, where alcohol is prohibited, so I had no way of knowing. Fortunately, we were drinking Águila Light. As time went on, our conversation verged on nostalgic, as it gravitated to the voyage we had shared. At one point, Nelson began calling some of the other crew members, passing each one to me for a hello. Nelson's spirits seemed to lift as we reconnected with these coworkers, especially the captain. Speaking to him gave Nelson the idea to introduce me to one of the captain's favorite haunts: a local bar where seafarers and their riverine counterparts congregate between voyages. Around 12:30 p.m. we arrived at the Silla Verde (literally the Green Chair, although the chairs were white), whose powerful sound system bathed the block in the heartrending sounds of *vallenato*. We settled into a table facing the street and another round arrived in seconds. The music, the beer, the bar: all the elements converged to create an atmosphere ripe for disclosure, and Nelson revealed what had been eating away at him.

Two days earlier, a towboat-and-barge convoy had arrived in the river port of Barrancabermeja. Its mission was to load the tanks of its barges at the Ecopetrol oil refinery and move them downriver for export within a specified time frame. But conditions were especially bad since the management and maintenance of the river for cargo transport had been perennially neglected, and a drought was exacerbating the situation. This made it impossible for the crew to safely perform the operation and forced them to dock at the refinery's pier

FIGURE 3.8. Loading dock at Ecopetrol oil refinery, Barrancabermeja, Santander. Source: photograph by author.

until conditions improved. There they were effectively trapped, since the oil refinery in Barrancabermeja is heavily guarded, and the crews of shipping companies hired to move its products are generally prohibited from setting foot on the property—they perform their work entirely on deck, while a team from the refinery handles all land-based tasks. In conditions like these, crews have no choice but to tie their boat up indefinitely along a concrete embankment abutting the refinery without permission to disembark (figure 3.8). The exact details of the case are inconclusive, but Nelson gave me the version he had heard.

After multiple days of inactivity, a handful of crew members, some of whom were known to Nelson, set off on an unauthorized nighttime excursion. Restless, claustrophobic, and desperate for diversion, they hired a local boatman with a motorized canoe to transport them to the city's public dock. From there they strolled through the waterfront cantinas to blow off steam. Sometime around 1:30 a.m., they phoned the boatman to say they were ready to return. The night was dark, the current was swift, and the men had been drinking. As they filed off the canoe and onto the towboat, the cook—a thirty-nine-year-old navy man from Barranquilla who was relatively new to riverboat work—lost his balance and plunged into the river. The towboat might have had a chance at rescuing him, but the current swept him toward the barges tied up just downstream, and he disappeared below their hulls. Six days later his body was found.

Nelson had not been close to the lost crew member, but the news nevertheless hit him hard. He did not condone the violation of company policy—leaving the vessel is prohibited except for official business the captain deems necessary—but he certainly identified with the victim and resented the incident's framing as a case of reckless rule breaking. Nelson also felt for the victim's family, who were unlikely to receive compensation from the employer or from insurance due to the breach of contract. What seemed to haunt Nelson most, however, were the conditions of possibility for the accident. The government's failure to manage and maintain the river had made it more difficult, even dangerous, for the crew to perform their work. Complicating matters further, the oil company's rigid security protocols had forced them into a precarious position. Both factors increased the risk to workers: if the river had been flowing smoothly, the crew would have been busy working, and if they had been granted access to land, they could have embarked more safely. Seen from this angle, the implications were hard for Nelson to stomach: by design, the logics governing his industry sacrifice lives like his to protect the circulation of cargo. Yet within a hierarchical order that differentially distributes injury, even death, the assertion of livingness, autonomy, and personhood continues.[25] As we said goodbye, Nelson confidently reminded me (and perhaps also himself) that this tragedy would only strengthen the resolve of *navegantes* to protect and care for themselves and each other.

25 Here I follow Katherine McKittrick's plea to attend not only to "how the premature death of Black people, and, more broadly, the acute marginalization of the world's most vulnerable communities, are entrenched in algorithmic equations" but also to how these equations are "continually interrupted by an assertion of life and therefore a new definition of livingness." McKittrick, *Dear Science*, 105–6, 144.

4

In the Wake of Logistics

I'm awakened by the piercing blast of a warning siren. A few moments later, two diesel marine engines begin to roar. My bunk starts to vibrate, its metal frame clanging against the wall. I quickly orient myself and then glance at my watch. It's just before five o'clock in the morning, and I'm lying in my berth on a commercial riverboat belonging to one of Colombia's oldest fluvial transport companies. I pull myself out of bed, throw on some clothes, and ascend to the upper deck. The captain, catching sight of me, barks out a friendly good morning: "Buen día, Profe. ¿Cómo amaneció?"

For nearly one hundred years, the shipping company he works for has been plying the Magdalena River, which connects Colombia's Andean interior to its Caribbean coast. The company owns a fleet of thirteen towboats, which guide convoys of barges upriver and down. These barges, when lashed together

---

A version of this chapter was published as "In the Wake of Logistics: Situated Afterlives of Race and Labour on the Magdalena River," *Environment and Planning D: Society and Space* 39, no. 3 (2021): 441–58.

by wire cables, resemble the landing strip of an aircraft carrier, and they can transport all manner of things, from dry bulk on their decks to liquid cargo in their tanks. The towboat I'm on, one of the company's most formidable vessels, frequently powers convoys of eight barges, sometimes more.

The crew consists of the captain, one helmsman, and three pilots, who take turns navigating and steering; six deckhands, who perform all manual labor, and one boatswain, who oversees their operations; four engineers responsible for the engines and other equipment; and two cooks, who prepare meals and manage supplies. These eighteen men (and riverboat crews are invariably male) live and work together in close quarters—the towboat is 10 meters wide by 36 meters long—for twenty-one day shifts, followed by seven days of shore leave. While onboard, crew members work from sunup to sundown or, when conditions permit, around the clock. Though most hail from the Magdalena River's lower reaches and not strictly the coast, all are *costeños*—the racialized category of regional affiliation attached to the inhabitants of northern Colombia's tropical lowlands.[1] The regional-cum-racial identity of these workers is not incidental to the work they perform—indeed, the articulation of race and labor has long been a defining feature of commercial transport along the Magdalena River.[2]

On days like these, the captain begins by issuing orders to the boatswain and head mechanic. While the crew's maneuvers follow a well-recognized chain of command, they are ultimately determined by the technological specifications of the vessel, the hydrological conditions of the river, and the commercial imperatives of the shipping company and its clients. This company is one of a handful moving cargo between Barranquilla and Cartagena on the

1 According to Colombia's geo-racial regime of identity and belonging, people from *la costa* (the Caribbean or Atlantic coast) are marked by difference from the assumed whiteness of the populations of the Andean interior, sometimes regardless of phenotypical similarities. And while *la costa* is commonly associated with Blackness, this association is ambiguous, especially relative to the Pacific Coast region. See Wade, *Blackness and Race Mixture*, 79–93.
2 Much of my analysis, including the concept of articulation and the conjunctural method, is indebted to Stuart Hall. See, for example, Hall, "Race, Articulation and Societies." For other scholarship on race and labor in the Black radical tradition, see Robinson, *Black Marxism*; Johnson, *River of Dark Dreams*; Kelley, *Race Rebels*, Du Bois, *The Souls of Black Folk*; Roediger, *The Wages of Whiteness*. Latin American decolonial thought also inspired the ideas advanced here. See Quijano, "Coloniality of Power." So, too, does work on race and space within the field of Black geographies. See Bledsoe and Wright, "The Pluralities of Black Geographies"; McKittrick and Woods, *Black Geographies*; Chari, "Critical Geographies"; Gilmore, "Fatal Couplings"; Hawthorne, "Black Matters Are Spatial Matters." For engagements with debates about race, capitalism, and infrastructure by labor geographers, see Strauss, "Labour Geography III." See also Stokes and De Coss-Corzo, "Doing the Work."

Caribbean coast and Barrancabermeja approximately 630 kilometers inland. A key component of the distribution network linking Colombia to overseas sites of production and consumption, the company's operations are calibrated by the logic of logistics, which seeks to control the movement of goods through space, on time. The work performed by the crew members onboard exemplifies the human labor that powers the logistics industry—an increasingly important domain of contemporary capitalism worldwide.

Today is an ordinary day for the riverboat crew, except that we're not yet on the river. We've spent the last two days floating in the Bay of Cartagena while our barges were being emptied of sixty thousand barrels of crude oil. We are now making our final trip between an anchor buoy, where we had tied up overnight, and the loading pier of Ecopetrol, the state oil company. Jutting out into the bay, the pier is an assemblage of hoses, pipes, valves, pumps, and walkways, which connects to a vast refinery complex—Colombia's second largest after the one in the river port of Barrancabermeja, where these barges were filled ten days ago. Now that the last drops of oil have been sucked out, the towboat will reassemble its convoy of empty barges and repeat the same journey again. The daily rhythms of riverboat work add up to an endless cycle of movement along the same stretch of river between Colombia's oil capital and its main transshipment port.

From my perch on the towboat's upper deck, I take one last look at this peculiar waterscape—a critical link in the petroleum industry supply chain. Immediately visible are the gas flares and distillation columns of the oil refinery and the maritime tankers being filled just offshore. Through the acrid haze, I can also make out other components of the logistics network connecting Colombia to international markets: the ship-to-shore cranes of nearby container terminals; the towering silos and floating docks of a cement plant; the refrigerated storage facilities of food importers; the gated offices and warehouses of a duty-free zone; a security checkpoint manned by the Colombian Navy's marine infantry. I can see Cartagena's skyline glistening on the horizon some 20 kilometers away, while the logistical infrastructures surrounding me here are nearly invisible from its exclusive hotels and luxury boutiques. The day there has yet to begin, whereas the crew onboard has been active for hours—a microcosm of the relationship between the capital accumulation expressed in the city's built form and the logistical labor on which it depends.

Our convoy of towboat and barges, once discharged and reassembled, begins to cross the bay and ascend the Canal del Dique—a waterway dug initially by the Spanish in the sixteenth century to connect the strategic seaport of Cartagena to the interior. As we navigate through the suffocating heat and dense vegetation, I'm reminded of the backbreaking work that went into digging the canal, whose chief objective was to reduce travel times between Spain's mainland colonial possessions and its transatlantic fleet. This work was performed initially by enslaved Indigenous and African laborers, and it was their descendants who powered the rafts going to upriver mines and plantations and returning with valuable goods to be loaded onto galleons bound for Europe. Along the banks, remnants of haciendas owned by white settlers testify to the importance of the river as a conduit for the expansion of racial capitalism in the Americas. Beginning in the colonial period and persisting to the present day, articulations of race and labor have structured the work of fluvial transport, which now occupies a central role in Colombia's burgeoning logistics industry.

Based on ethnographic fieldwork conducted aboard a commercial riverboat, and on historical accounts of riverboat work, this chapter examines the racial formations on which logistics depends.[3] Logistics is organized around the flows of goods, vessels, and workers at the heart of capitalist modernity, and these flows are made possible by labor regimes whose racial underpinnings have both persisted and changed over time. Tracking continuities and divergences in the domain of fluvial transport along Colombia's Magdalena River, I propose that our understanding of logistics is enriched by attending to historical articulations of race and labor. My analysis is inspired by scholars who reckon with the afterlives of racial slavery, as well as by those who track precisely how that legacy unfolds in geographically and historically situated ways.[4] Rather than pitting these perspectives against each another, I engage them simultaneously through the analytic of situated afterlives, which focuses attention on the constitutive relationship between systems of racial hierarchy and capital accumulation on a world-historical scale; and the shifting contours of this relationship across space and time.[5] How are race and labor articulated historically along the Magdalena River, and how do these historical articulations shape the work of fluvial transport today?

---

3 Lara, *Inland Shift*; Khalili, *Sinews of War and Trade*.
4 Hartman, *Lose Your Mother*; Sharpe, *In the Wake*; Mbembe, *Critique of Black Reason*; McKittrick, "Plantation Futures." For approaches that highlight geographical and historical specificity, see Hall, "Race, Articulation and Societies"; Hart, *Disabling Globalization*; Chari, "Three Moments of Stuart Hall"; Arias and Restrepo, "Historizando raza."
5 I borrow the concept of *afterlives* from Saidiya Hartman and others using it to confront the legacy of racial slavery and anti-Blackness. See Hartman, *Lose Your Mother*, 6. The term *situated* refers to Donna Haraway's "situated knowledges" and to the wider epistemological commitment her work (and other feminist critiques) made possible. See Haraway, "Situated Knowledges."

* * *

USUALLY LOCATED AT the periphery of cities or in the transport corridors connecting them, logistical infrastructures are often less visible than other hubs of capitalist activity. Drawing on fieldwork conducted along the shipping route connecting the interior of Colombia to overseas markets, I argue that our understanding of capitalism shifts when logistical infrastructures become the point of reference.[6] For example, the social world of the vessel I boarded disrupts conventional representations of the global economy, which often depict a network of nodes and vectors through which things move quickly and smoothly. Locating ourselves amid the logistics industry, we see that this frictionless space of continuous circulation is a fantasy of the industry itself.[7] Stefano Harney and Fred Moten call this "the fantasy that capital could exist without labor."[8] According to this fantasy, they argue, "logistical populations will be created to do without thinking, to feel without emotion, to move without friction, to adapt without question, to translate without pause, to connect without interruption."[9] Though this logistical fantasy may be partially fulfilled in certain sites and situations, from the deck of the riverboat it appears more an aspirational goal than an accomplished fact.

The importance of paying critical attention to logistical infrastructures is underscored by Charmaine Chua, Martin Danyluk, Deborah Cowen, and Laleh Khalili, who argue that—in "its pursuit of speed, efficiency, reliability, and flexibility"—logistics draws upon historical configurations of power that have long underpinned capitalist modernity, or what Aníbal Quijano calls "coloniality."[10] They note that although the "logistics revolution represents a paradigmatic shift in the operations of capital, it also marks the continuation of centuries-old processes of imperial circulation and colonization."[11] In particular, the "Atlantic slave trade, which depended on a network of intercontinental commodity chains, was a precursor to present forms of large-scale, integrated capitalist production."[12] Achille Mbembe goes further, stating that "the systematic risks experienced specifically by Black slaves during early capitalism have now become the norm for . . . all of subaltern humanity," in a

---

6 Toscano and Kinkle, *Cartographies of the Absolute.*
7 Chua, "Logistics."
8 Harney and Moten, *The Undercommons,* 90.
9 Harney and Moten, *The Undercommons,* 91.
10 Chua et al., "Introduction," 625; Quijano, "Coloniality of Power."
11 Chua et al., "Introduction," 619.
12 Chua et al., "Introduction," 620.

FIGURE 4.1. J. M. W. Turner, *The Slave Ship,* or *Slavers Throwing Overboard the Dead and Dying, Typhoon Coming On,* 1840.

process he calls "the becoming Black of the world."[13] If Mbembe's point has validity, then histories of Atlantic slavery bring into fuller view the articulation of race and labor inherent to modern logistics.

Works of art and literature have long opened critical perspectives on the racial underpinnings of capitalist modernity. Frequently cited is the 1840 painting by J. M. W. Turner commonly known as *The Slave Ship* (figure 4.1), but originally titled *Slavers Throwing Overboard the Dead and Dying, Typhoon Coming On.* This painting was based on the true story of the *Zong*—an eighteenth-century slaver whose captain dumped his perishing human cargo overboard so he could collect insurance money. This painting's initial exhibition coincided with an antislavery convention held in London, and has ever since, as

13 Mbembe, *Critique of Black Reason,* 4–6. Deborah Thomas argues that "modern western political economy has been structured on the basis of a sovereign violence—grounded in the plantation—which works through racialized categories of personhood." Thomas, "Time and the Otherwise," 179. For Thomas, the plantation is a foundational space for capitalism; so, too, is the region in which the plantation was most fully developed.

FIGURE 4.2. Kara Walker, *Fons Americanus*, 2019.

Paul Gilroy puts it, "provided so much moral ballast for the indictment of racial capitalism."[14] Likewise, Cedric Robinson argues that the Africans who died on slave ships like Turner's represented "one profoundly tragic measure of the extent to which the development of the capitalist world system depended on labor its metropolis could not produce."[15]

From Herman Melville's *Moby-Dick* and *Benito Cereno* to C. L. R. James's *Mariners, Renegades and Castaways*, ships transporting human and other cargo have given rise to radical perspectives on capitalism and its dark underbelly— racial slavery.[16] The same is true for images like Turner's, or recent artistic engagements with related themes, such as Sondra Perry's *Typhoon Coming On*, which in the words of a critic "reboot[ed] the Zong massacre for the present

---

14 Gilroy, "'Where Every Breeze Speaks,'" 17; cf. Gilroy, *The Black Atlantic*, 13–14.
15 Robinson, *Black Marxism*, 118.
16 Melville, *Moby-Dick*; Melville, *Benito Cereno*; James, *Mariners, Renegades and Castaways*; Linebaugh and Rediker, *The Many-Headed Hydra*.

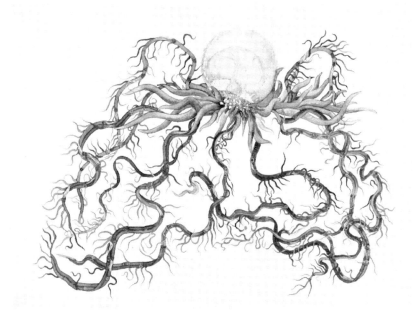

FIGURE 4.3. Ellen Gallagher, *Watery Ecstatic*, 2003.

day," or Kara Walker's *Middle Passages* and *Fons Americanus* (figure 4.2) and Ellen Gallagher's *Watery Ecstatic* (figure 4.3) and *Bird in Hand* (figure 4.4).[17] By aesthetically immersing us in the racialized depths of hydro-history, these writers and artists perform "wake work," the analytic Christina Sharpe gives us for interrogating "the continuous and changing present of slavery's as yet unresolved unfolding."[18] Following Sharpe, I ask what a view from a commercial riverboat "calls on 'us' to do, think, feel in the wake of slavery."[19]

Returning to the logistics industry at the heart of the global economy, we might then recognize its genealogical antecedents. According to Harney and Moten:

> Modern logistics is founded with the first great movement of commodities, the ones that could speak. It was founded in the Atlantic slave trade, founded against the Atlantic slave. . . . From the motley crew who followed in the red wakes of these slave ships, to the prisoners shipped

17 For a review of Sondra Perry's work, see Rosanna McLaughlin, "Sondra Perry."
18 Sharpe, *In the Wake*, 14; Hartman, *Lose Your Mother*, 6.
19 Sharpe, *In the Wake*, 20.

FIGURE 4.4. Ellen Gallagher, *Bird in Hand*, 2006.

to the settler colonies, to the mass migrations of industrialisation in the Americas, to the indentured slaves from India, China, and Java, to the trucks and boats leading north across the Mediterranean or the Rio Grande, to one-way tickets from the Philippines to the Gulf States or Bangladesh to Singapore, logistics was always the transport of slavery, not "free" labor.[20]

If indeed one of the foundational moments of modern logistics entailed the extraction of value from racialized bodies across transcontinental networks of exchange, logistical infrastructures remain key sites for analyzing the global economic order. Pursuing this line of inquiry onboard cargo vessels allows us to position ourselves analytically, to paraphrase Sharpe, in the wake of logistics—that is, to examine the linkages between the logistics industry and the ongoing history of racial capitalism in the Americas. The centrality of fluvial transport along the Magdalena River to that history cannot be overstated, but the connections between racial slavery in the past and logistical labor in

20 Harney and Moten, *The Undercommons*, 92.

the present are not straightforward. While the slave ship works symbolically to focus attention on the constitutive relationship between systems of racial hierarchy and capitalist economic orders, it does not entirely illuminate the labor regimes that figure centrally here.[21]

In contrast, riverboat histories in the Americas—while also deeply entangled with settler colonialism, plantation economies, and unfree labor—shed light on aspects of logistical labor that transatlantic slavery and its oceanic itineraries do not. For example, Mark Twain's autobiographical account of his days piloting steamboats on the Mississippi River, as well as his fiction, both center on fluvial (not maritime) vessels to highlight the imbrication of localized racial orders and transnational circuits of capital.[22] Likewise, historians demonstrate the centrality of riverboats to the racialized political economy of American imperial expansion and reveal the racially structured forms of oppression and solidarity among their crews.[23] Riverboat histories also point to the paradoxical mix of movement and stasis, of circulation and fixity, of freedom and confinement, that frequently characterizes the lives of transport workers.[24] While seafarers experience similar working conditions, the comparatively understudied world of riverboat workers deserves further consideration.[25] Moreover, if the transoceanic container ship commonly epitomizes global logistics, the commercial riverboat floats along the margins—that is, at a distance from "the heart . . . of the contemporary logistical order"—but is just as central to the operations of capital.[26] What follows is a historical and ethnographic account of fluvial transport along the Magdalena River that examines the racial underpinnings of logistics, their historical foundations, and their contemporary manifestations. The analytic of situated afterlives helps illuminate how the constitutive relationship between race and capitalism both persists and changes over time.

* * *

FROM THE EARLY sixteenth century to the mid-twentieth, Colombia's Magdalena River was the primary artery of trade and travel between the Andean

---

21 Mezzadra and Neilson, *The Politics of Operations*, 41–43.
22 Twain, *Life on the Mississippi*; Le Menager, "Floating Capital."
23 Johnson, *River of Dark Dreams*; Buchanan, *Black Life on the Mississippi*.
24 Peters and Turner, "Carceral Mobilities."
25 Anim-Addo, Hasty, and Peters, "The Mobilities of Ships," 344.
26 Schouten, Stepputat, and Bachmann, "States of Circulation," 780. See also Mezzadra and Neilson, *The Politics of Operations*.

interior, where the major cities of Bogotá, Medellín, and Cali are located, and the Caribbean coast, the main gateway to Europe and North America.[27] For over four hundred years, the river was fundamental to the modern/colonial project in the Americas, which depended on the ability to move people (laborers, merchants, travelers, settlers) and goods (gold, silver, sugar, tobacco, coffee, bananas, oil) between the mainland and the sea. Most imports also entered Colombia through the river's mouth and were distributed from the ports lining its banks, which for a time were some of the most dynamic and prosperous places in the Americas.[28]

Beginning with the initial Spanish expeditions of the 1530s, however, those seeking travel or transport along the river encountered *un río difícil* (a difficult river), due to its suffocating climate, winding course, shifting channels, seasonal variations, rapid current, and abundant obstructions.[29] Along with some technological solutions, such as new watercraft, the main strategy for overcoming these difficulties was an exceptionally brutal labor regime. While the Indigenous inhabitants of the river basin had utilized simple canoes, or *piraguas*, the Spanish colonizers introduced a larger vessel called the *champán*, a covered dugout, and the *bongo*, a wooden raft, both of which could carry greater volumes of goods.[30] These were manned by teams of boatmen (*bogas*) conscripted through the *encomienda* system, which the Spanish used throughout their empire to control Indigenous labor.[31] *Bogas* were forced to pole and row for hours on end in impossibly harsh conditions, and in no time the Indigenous population along the river had almost entirely died out.[32]

Once the Indigenous boatmen had succumbed to what Orlando Fals Borda calls their "fatal service," Spanish colonizers began importing enslaved Africans to replace their now-decimated workforce.[33] However, the same conditions were endured by the *bogas negros*—the "Black boatmen" who dominated the vocation from the seventeenth century onward—and many of them eventually met the same fate as their Indigenous predecessors. Yet the labor supply could now be replenished by the steady flow of human chattel crossing

27 Zavala, "Los aspectos geográficos"; Alvear Sanín, *Manual del Río Magdalena.*
28 Bocarejo Suescún, "Lo público de la Historia pública"; Posada-Carbó, *The Colombian Caribbean,* 6.
29 Márquez Calle, "Un río difícil."
30 Posada-Carbó, "Bongos, champanes y vapores."
31 Gilmore and Harrison, "Juan Bernardo Elbers."
32 Fals Borda, *Historia doble de la Costa,* 45A.
33 Fals Borda, 45A; Márquez Calle, "Un río difícil," 35.

the Atlantic and arriving in Cartagena—the leading slave port in New Granada.[34] With its insatiable appetite for cheap labor and its propensity for destroy-
ing bodies with extraordinary speed, transport and trade along the Magdalena
River was foundational to the long, bloody history of racial capitalism in the
Americas. Transoceanic exchanges of enslaved people and the commodities
they produced were closely tied to the movement of bodies and goods up and
down this inland waterway.

Despite the importance of bonded labor to early colonial fluvial transport,
by the late eighteenth century the work of *bogaje* was performed mostly by free
people of African descent, who had concentrated in large numbers along the
Magdalena River.[35] Though some had escaped slavery, most had been granted
or had purchased their freedom through lawful means, and yet their racialization as *negros* (Blacks), *mulatos* (mixed African and European ancestry), or *zambos* (mixed African and Indigenous ancestry) gave them uncertain legal and
political status.[36] *Bogas* also suffered harsh discrimination in colonial society at
large: in the early 1800s, Sergio Solano notes, "*bogas* occupied the lowest level
on the scale of social recognition and prestige."[37] This continued throughout the
nineteenth century, as *bogas* were routinely subjected to what Rory O'Bryen
calls "ritual dehumanisation" in cultural and political discourse.[38] They were
accused of living outside the norms of society and in violation of the authority
of Church and Crown, since *bogas* led itinerant lives along a notoriously ungovernable river, were ambiguously subject to legal jurisdictions, and mostly
escaped the control of colonial authorities.[39] However, as Katherine Bonil-
Gómez shows, the legal and political status of *bogas* was a contested affair, and
one they themselves had a hand in shaping.[40] In advocating for their collective
interests on the basis of their occupation, "*bogas* were trying to forge and defend their personal autonomy in the form of spatial mobility, and the time to
cultivate social relations."[41]

---

34 Barbary and Urrea, *Gente negra en Colombia*, 72.
35 Bonil-Gómez, "Free People of African Descent."
36 Bonil-Gómez, "Free People of African Descent."
37 Solano, *Puertos, sociedad y conflictos*, 41.
38 O'Bryen, "On the Shores of Politics," 465. See also Villegas, "El valle del río Magdalena";
    Martínez Pinzón, "Tránsitos por el río Magdalena"; Arias Vanegas, *Nación y diferencia*.
39 Solano, *Puertos, sociedad y conflictos*; Bonil-Gómez, "Free People of African Descent."
40 Bonil-Gómez, "Free People of African Descent," 188.
41 Bonil-Gómez, "Free People of African Descent," 190.

Bogas fought for spatial and temporal freedoms, as these freedoms were inherent to their work. They were accustomed to moving fluidly between towns along the riverbank, sometimes stopping even for weeks at a time.[42] Accounts written by travelers commented uniformly on the interminable hours of grinding physical work but also on the flexible timetable of riverboat journeys.[43] Solano argues that *bogas* did not draw boundaries around work and leisure: they sang and drank while they navigated, and often stopped midjourney for rest or pleasure irrespective of their clients' wishes.[44] The autonomy possessed by *bogas* was related to the fact that they customarily received payment for their services in advance, which allowed them to complete their contract on their own terms, since only they possessed knowledge of the complex environment in which they worked. This afforded *bogas* a sense of superiority over their patrons, whom they could easily manipulate to ensure their work was valued properly.[45] Indeed, the entire viceroyalty depended heavily on the boatmen of the Magdalena River—without their labor, the colonial economy would have ceased to function.[46]

Fluvial transport took on renewed importance in the movement for independence from Spain. In recognition of the river's importance for the nascent nation's future, Simón Bolívar issued an early decree granting a Colombian engineer of German origin, Juan Bernardo Elbers, a monopoly concession to develop steamboat navigation.[47] At a moment marked by what Francisco Ortega calls the sense of "precarious time," improving river transport was seen as an urgent project of political consolidation that could integrate a sharply divided young country.[48] That project was both a geographical and a racial one, as political and intellectual elites sought to create not only a unified territory out of a fragmented collection of regions but also a unified identity for a nation composed mainly of people of heterogenous mixtures of Indigenous, African, and European ancestry.[49] Though *mestizaje* (or hybridity) was often espoused, it was based on an underlying racial and regional hierarchy that

---

42 Peñas Galindo, *Los bogas de Mompox.*
43 Solano, *Puertos, sociedad y conflictos,* 42.
44 Solano, *Puertos, sociedad y conflictos,* 42.
45 Solano, *Puertos, sociedad y conflictos,* 43.
46 Villegas, "El valle del río Magdalena," 157; Bonil-Gómez, "Free People of African Descent," 186.
47 Gilmore and Harrison, "Juan Bernardo Elbers."
48 Ortega, "Precarious Time"; Villegas, "El valle del río Magdalena," 151-52.
49 Wade, *Blackness and Race Mixture,* 8-11.

privileged the lighter side of the mestizo spectrum and the Andean highlands over the coastal lowlands.[50]

These racial and regional anxieties were fundamentally linked to aspirations of progress, development, and modernity.[51] And due to its strategic importance as a conduit between Colombia and the wider world, the Magdalena River and its peoples featured prominently in these debates.[52] Flowing from the characteristically white temperate highlands to the predominantly Black and mestizo tropical coast, the river was seen as both a racialized measure of civilization and an infrastructural fix for underdevelopment.[53] Nineteenth-century *letrados* (members of learned society), such as Liberal parliamentarian José María Samper, saw the *boga* as both a hindrance to civilizational advancement and an obstacle to the flow of commerce, and sought ways to "erode the *boga*'s monopoly over river transport" and erase these humiliating "reminders of Colombia's 'barbaric' past."[54] According to the economic and political imperatives at the heart of early nation-building efforts, interventions that sought to improve fluvial transport were inseparable from prevailing racial taxonomies and regional inequalities.[55]

Invoking free-market doctrines, private merchants and public officials united in their attempts to remove hindrances to industry and trade, "fixat[ing] on boatmen's dominion over navigation as a major obstacle to commercial progress."[56] As in the colonial period, *bogas* in the mid-nineteenth century continued to exercise control over timing and compensation, effectively setting "the tempo of the nation's commerce" through work stoppages and strikes, while enjoying spatial mobility and rejecting the deference expected of racially subordinated populations.[57] To temper *bogas*' grip on navigation, commercial boosters lobbied the national government to institute a regulatory system that, according to Jason McGraw, "rendered boatmen the country's most heavily policed workforce."[58] Although this system was eventually dismantled

---

50 Wade, *Blackness and Race Mixture*; Appelbaum, *Mapping the Country of Regions*.

51 Wade, *Blackness and Race Mixture*; Appelbaum, *Mapping the Country of Regions*.

52 Leal, "Usos del concepto 'raza'"; Martínez Pinzón, "Tránsitos por el río Magdalena"; O'Bryen, "On the Shores of Politics."

53 Leal, "Usos del concepto 'raza'"; Villegas, "El valle del río Magdalena."

54 O'Bryen, "On the Shores of Politics," 465–66; Martínez Pinzón, "Tránsitos por el río Magdalena," 22.

55 Villegas, "El valle del río Magdalena," 155.

56 McGraw, *The Work of Recognition*, 73.

57 McGraw, *The Work of Recognition*, 77–79.

58 McGraw, *The Work of Recognition*, 74.

by the abolitionist movement, which saw it as constricting labor freedoms, the racially inflected regulation of boatmen was simply devolved to local authorities. Their jurisdiction was always limited, however, and river merchants eventually resorted to steam technology to resolve the problem *bogas* supposedly posed for free trade.

Steamboats, once introduced, did come to play an important economic role by facilitating the trade of tobacco and quinine, the nation's first export crops, and eventually coffee—the commodity that would fuel Colombia's modernization drive.[59] Though the *vapores*, as they were called, were not immune to the river's navigational obstacles and by no means replaced the older vessels, they reduced freight costs and shipping rates by increasing the pace of commerce and communication, thereby boosting exports and profits.[60] They also brought with them an air of sophistication: as one observer put it, the "luxurious and comfortable" steamboats were "objects of modern civilization" compared to the canoes and rafts, which for him were "memories of the past."[61] So, too, republican elites hoped that the consolidation of steamboats in the 1870s and 1880s would displace "the coarsest of our national types, the boga . . . a tall, muscular man of colour, savage in his customs, and sole rival of the caiman."[62] Throughout this period, Colombia's hopes of becoming a modern, independent nation were inextricably bound up with fluvial transport and with the racialized labor on which it depended.

At first, the arrival of *vapores* did not greatly change the labor regime along the river. Most steamboat companies were based in the port of Barranquilla at the mouth of the Magdalena and hired crews from there or from upriver towns.[63] Though some were recruited from Cartagena's maritime workforce, the majority descended from *bogas* with extensive experience in fluvial transport and an established ethos of spatial and temporal flexibility.[64] These continuities were strengthened by the fact that, to be hired, one had to be endorsed by (or related to) an existing crew member. And while it was common for *bogas* to affiliate with specific steamboats, as before, they were contracted only for a single voyage. Equipment repairs, commercial fluctuations, and environmental conditions could leave them temporarily idle, but this afforded them time

---

59 Horna, "Transportation Modernization and Entrepreneurship," 35–36.
60 McGraw, *The Work of Recognition*, 91.
61 Cited in Posada-Carbó, "Bongos, champanes y vapores," 3.
62 Vergara y Vergara [1867] 1957, cited in O'Bryen, "On the Shores of Politics," 465.
63 Solano, *Puertos, sociedad y conflictos*, 38.
64 Solano, *Puertos, sociedad y conflictos*, 36.

to dedicate to other economic activities.[65] During this moment of significant technological change, the articulation of race and labor along the river remained relatively stable.

Things began to shift around the turn of the twentieth century as the Colombian state sought again to regulate riverboat work amid a rapid increase in people employed in the trade.[66] Decrees were issued that endowed steamboat captains with increased authority and that deployed fluvial inspectors to enforce equipment and labor standards and to keep detailed records of commercial activities.[67] These regulatory requirements, which increased steadily throughout the first half of the twentieth century, aspired to transform notoriously capricious riverboat workers into reliable contributors to the national good. The capital-intensiveness of steamboats also altered the relationship between *bogas* and vessel owners, who were now members of the white elite and, in some cases, English, German, or American investors.[68]

At this point, a new labor regime began to unsettle the one that had been in place since the late eighteenth century, when *bogaje* became the province of free persons of African descent.[69] Whereas *bogas* had never been under direct supervision of boat owners, captains and officers now served as representatives of steamboat companies and began to impose strict discipline, establish regimented schedules, and limit time in river ports. Though some payment was still doled out to crews in advance, the majority was distributed once the vessel reached its destination, which significantly reduced workers' bargaining power and temporal flexibility. Steamboat technology added another dimension of labor control, since it required less contact between crew members and riverine populations, especially after wood-burning boilers were replaced by internal combustion engines, and fuel was made readily available along the riverbank. Riverboat work remained exceedingly strenuous but now demanded less knowledge of the river, which made the job accessible to a wider population.

---

65 Solano, *Puertos, sociedad y conflictos*, 44–45.

66 For statistics on riverboat workers (1872–1928), see Solano, *Puertos, sociedad y conflictos*, 36. Jason McGraw estimates that the average steamboat employed thirty to forty deckhands. McGraw, *The Work of Recognition*, 93. For a detailed account of regulatory statutes, see Solano, *Puertos, sociedad y conflictos*, 47–49.

67 Solano, *Puertos, sociedad y conflictos*, 40.

68 Solano, *Puertos, sociedad y conflictos*, 52.

69 The changes outlined here summarize a more detailed inventory complied by Solano, *Puertos, sociedad y conflictos*, 46.

The racial articulation of this new labor regime also shifted, as the category of *boga* itself began to disappear. This was partly due to the change in physical activity; the term, after all, had referred to the act of rowing. But this shift also reflected a wider trend after Independence, whereby racial taxonomies were increasingly supplanted by regional typologies.[70] The latter, while continuing to signify racial and cultural difference as well as occupational aptitudes and to enable subtle forms of discrimination, nevertheless held out the promise of liberal values, such as equality and inclusion.[71] Indeed, steamer crews themselves advocated for new monikers that carried less negative connotations, opting instead for labels mainly derived from seafaring, such as *tripulante, navegante, marinero,* and *buquero*.[72] These designations, they hoped, would distance their vocation from its racialized proximity to Blackness—a shift they had reason to think would translate into less discrimination, if not higher wages. Many also emphasized their identities as *costeños* or *ribereños* (from the Caribbean coast or Magdalena valley), but these regional categories still positioned riverboat workers within a geo-racial hierarchy that implied disadvantages within the labor market and in Colombian society at large.

Despite expectations, steamboats continued to struggle with the river's physical conditions, and shipping traffic regularly ground to a halt. A series of bloody civil wars throughout the nineteenth century had also regularly hampered navigation, as vessels were seized by opposing factions, converted into warships, and subsequently damaged or destroyed.[73] But the real downfall of steamboat transport—indeed of commercial shipping in general along the river—came in the mid-twentieth century as navigation was hampered by complex socio-ecological factors, investment was directed to roads and railways, and the Pacific port of Buenaventura took precedence for key exports.[74] This was also the beginning of Colombia's long and bloody armed conflict, which made the movement of cargo along the river all the more difficult. Nevertheless, a few shipping lines managed to sustain their operations, albeit with new equipment, and the experience of riverboat workers during this period reflects the historical articulations of race and labor in the world of fluvial transport.

70 Appelbaum, *Mapping the Country of Regions.*
71 Arias Vanegas, *Nación y diferencia.*
72 Solano, *Puertos, sociedad y conflictos,* 49.
73 Safford, "Foreign and National Enterprise," 525.
74 Posada-Carbó, *The Colombian Caribbean,* 5.

THE ARMED CONFLICT is often said to have begun in 1948 with the assassination of popular presidential candidate Jorge Eliécer Gaitán on a street in downtown Bogotá. Gaitán's murder sparked mass rioting throughout the capital, as well as in smaller cities and towns across the country, which marked the onset of La Violencia—a decade of political violence lasting until 1958. This coincided with the decline of commercial shipping on the Magdalena, which created an opening for armed groups to use the artery to pursue their political and economic objectives.[75] Navigating the river became increasingly dangerous, with revolts erupting in riverside cities and towns, partisan checkpoints appearing at strategic locations, and confrontations between Liberal and Conservative factions occurring along the waterway.[76] Testimonies from commercial riverboat crews attest to the impact this period of violence had on river navigation: the routes they followed, the precautions they took, and the timing of their journeys were all dictated by the logic of survival.[77] Riverboat workers also began to witness the artery filling up with corpses of combatants and civilians—a phenomenon that would recur throughout subsequent stages of the conflict well into the twenty-first century.

As the war raged on, the Magdalena Medio (or Middle Magdalena)—an extensive swath of interior bisected by the eponymous waterway—suffered some of the most horrific and protracted periods of fighting. An epicenter of violent clashes between guerrilla insurgents, paramilitary groups, drug cartels, and state security forces, the region came to be known as one of the most conflict ridden. While much of the bloodletting took place on solid ground, the river played a major role. Initially enabling the movement of armed actors, the Magdalena became a strategic corridor for the expansion of territorial control and for capital accumulation through drug trafficking and resource extraction.[78] Remote areas accessible only by boat were ideal for coca cultivation and cocaine processing, and the waterway served as a clandestine route to the Caribbean Sea and to Venezuela, where the finished product could be exported to consumer markets overseas.[79] By the 1980s, it was common to find corpses

75 See the 2021 virtual conference given by Muriel Jiménez Ortega, "Las violencias y el río Magdalena."

76 Guerra, "El imaginario oficial," 149–50.

77 Guerra, "El imaginario oficial," 149–50.

78 Duarte et al., *Entre paramilitares y guerrillas*, 67. See also Beltrán and Cuervo, "Pentecostalismo en contextos rurales"; Moreno Sarmiento and Zamora Aviles, "Acumulación capitalista."

79 Echandía Castilla, *Dos décadas de escalamiento*, 165.

floating in the channel, while eddies downstream of riverside towns gained infamy for accumulating human remains.[80] Armed groups devised gruesome techniques for disposing of bodies underwater, such as cutting open a victim's stomach and filling it with stones, and crocodiles were enlisted as proxy killers.[81] Islands in the river housed covert torture sites, and fishermen were consulted when families went searching for loved ones gone missing.[82] Scientists have even developed a mathematical model for predicting how lifeless bodies drift in waterways to aid in the search for the disappeared.[83]

The lower reaches of the river have experienced relatively less violence, according to regional analyses, since guerrilla presence was weaker toward the Caribbean coast, and paramilitary groups met little resistance.[84] An exception was the Canal del Dique, the canal linking the river to Cartagena, where the bodies of thousands killed by paramilitaries were unceremoniously dumped.[85] Victims were brought from other parts of the country, according to testimony received by the Truth Commission—a practice encouraged by local authorities.[86] An amphibious expanse called La Mojana was also terrorized by armed groups hell-bent on desiccating wetlands and forcibly consolidating them into land for cattle ranching, mining operations, and plantation agriculture.[87] Here accumulation by dispossession reconfigured the land-water boundary and further violated fluvial ecosystems by channeling agricultural and industrial discharge: mercury from mines, waste from ranches, and pesticide from plantations.[88] And Montes de María, an area running from the western bank of the Magdalena to the shores of the Caribbean Sea, became a front line in the battle between guerrillas and paramilitaries. This is an upland area, but its strategic value for armed groups derives from its proximity to the region's two major water bodies and the connectivity afforded by its network of roads, streams, and swamps.

---

80 Rutas del Conflicto, "El silencio del río grande." ; Sáez, "El pueblo que adopta cadáveres."
81 Rutas del Conflicto, "El silencio del río grande"; VerdadAbierta.com, "'A su hermano lo lanzaron vivo a los cocodrilos.'"
82 Rutas del Conflicto, "El silencio del río grande."
83 Millán Valencia, "El modelo matemático."
84 González G. et al., *Territorio y conflicto*, 8.
85 Maldonado Rozo, "Canal del Dique."
86 Maldonado Rozo, "Canal del Dique."
87 Gutiérrez Campo and Escobar Jiménez, "Territorio anfibio y despojo." See also O'Bryen, "Untangling the Mangrove."
88 Camacho, "Acumulación tóxica."

In places like Montes de María, an area historically inhabited by campesinos of African descent, violent spatial politics took explicitly racialized form. While these territories had been persistently threatened since the colonial period, further cycles of dispossession began in the 1960s, when a state-led project of agrarian reform began undermining relatively autonomous Black communities by refusing to recognize their political subjectivity, agricultural economies, and territorial rights.[89] The area subsequently underwent multiple upheavals, with guerrilla incursions and land occupations followed by waves of paramilitary violence, land dispossession, and agro-industrial expansion.[90] The paramilitary groups controlling the area "consolidated a hierarchical social order in terms of ethno-racial belonging, sex and gender," whereby people of African descent, especially Black women, were punished most cruelly for resisting armed occupation.[91] They were subjected to dehumanizing and degrading treatment, including physical and psychological torture, and these racialized manifestations of violence were countered by the strategic deployment of Black political subjectivity and embodied territorial practices in defense of autonomy and place.[92]

Prior to emancipation in the mid-nineteenth century, Eloisa Berman-Arévalo notes, the waterways between the Caribbean coast and Montes de María were "natural escape routes for maroon slaves" who established settlements in the general vicinity.[93] There they set up *palenques*—communities of formerly enslaved people who had escaped bondage or attained freedom by other means—and these areas continue to host majority Black populations.[94] These settlements ranged across the lower Magdalena valley, clustering around waterways such as the Canal del Dique and the floodplains of La Mojana, which would eventually become hotspots of violent conflict. Many of the paramilitary groups that imposed regimes of terror on these terraqueous spaces came from the interior highlands; they took pride in their regional pedigree and its implicit association with whiteness. Some analysts have even identified a pattern whereby violence was highest in areas "located on the

---

89 Berman-Arévalo, "Mapping Violent Land Orders." See also Berman-Arévalo, "Geografías negras del arroz."
90 Berman-Arévalo, "Mapping Violent Land Orders," 350.
91 Universidad ICESI and Centro de Estudios Afrodiaspóricos, "Racismo, patriarcado y conflicto armado," 32, 115.
92 Berman-Arévalo, "Geografías negras del arroz"; Berman-Arévalo, "El 'fracaso ruinoso.'"
93 Berman-Arévalo, "El 'fracaso ruinoso,'" 128.
94 Fals Borda, *Historia doble de la Costa*, 52B.

FIGURE 4.5. Puerto Plomo as seen from the boat, 2018. Source: photograph by author.

border between Caribbean and Andean worlds."[95] According to predominant geo-racial regimes, these worlds occupy different positions within a social and spatial order organized around anti-Blackness and white supremacy, and perhaps unsurprisingly a "different logic" of violence prevailed along the boundary between them.[96] In both terrestrial and fluvial manifestations, the armed conflict reflected and reinforced the hierarchical orders of difference governing the limits of being and belonging in Colombia.

Throughout the conflict, commercial riverboat captains and crews have had simultaneously to navigate both violent environments and entrenched hierarchies. They have witnessed all types of social and ecological depredation, and they possess extensive knowledge of the armed conflict and its aquatic geographies. This became clear during my time spent onboard. I was reluctant to pry, since years of fieldwork in Colombia had taught me not to push people to relive traumatic pasts, yet the conflict had a way of entering conversations throughout my river journey. On hot, slow afternoons I often gravitated to the

95 González G. et al., *Territorio y conflicto*, 8.
96 González G. et al., *Territorio y conflicto*, 8.

control bridge, where I could usually find a willing interlocutor in the on-duty helmsman (the air conditioning was also a draw). With time elongated by the sluggish pace of travel, seemingly infinite stretches of silence went unbroken until something on the horizon sparked a comment. Such comments usually sought to educate me in the finer points of fluvial navigation, and given my inexperience there was no shortage of teachable moments. To my surprise, however, crew members often reached back to the past and dredged up memories from the armed conflict's darkest days.

"See that spot," Ángel asked while gesturing to a clearing along the riverbank. "We used to call it Puerto Plomo [Lead Port]," he informed me, explaining the guerrilla's penchant for launching attacks on towboat-and-barge convoys from this location (figure 4.5). "*Pura trinchera*," he exclaimed: pure trench warfare. I could make out low hills surrounding the clearing, which I imagined once offered clear sight lines, as well as waist-high brush that would have provided natural cover, but Ángel added his own account of what made this site strategic. The nearby San Lucas mountain range was a guerrilla stronghold, and combatants could reach this desolate stretch of river with relative ease. Hydrological conditions were also a factor, he said, as extensive sedimentation in the main channel complicated navigation, and this forced convoys to hug the riverbank, making them especially vulnerable. "The guerrilla would dig in and fire off round after round as we floated slowly by," Ángel recalled. The honorific title *veteran*, given to crew members who had survived that era, was not metaphorical.

The captain, standing watch, chimed in. I had come to know him as a serious character with no patience for gossip or banter, but both men were now animated, as if they relished recounting stories from this tragic chapter of Colombian history. "We had to travel with armed personnel from the marine infantry onboard," he recalled, "but they [the guerrilla] still attacked us constantly, especially above kilometer 506." The captain then described the so-called Popemobile that was built to protect the pilothouse: "The shipping company installed an armored shell around the control bridge: sheets of iron backed by sandbags. The only opening was a narrow slot through which to see. The pilot had to lock himself up completely to be able to navigate safely." The captain then compared the past to the present: "The biggest concern now is whether water levels will allow us to pass through this stretch," he reported. "We used to be terrified that an ambush was always waiting around the next bend." But as Ángel had mentioned, hydrology was also relevant: "Sedimentation forced us to move slowly and to concentrate intensely on our technical maneuvers, which played right into the hands of the guerrilla." I learned later that the topographic features of this riverbank were also the result of hydrological management. "There are piles of sand there," a mechanic told me, "which the guerrillas used to entrench themselves." These sandpiles were dredge spoil that had been removed from the shipping channel to improve navigation. The dredger dumped the sediment along the riverbank, giving the guerrillas an advantageous position for their assault.

Along the journey, crew members often pointed to sites of repeated confrontations, some of which were at the mouths of tributaries joining the Magdalena's main stem. Ángel mentioned a waterway called Caño Corea (Korea Canal), presumably named after the other twentieth-century conflict "where they also fired at us [*nos dieron plomo*]." The guerrillas would descend from their mountain encampments, initially on foot and then onward by boat through small streams feeding the river. Their objective was simple—force shipping companies to pay *vacunas* (fees for protection and safe passage)—and although some complied, others refused. The company that employed Ángel appealed to the government for military protection and was successful (their main client was Ecopetrol, the state-owned oil company). "This infuriated the guerrillas," Ángel recalled, "and they responded with campaigns to damage, even sink, our vessels." Ángel's uncle worked on one of the boats that was targeted. "This was back in 1997," he told me, "up in Bocas del Rosario, Santander [the Magdalena Medio]. River conditions forced them to stop for the night, so they had to tie up in a desolate area [*puro monte*] that was notoriously dangerous [*caliente*]. In the early morning hours, the guerrillas arrived by canoe and strapped dynamite to the towboat's hull. Nobody saw anything. They rowed to the opposite bank and boom! Some of the crew managed to jump overboard, but the vessel sank quickly. That was their goal." In contrast to the guerrillas' terrestrial objectives, which often centered on the occupation and redistribution of land, in fluvial environments they sought to disrupt the flow of commerce. The same rationale motivated their attacks on other transport corridors, such as highways, but over water the material conditions were different. The vastness of the waterscape made it impossible for the state to establish dominion, and this created openings for guerrillas. The same constraint applied in reverse, however, which forced the rebel groups to resort to tactical strikes in pursuit of more limited ends. Relative to conflicts over land, the river was harder to control.

A primary target of guerrilla aggression was Ecopetrol, one of the Colombian state's most valuable assets, and this put the crews of riverboats contracted by the oil company perpetually in harm's way. According to Edwin, a mechanic, "we were civilians in the middle of a crossfire. We tried to maintain our distance from military personnel onboard . . . to make it clear who was a soldier and who was a worker." The subtle distinction was not always appreciated, Edwin noted, by those lobbing grenades from the riverbank. And the problems continued even after the guerrillas began losing strength in the early 2000s, Edwin told me: "The guerrillas left when the *paracos* [paramilitaries] arrived, and they were just as bad. The remedy was worse than the illness." Paramilitaries took control of points along the shoreline where the guerrillas once reigned, which meant that riverboats were attacked less frequently. "But we had to be just as careful," Edwin reported, "maybe even more so, not to get mixed up with them." He told the story of a recent stop in a town occupied by armed groups to emphasize that this pattern continues. "We got out of there as quickly as possible," he remembered. "We didn't wait around to see who was in control—the ELN [leftist guerrillas] or the AUC [right-wing paramilitaries]." Either way, he and his colleagues risked becoming casualties of a conflict between warring factions, none of which represented them.

Declaring allegiances is a dangerous game in Colombia, and civilians generally refrain from playing it, especially outside their immediate circle of trust. Riverboat workers, while generally professing neutrality, can often speak quite candidly. Many admitted to sympathizing with the ostensible goals of guerrilla groups—land redistribution, democratic accountability—but they also opposed their violent tactics and lamented the eventual abandonment of their social and political ideals in pursuit of economic gain. Some felt indebted to the ELN for defending the oil workers union, which also represented some fluvial transport workers, when its leaders and members were being targeted systematically by right-wing paramilitaries. Others felt that this association was damaging, however, and criticized the hypocrisy of leftist groups for attacking infrastructures manned by low-paid workers. Paramilitaries were famed for neutralizing threats from the guerrillas—an attractive goal to riverboat workers—but their loyalty to large landholders and wealthy businessmen did not sit well. Moreover, crew members occasionally described the paramilitaries as an occupying force that has subjected territories long inhabited by friends and families to brutal regimes of terror. Some also harbored distrust for the police and the armed forces, who they said were prone to corruption and capitulating to paramilitary rule. None of these parties to the armed conflict seemed to align well with the interests and values of riverboat workers.

In addition to their knowledge of the aquatic geographies of violence, these men were also intimately familiar with Colombia's geo-racial regimes and their role within the armed conflict. "We're lovers, not fighters," one deckhand quipped, referring to an essentialized depiction of *costeños* as intrinsically nonviolent. This whimsical comment dovetailed with other, more serious allegations that violence has often spread from the Andean interior to the Caribbean coast, and that those who have perpetrated it "don't look like us and aren't from our communities," in the words of a crew member from the Lower Magdalena whose hometown had suffered paramilitary killings and disappearances. This charge equated riverboat workers—coded historically as Black and mixed-race men from the Caribbean coast region—with victims along lines of place and identity, and in opposition to those responsible for violence, who were assumed to belong to other racial and regional designations. While some degree of generalization is possible when it comes to the demographic profile of armed groups—paramilitaries were frequently associated with whiteness; the guerrillas were known to have been more hospitable to Black and Indigenous recruits; and the armed forces were said to resemble the poorer strata of Colombian society at large—this varied by region, and the rank-and-file members of each were internally diverse.[97] In practice, this made clear-cut distinctions difficult; there was no way to socially differentiate riverboat workers from the people enacting violence against them.

In the fluvial transport industry, hierarchical values attached to region, class, color, and other markers of difference are reflected in the ranks of crew members, as well as in the gap between workers onboard and management on land. During the armed conflict, nonwhite working-class men laboring on the water were frequently caught in the crossfire and often fell prey to confrontations between factions that did not represent them, whereas those whose economic interests were threatened occupied another position entirely. Such differences often corresponded to physical appearance, though not necessarily; regardless of phenotype, riverboat workers could be racialized in subtle ways. For example, a pilot who presented as white was nevertheless nicknamed *golero* (black vulture), indicating his position on the darker end of the racial spectrum. He said he received this handle for other reasons, but nicknames derived from racialized identities are extremely common (*negrita*, or "blackie," for the darkest woman in town), and references are often made to animals (the ubiquitous term for "white guy" is *mono*, or "monkey"). While class background, regional origin, and linguistic markers likely trumped skin color in this case, that did not always hold true. A deckhand who identified as Black

---

97 A telling exception comes from Teo Ballvé's interviews with the paramilitary commander Freddy Rendón, alias El Alemán, who boasted of the racial diversity of his bloc in defense of its legitimacy in territories with large Afro-descendant and Indigenous populations, such as Urabá. See Ballvé, *The Frontier Effect*, 87.

once joked that if he tried to pass as a gringo (the term for a light-skinned foreigner), he could only hope to be branded *gringo quemado* (burned gringo) on account of his dark skin. The status of riverboat workers within the geo-racial regimes of difference structuring Colombian society and space—as people racially coded as Black, regardless of physical appearance or self-identification— shaped their position within the armed conflict: as people whose injuries and mortalities could be classified as collateral damage.

* * *

DURING THE SEVEN days it would take us to reach our upriver destination, and in subsequent interviews, I spoke at length with crew members about their work. While onboard, most conversations took place in the towboat's wheelhouse. This is the domain of the captain and his pilots, and the shipping company's head office had instructed me to remain there during waking hours. I could visit other parts of the vessel, with permission and if accompanied, though my options were limited. The towboat's engine room, where the mechanics work, was deafeningly loud and oppressively hot. The flat expanse of the barge convoy, where the deckhands perform most of their tasks, was off-limits on account of safety protocols. An obvious place to chat—or so I thought—was the galley where everyone eats, but meals are taken mostly in silence under the grainy glow of a wall-mounted television. Fortunately, the wheelhouse provided ample opportunity to converse with crew members, and not only the captain and pilots, as others frequently passed through. The room was air-conditioned, protected from both blazing sun and torrential rain, and a stack of plastic chairs beckoned visitors. Despite these modest comforts, the more time I spent in the wheelhouse, the more I came to understand the paradoxical combination of freedom and confinement riverboat workers often spoke about when discussing their jobs.

The crews laboring on the Magdalena River's shipping lines live itinerant lives, spending much more time on the boat than they do anywhere else. "This is our home," the first pilot told me. "For twenty-one days straight we live and work on the boat, moving upriver and down. Don't get me wrong—I look forward to shore leave. But when I go home [switching now to the river town of Malambo] I feel lost, unsure what to do with myself. When we're working, we're constantly in motion." Though crew members frequently lamented their separation from family and friends, many described their perpetual state of movement with words like *flexibility* and *freedom*. Their mobility is highly constrained, however, and the tight quarters of the vessel are only the beginning. Leaving the boat is prohibited, unless authorized by the captain for a specific task, and no stops are allowed in river towns or ports during the journey. The head mechanic once referred to this as being "trapped on the move."

The simultaneous itineracy and immobility inherent to this labor regime reflects the historical linkages between fluvial transport along the Magdalena River and the manpower of enslaved Africans and their emancipated descendants. These workers were both infinitely transportable and tightly controlled; they could be moved anywhere but were everywhere subjected to extreme discipline. On the river, they were made to travel incessantly but according to strict limitations. The emancipated people of African descent who powered riverboats in later years also experienced a contradictory mix of freedom and confinement. They enjoyed spatial mobility and temporal flexibility, and yet they were fixed socially within rigid and discriminatory racial hierarchies. Though riverboat work changed significantly throughout the twentieth century, the logistics industry remains indebted to the articulations of race and labor that have powered fluvial transport for centuries.

My time spent in the wheelhouse gave me insight into the constrained mobility of riverboat workers, but it insulated me from many of the everyday dangers they face. Accidents and injuries are common, and multiple health and safety hazards are ever present. The tanks of the barges are filled with highly flammable liquid cargo. The convoy is lashed together by heavy steel cables winched to extreme tautness (figure 4.6). The heat and humidity of these tropical lowlands are extreme. The filtered river water consumed onboard is potentially toxic (*muy pesado*, or "very heavy," they warned me). A casual misstep around the vessel's edge will lead to almost certain death. Riverboat work is most physically taxing for the deckhands, who perform all onboard manual labor, and its grueling demands clearly take a significant toll on their bodies. The two oldest deckhands are in their fifties; their coworkers, decades younger, marveled at how they had lasted so long. The mechanics working below deck in the towboat's engine room face other adversities, such as asphyxiation and deafness. When asked about these conditions, many expressed concerns, but always alongside a sense of pride. "No one else can do the work we do," an experienced deckhand told me. "It's in our blood."[98]

---

98 For early modern epistemologies of race and blood purity, which conceived of race as an invisible essence passed down through the generations, see Rappaport, "Colombia and the Legal-Cultural Negotiation." For similar claims made by Italian fashion managers relative to their Chinese counterparts, see Rofel and Yanagisako, *Fabricating Transnational Capitalism*, 64. Notably, Rofel and Yanagisako interpret the claim that fashion is "in our DNA" as metaphorical, rather than about biology and genetics (or race).

FIGURE 4.6. *Marineros* (deckhands) maneuvering the cables that bind the barges to the towboat. Source: photograph by author.

In conversations with crew members, and with managers back on land, I was often struck by frequent connections drawn between the peculiar qualities of riverboat work and the physical composition of those who perform it. According to long-standing racial ontologies, which once determined questions of value in slave markets throughout the Americas, the bodies of riverboat workers are assumed to be naturally suited to enduring extended periods of time in harsh conditions. The category of *boga*, which for centuries was used to identify boatmen, referred simultaneously to their professional occupation, geographical origin, and racial extraction. *Bogas* were typed by Spanish colonizers as genetically predisposed to riverine labor and its associated hardships. Though that category is uncommon today, the vocation of riverboat worker remains tied to the same river towns and the associated regional-cum-racial identity of their inhabitants (boatmen still generally self-identify as *costeños* or *ribereños*). As before, they are widely believed to be constitutionally fit for riverboat work.

This strategy of labor exploitation and control is also a point of distinction invoked by workers themselves. After all, it keeps the profession in the family, often quite literally. New recruits must still be vouched for by current crew members, and strong kinship ties exist among the crew. On the boat, over a quarter of the workers hailed from the river town of Yatí (in the area *bogas* once called home) and considered themselves relatives. The strict association of boatmen with Blackness, condensed in the category of *boga*, has loosened, and riverboat workers are no longer uniformly dark skinned or of African descent, nor are they necessarily subject to the same level of discrimination. Yet their geo-racial identity remains central to their occupation—both in practices of labor recruitment and management, and in the experience of committing one's body to this arduous vocation. These genealogical systems of kinship and capability continue to support the articulation of race and labor along the Magdalena River.

The work of the captain and his pilots, though less physical, is considered equally hereditary. Detailed knowledge of hydrological conditions and navigation techniques is said to be the inborn property of river people, passing automatically through generations. Though one hones these skills on the job, the inherent capacity to master the vocation is believed to be inherited from an older male relative (a father or an uncle). The captain I came to know is an exception to this rule: he was born in a coal mining village and raised in a regional capital far from the river. His upbringing, accent, and appearance all marked him as broadly *costeño* but not *ribereño*, as he lacked fluvial pedigree; indeed, his prodigious aptitude for commanding the vessel was seen as an anomaly. Like his team of helmsman and pilots of riverine origin, however, the captain relied upon his intrinsic talent for navigation and made infrequent use of charts, radar, and other technological aids. *Navegamos a lo empírico*, they often told me, referring to the inherent knowledge and skills inherited from elders and refined through experience.

Locating the capacity for certain types of work in the hereditary body is fundamental to the labor regime structuring the logistics industry along the Magdalena River. However, it also makes riverboat workers relatively difficult to replace and affords them some control over their time. Until recently, they were given three days of shore leave every two months. Their trade union, Sintranaviera, fought for better conditions, and they are now entitled to seven days off for every twenty-one days of work, though holidays are nonexistent (operations continue on Easter and Christmas, as I discovered during Semana Santa, or Holy Week). And while the speed and predictability of riverboat journeys are central preoccupations of the shipping company, as throughout the logistics industry, riverboat workers are rarely held responsible for slowdowns or stoppages. Difficult stretches of river might delay the convoy significantly;

traversing just a few kilometers per day is not uncommon when water levels are low or where sedimentation is pronounced. In these cases, the captain and crew use their intimate relationship to the river and inimitable command of the vessel to rebuff pressure and avoid sanctions from the head office in Barranquilla. Not only do they refer to their ability to see the sandbars impeding navigation and feel the boat as its hull runs aground. They also assert their intrinsic talent for determining whether the convoy's draft is shallow enough, the towboat's propellers strong enough, and the water levels steady enough for the journey to proceed. According to the articulation of race and labor at work along the river, their lighter-skinned, land-bound managers are inherently unable to object.

That said, the bargaining power and temporal flexibility possessed by earlier generations of *bogas* have been significantly reduced. The timetables of riverboat journeys are now dictated by the management of the shipping company rather than by rivermen's ability to determine the pace and rhythm of their work. When temporal fluctuations do occur, they are due to factors beyond the control of the captain and crew. Opportunities for rest or diversion are limited to the time between shifts or to the moments in which their labor is not needed. The latter is especially true for deckhands, who can be called upon at any time to perform specific maneuvers, whereas the captain and pilots take turns at the helm, as do mechanics in the engine room. Deckhands are always on call, and when the vessel goes into twenty-four-hour operation, they are effectively on duty around the clock. During my journey onboard, I often engaged in exchanges on the passageways of the towboat's upper deck or in the kitchen—two places crew members linger during breaks—only to find the conversation interrupted abruptly by a call from the captain conveying an order. The towboat is under constant CCTV surveillance, and the captain (or whoever is at the helm) has a live feed of what is happening in key locations around the boat. The video transmission (or at least a record of it) is also available to the shipping company's main office, giving management near-total oversight of its workforce. Only in small ways are riverboat crews able to manipulate time for their own benefit.

This is especially evident in riverboat workers' orientations toward the future. During my journey, formal interviews and casual conversations frequently touched on the impossibility of predicting or determining what would happen next. Hopes for advancement do exist for some, especially those like a young helmsman who has quickly worked his way up through the ranks. Most crew members got their start as deckhands, or in the company's shipyard, and were eventually tapped for promotion. They are grateful to their employer for the possibility of a decent life and trust that this will continue. But the rhythms of work lie mainly beyond everyone's control; hence, crew members constantly invoke the will of God (*si Dios quiere, con el favor de Dios*) when discussing the future. These phrases are used commonly throughout Colombia to reference temporal horizons that lack certainty and are not unique to riverboat work. But for crew members, almost all work-related events are of this sort. Will we arrive in port tomorrow? Will you visit family during your next leave? Will you be promoted to captain? Will you eventually earn enough to build a house? Consistently, the answers to questions like these reflect uncertainty and unpredictability. To the extent that the future can be anticipated, it contains more of the same: journeying up and down the same stretch of river, transporting the same products, adhering to the same schedule.

Meanwhile, the Colombian state sees fluvial transport and the logistics industry as keys to future prosperity. While the economy depends less than it once did on the Magdalena River (the trucking industry has dominated the logistics of trade since the mid-twentieth century), development plans increasingly hinge on its port terminals and shipping channels.[99] Echoing earlier moments in which imperial or national fortunes were tied to the river, the plan to improve navigation and increase trade now promises to advance Colombia forward to a new stage of history.[100] When the plan was announced in 2012, President Juan Manuel Santos invoked the founder of the nation, Simón Bolívar: "He knew that the Magdalena River should be the main axis for the country's development, and we're making that dream come true."[101] The vice president, Germán Vargas Lleras, then the government's standard-bearer for infrastructure, was equally optimistic in his regular Tweets, while other officials used words like "revolutionary," "transformative," and "salvation."[102] Jorge Barragán, president of the consortium initially awarded the contract, called it "a pact to create a new country."[103] While some critical perspectives were voiced by academics and environmentalists, the mainstream media has covered the navigability plan in similar terms.[104] Seen from the capital city, and in the eyes of the political and economic elite, the country's future appears to depend on logistical labor even as riverboat workers themselves fit awkwardly within that

---

99 Corredor and Díaz Barragán, "Navegabilidad del río Magdalena."
100 Delvalle Quevedo, "El proyecto de Recuperación."
101 *El Heraldo*, "Santos anuncia inversión."
102 *Semana*, "Cobra vida el río Magdalena."
103 *Semana*, "'Recuperar el río.'"
104 Rodríguez Becerra, *¿Para dónde va el río Magdalena?*

future. Government and industry experts I spoke with argued that these workers rely on outdated, unprofessional, and inefficient navigational techniques; they must be retrained or replaced if fluvial transport is to meet ambitious projections. In official imaginaries of the future, riverboat workers are both essential and expendable: the promise of prosperity is predicated on their labor, but this prosperity may well pass them by.

Madre Magdalena

Along the banks of the Magdalena River lives a mythical creature—half man, half alligator—known as the *hombre caimán*. According to legend, he began as Saúl Montenegro: a fisherman possessed by the desire to spy on women washing and bathing in the waterway's adjacent streams and swamps. This desire leads Saúl to solicit help from an Indigenous shaman, who supplies him with two magic potions: one empowering him to assume reptilian form, the other to reverse the transmutation. The first potion enables Saúl to fulfill his desire single-handed, but the second requires an accomplice. A trusted friend complies until, on one occasion, he fumbles the bottle containing the counteragent, spilling some of the liquid on the alligator's head and torso and losing the rest, leaving Saúl in a permanently hybrid state—straddling the boundary between man and beast. Horrified by his accursed fate and shunned by his community, the *hombre caimán* goes into hiding under the water hyacinth carpeting the riverbanks. His mother, ever loyal, sustains him with a diet of cheese, cassava, and rum-soaked bread, but in desperation the *hombre caimán* eventually flees, letting the river's swift current carry him downstream and out to sea.

The *hombre caimán* is a popular myth that circulates widely in the form of songs, stories, monuments, murals, and festivals (figure 5.1). Although the mythical creature often appears without reference to the backstory, the legend is clearly an allegory about heterosexual male desire. When directed at men, the didactic emphasis falls on the unbridled pursuit of sexual gratification, especially of a voyeuristic sort. Desire itself is not to blame, however, since Saúl's reliance on and misuse of magic are what ultimately leads to his demise. When women and girls are on the receiving end of the story, the moral imperative shifts to the dangers of exposing oneself in public. Desire is again exempted, since the burden falls on the sexualized objects themselves to avoid certain places or activities. On the whole, the legend can be read as naturalizing a lascivious and predatory masculinity, which men must work to control and women must learn to endure.

When place is considered, the *hombre caimán* appears to implicate a certain type of man. The story unfolds on the banks of the Magdalena River, suggesting that hypersexualized masculinity is especially prominent among men of the region (*ribereños* or perhaps *costeños*). In some versions of the story, Saúl Montenegro is identified as a fisherman, which implies an even closer relationship to the Magdalena valley's aquatic geographies. In visual depictions of the legend, such as statues and murals, the *hombre caimán* is often given features stereotypically associated with people of African descent. This makes the legend's interspecies transmutation all the more significant, since depictions of Black men containing "continuous references to animals considered wild, such as the ape or the alligator," have been common among travelers to the region since the nineteenth century (figure 5.2).[1] This tradition lives on in legends like the *hombre caimán* and its allegorical portrayal of a man whose deviant sexuality is cause for his very humanity to be called into question. As with the serpent and iguana in the preface, the *hombre caimán* blurs the ontological boundary between human and nonhuman, again revealing the intimate relationship between ideologies of race, gender, and nature.

Another interpretation of the legend was proposed in the 1970s by renowned sociologist Orlando Fals Borda, who suggested that the *hombre caimán* is the "mythological idealization of the amphibious culture" possessed by people who live and work at the interstices of land and water.[2] This interpretation has influenced more recent efforts to celebrate and defend the

---

1 Deavila Pertuz and Guerrero Mosquera, "La imagen de las personas," 298.
2 Fals Borda, *Historia doble de la Costa*, 26B.

FIGURE 5.1. Monument to the *hombre caimán* in the town of Plato, Magdalena.
Source: Wikimedia Commons.

distinctive lifeworlds of the *ribereño* communities of the Magdalena basin.[3]
For example, Germán Márquez Calle invokes the *hombre caimán* to recall the
"peaceful coexistence" of man and nature that once characterized the terraqueous environments of the Caribbean coast.[4] For Fals Borda, amphibious
culture emerged out of enduring regimes of colonial exploitation and capitalist

---

3 Bocarejo Suescún, "Lo público de la Historia," 77.
4 Márquez Calle's version is heavily romanticized: "In the Caribbean, meanwhile, evolves
the Hombre Caimán, which develops an amphibious culture, both terrestrial and aquatic,
that takes advantage of fishing, hunting, agriculture, and livestock. In principle, nothing
is lacking, but this abundance does not lead to accumulation: where no one is poor, no
one can be rich, it seems, since there is no need to abuse. The basic needs are satisfied,
daily sustenance is not lacking. Working in excess, more than undesirable, is unnecessary; conserving food is difficult and there is no need to save, in the face of an invariable

FIGURE 5.2. *Cayman Hunting.* Source: Charles Saffray, *Voyage à la Nouvelle Grenade*, 1869.

accumulation, and the legend memorializes its precarious existence in the face of multiple pressures.[5] Márquez Calle also sees this virtuous version of the *hombre caimán* as an endangered species threatened by impoverishment, extractivism, and climate change. In these accounts, the figure comes to symbolize a social and environmental order militating against a political economy pushing it toward extinction. Such interpretations de-emphasize the legend's moral lessons and precautionary warnings, as well as its gendered and sexualized connotations. However, both derogatory and celebratory renditions traffic in ideas about men—especially men of certain geo-racial designations—and their relationships with the nonhuman world.

The transmutation between man and alligator is not the only interspecies phenomenon attributed to the lower Magdalena valley and the Caribbean coast.[6] Consistent with a national imaginary that maligns these areas as uncivilized and immoral relative to the highland interior, men of the region are stereotypically associated with bestiality.[7] The presumed object of their zoophilic desire is the female donkey (*burra*) to whom adolescent boys are said to lose

<hr />

future." Márquez Calle, *El hábitat del hombre caimán*, 152–53. Although the concept of *cultura anfibia* appears throughout this text, Fals Borda is curiously not referenced.

5 Fals Borda, *Historia doble de la Costa*.

6 Other popular myths related to the lower Magdalena valley are the *mohán* and the *hombre hictoea*.

7 My approach to bestiality/zoophilia is inspired by Bourke, *Loving Animals*.

their virginity and with whom older men may enjoy the occasional tryst. The popular slang for those who engage in human-equine love is *burrero*, which translates loosely to "he who has sexual intercourse with donkeys," and it can be used to slander people from the region, or within the region to ridicule those of humble, rural origins.[8] The trope is so prevalent that it even made an appearance in the 1969–70 presidential campaign.[9] When the two candidates, Evaristo Sourdis and Misael Pastrana Borrero, were interviewed on radio in the United States, an interviewer with rudimentary Spanish garbled Pastrana Borrero's second surname. Pastrana Borrero replied that the proper pronunciation is "Borrero" (emphasizing the first *o*) and that the *burrero* was Sourdis, a lawyer of Sephardic Jewish descent from the town of Sabanalarga, in the department of Atlántico on the Caribbean coast.

Indeed, Fals Borda himself saw these sexual mores as characteristic of *costeño* men, which he linked to their mixed racial composition. "Let's look at ourselves, those of us who are sitting in this house," Fals Borda wrote, referring to a gathering of men from the Caribbean coast: "we are a true cosmic hodgepodge [*mescolanza cósmica*]."[10] Here he was thinking with the Mexican intellectual José Vasconcelos and extending his argument about the superiority of the *raza cósmica* (cosmic race) to the Colombian Caribbean. Fals Borda continued, "It cannot be said that there is any pure race here, which is undoubtedly a factor in shaping our culture as it currently exists. . . . One source of this dynamic coastal culture has been our attitude toward sexuality. On balance, sex was not and is not a problem among us *costeños*, not even in relation to the well-known customs of childhood games."[11] Reflecting on the widespread acceptance of bestiality, Fals Borda emphasized the practice as intrinsic to the development of heterosexual masculinity, resorting not coincidentally to homophobic slang: "*Marica* [fag], we know that *el burrear* [sex with donkeys] helps man develop. The *maricón* [faggot] who doesn't do it is lame!"[12] His final flourish was to praise *costeño* culture for its sexual honesty: "All levels of our society

---

8 One study that sought to measure popular opinion about zoophilia and bestiality in Barranquilla found that the vast majority of respondents saw the practice in a positive light. Notably, this study associated the arrival of the practice in the city with the migration of riverine populations from the lower Magdalena valley. Núñez Navarro, "Evaluación de la conducta sexual," 22.

9 Núñez Navarro, "Evaluación de la conducta sexual," 90–91.

10 Fals Borda, *Historia doble de la Costa*, 151B.

11 Fals Borda, *Historia doble de la Costa*, 151B.

12 Fals Borda, *Historia doble de la Costa*, 151B.

accept the maturing function of *burreo* [sex with donkeys], with the difference being that here we are frank enough to admit it."[13]

Along the Magdalena River, riverboat workers of days gone by were said to have had their own interspecies romance with an animal native to Caribbean coastal waters: the Antillean manatee. These enigmatic aquatic mammals were mythologized for centuries by seamen of many cultures, who compared them with mermaids and fantasized about their voluptuous shape and their uncanny humanlike qualities.[14] Fals Borda documented similar references in his interviews with veteran *bogas* (boatmen) who recounted a time when zoophilia was routine: "We took a short siesta at noon, and when night came, we docked the canoe, after having traveled about 20 kilometers in twelve hours navigating upriver. We disembarked with our mat and tent and lay down to rest not far from the fire we lit to keep away mosquitoes and jaguars. Some companions buried themselves in the sand to sleep better. Others would sneak away in search of some big manatee to fuck, because, as you know, this animal has a vagina and breasts, and it leaves the river for three days each month during menstruation."[15] Manatees are now rare, having been hunted to near extinction, as are tales of their irresistible allure to men working along the river. However, the association of *bogas* with bestiality belongs to a host of assumptions about gender, sexuality, and race that have long attached to riverboat workers. Beyond fantastical fables, for centuries *bogas* were hypersexualized in the national imaginary, and this contributed to their subhuman status—much like the *hombre caimán*.[16] The form of masculinity attributed to them also dovetails with pervasive stereotypes of crass, lecherous, hard-drinking men who work on ships and boats. Fals Borda and the *bogas* he quoted sought to recuperate rather than reject these stereotypes, resignifying them as characteristic of a unique lifeworld devalued by the dominant culture. Yet again, the ontological boundary between human and nonhuman nature inheres in both racial taxonomies and gender norms.[17]

This chapter follows the gendered idioms circulating along the river in order to grasp forms and practices of masculinity in the world of fluvial trans-

---

13 Fals Borda, *Historia doble de la Costa*, 151B–52B.

14 Davis, *Magdalena*, 227–28.

15 Fals Borda, *Historia doble de la Costa*, 47A.

16 For a comparison between the *boga* and the jaguar, see Gómez Picón, *Magdalena, río de Colombia*, 309.

17 For the mutual constitution of gender and nature in feminist cultural analysis, see Yanagisako and Delaney, *Naturalizing Power*; Haraway, *Simians, Cyborgs, and Women*.

port and logistics. It examines with the attribution of femininity to the water body, from its initial naming by Spanish explorers to recent environmental campaigns that seek to defend the "mother" of the nation. The chapter then moves to the gendering of human-environment relations, whereby certain activities (washing clothes, bathing children) are associated with women and others (fishing, navigation) with men. But the river's vulnerability and volatility in the face of climate change challenge these stereotypes: the waterway becomes an angry man to be feared as well as a defenseless woman to be saved. Likewise, an analysis of gender roles in fluvial transport and logistics highlights the divergent forms of masculinity between management and workers, the relations of intimacy and practices of care among all-male crews, and the vital work performed by women in an industry that presumes their absence. The goal is to advance an understanding of logistical capitalism that avoids reifying the male-female binary and essentializing gender roles, norms, and values.[18]

* * *

IN 1501, THE Spanish conquistador Rodrigo de Bastidas sailed across the mouth of a great river. Inspired by the timing of his arrival, he named the waterway after the saint whose conversion was celebrated on that day: María Magdalena, or Mary Magdalene. Whereas earlier names, such as Yuma (land of friends), reflected Indigenous cosmologies, baptizing the river Río Grande de la Magdalena imposed upon it a religious order with gendered overtones. At the time of conquest, Mary Magdalene had not yet been exonerated by the Catholic Church and was still a figure of repentant female promiscuity—an allegory that may have seemed fitting for a bountiful water body in a treacherous land. Her reputation later cleared by papal decree, Mary Magdalene eventually became unequivocally endowed with the virtues of strength, loyalty, and conviction. This reversal of fortune subtly shifted the river's ideological valence, but the association with an iconic figure of gendered religiosity remained. Whether signifying repentant depravity or unsullied devotion, the waterway's personification has consistently reflected the symbolic linkages between nature, femininity, and morality.

The transformation of Mary Magdalene's reputation has been invoked recently to represent shifting attitudes toward environmental protection. The

---

18 Of the rich and diverse field of feminist cultural analysis and masculinity studies, I am especially indebted to the theoretically sophisticated and contextually sensitive work of Mara Viveros Vigoya. See Viveros Vigoya, *De quebradores y cumplidores*; Viveros Vigoya, "Más allá del esencialismo."

anthropologist Wade Davis, for example, concludes his impassioned travelogue with lofty musings about the story's contemporary relevance. He quotes Xandra, a Colombian travel companion, who finds hope in the comparison between a slandered woman and a soiled river: "María Magdalena was condemned until history took an unexpected turn. Now she's a symbol of love, loyalty, and grace. Can't we do the same for the river?"[19] Davis's account is peppered with gendered references to the waterway and its cultural significance. For example, a popular musician from the riverside town of El Banco refers to the "duty to protect the Madre Magdalena. . . . We cannot survive without her. She is the source and fountain of our culture."[20] Throughout the book, Davis himself adopts similar rhetoric, frequently endowing the river with feminine personhood in his quest to convince Colombians to embrace an ethos of stewardship. To be worthy of protection, Davis and his interlocutors seem to imply, the river must find its place within a patriarchal order that figures the Magdalena as mother of the nation.

In parallel to the gendering of the waterway itself, riverine activities have been divided historically between those assumed to be the domain of women and others conventionally associated with men. For example, using river water to wash clothes, bathe children, and mop floors is commonly linked to women's responsibility for reproductive labor in riverside communities.[21] However, if human-environment relations along the river are marked by the feminization of caring practices, such practices are not limited to the domestic sphere. In some riverside communities, the role of *cuidadoras* is adopted by women who dedicate themselves to the conservation, defense, and protection of water bodies.[22] In the municipality of Puerto Boyacá, these self-appointed caretakers perform stewardship activities in the swamps and floodplains surrounding the town, clearing vegetation that adversely affects critical habitat for fish and other aquatic species, such as turtles and iguanas.[23] Women's care for fluvial ecologies also extends to the national political arena. A prominent example is the case of Sandra Vilardy, professor at the Universidad del Magdalena and member of the Humboldt Institute's scientific council. Beyond her research into the socio-environmental dynamics in northern Colombia's wet-

19 Davis, *Magdalena*, 347.
20 Davis, *Magdalena*, 270.
21 Rutas del Conflicto, "Las mujeres y el río."
22 DW Pía Castro, "Las mujeres de Puerto Boyacá."
23 Noticias NCC, "Mujeres luchan por la conservación." See also Salama, "Inside the Local Movement."

lands, Vilardy has been active in campaigns to prevent roadbuilding through ecologically sensitive areas, which she understands in a distinctly gendered key: "Women within the university have tried to give voice to local women leaders, to the fisherwomen, and although it has not been easy in an environment as macho as that of fishermen, there are women who are empowering themselves and the men are making space for women leaders; we are in a moment of leadership change and it's up to us women to promote this."[24] The environmental activist Francia Márquez is an even more remarkable case. Hailing from a town on the banks of the Río Cauca in southwestern Colombia, Márquez cut her teeth in campaigns to defend waterways against resource extraction and dam construction, and she now serves as Colombia's first Afro-Colombian and second woman vice president.

This work comes with certain risks, since environmental advocates in Colombia are regularly targeted by armed groups with ties to extractive industries, such as mining and oil.[25] The leadership of women in campaigns to protect water bodies from exploitation and contamination adds another dimension to the gendered dynamics of the armed conflict, but it also opens new possibilities for thinking about peace. In the words of Yurani Cuéllar, a leader who has been instrumental in the creation of a forest reserve in the Middle Magdalena, "Peasant organizations, and women specifically, will continue to fight to achieve the peace we so long for. . . . We hope for a territory where the peasant men and women who fled can return and those who are making war will leave, because we want a peaceful life, a healthy forest, clean rivers, a productive territory."[26] The linkage between ecology and violence implicit in Cuéllar's statement reflects a longer history of gendered relationships to the river during the armed conflict. Since the early 2000s, women have played an active role in the search for bodies of the murdered and the disappeared in the country's waterways. The most iconic example of this tradition comes from the riverfront town of Puerto Berrío, where a group of female leaders has assumed responsibility for honoring the remains of victims recovered from the Magdalena. In addition to caring for the dead and their watery graves, these women convene victims' family members in fluvial ceremonies featuring boats adorned with candles and flowers.[27] The gendered relationships between

---

24 ONU Mujeres, *Mujeres que cuidan la naturaleza*, 101.
25 Mejía Moreno, "'Nos están matando.'"
26 ONU Mujeres, *Mujeres que cuidan la naturaleza*, 160.
27 Rutas del Conflicto, "Las mujeres y el río."

people and nature along the river position women as caretakers of both human bodies and water bodies.

Yet women's engagements with the fluvial world go far beyond practices of care work. Indeed, many also participate in traditionally masculinized activities, such as fishing, hunting, and navigation, although in specifically gendered ways. Whereas men tend to fish in motorized boats using cast nets, women are more likely to travel on foot along the riverbank sporting handheld lines and hooks.[28] And these feminized practices are often concentrated in feminized spaces: the Magdalena's auxiliary swamps, channels, and tributaries, whose waters "are considered more peaceful and less dangerous" than those of the river itself.[29] In contrast, men travel long distances within the river's main channel to deeper-water locations known to be abundant with fish. The tools and techniques of catching fish are not the exclusive property of men, however. As Judith Nieto, community leader and member of the women's fishing association of Rioviejo, Bolívar, recalls, "Here women learn to fish from generation to generation, it's in our blood, I have known homes where the grandmother, the mother, and the daughter are all fishers and now the granddaughters. They don't learn from their husbands, but by tradition."[30] Further complicating the gendered division of riverine activities, male fishers are themselves actively involved in care work of various kinds. Alongside the masculinist assertion of control over the natural world and productive labor, men also engage in practices, such as sowing and weaving, that are conventionally feminized.[31] These practices are essential to the labor of fishing, as they are necessary for making and mending nets, and constitute an activity that is socially valued as necessary for providing sustenance to the family (figure 5.3).

If gendered relationships with fluvial ecologies are neither binary nor static, this is underscored by the fact that nature itself is actively being transformed by climate change. Along with shifts in the river's geomorphologic properties come changes to the anthropomorphic idioms in which its personhood is expressed. As hydrological patterns become increasingly unpredictable and extreme events, such as droughts and floods, intensify, the Magdalena's volatility and vulnerability are expressed in alternating, even opposing, gendered terms. During the rainy season, when the river frequently overflows its banks and floods adjacent towns, farms, and ranches, the waterway is depicted as an

28 García Becerra, "Mujeres," 5.
29 García Becerra, "Mujeres," 5.
30 García Becerra, "Mujeres," 5.
31 Museo del río Magdalena, "Sabiendas y subiendas."

FIGURE 5.3. "The fisherman mends his net with care [*con cariño*] in the yard of his house." Source: Rafael Gómez Picón, *Magdalena, río de Colombia,* 1948.

angry man to be feared in phrases such as *el río está muy bravo.* Meanwhile, as sedimentation, erosion, and other threats to the watershed's ecological health become heightened, the river is instead figured as a defenseless woman to be protected. Contributing to the gendered frames of volatility and vulnerability are the cyclical meteorological phenomena known as El Niño and La Niña, which have a major impact on weather patterns in Colombia and are also being altered by climate change.[32] As the hot, dry spells associated with El Niño are expected to increase in strength and duration, so too the cooler, rainy

---

32 IDEAM-Cormagdalena, "Estudio ambiental."

periods that typify La Niña are likely becoming magnified. On the one hand, this makes the distinction between the two phenomena more pronounced; on the other hand, as they become less patterned and predictable, the ability to definitively differentiate masculine dryness from feminine wetness is thrown into question. Though the association of atmospheric and hydrological patterns with gendered personhood traffics in conventional stereotypes, these stereotypes are becoming increasingly indeterminate in an era of ecological uncertainty.

Climate change is also compounding the violence underpinning human-environment relationships in the Magdalena valley, as fluctuating weather patterns and erratic water flows intensify the conflicts over land and water that have persistently impacted northern Colombia's amphibious territories.[33] Acute droughts and prolonged floods, for example, intersect with processes of dispossession and displacement linked to paramilitary land grabs—violent appropriations of nature that have plagued the region for decades, and that continue to influence the way local populations relate to dryland and wetland environments. At the intersection of climate change, armed conflict, and resource extraction are gendered caring practices that both sustain and disrupt violent territorial regimes.[34] Water provision is one of the key domains in which women are entangled with the ecology of war, as springs, canals, marshes, and streams serve both as resources for collective life and as sites of violent encounter.[35] As these water bodies become increasingly threatened or transformed by illegal mining, cattle ranching, and plantation agriculture, women are forced to seek out other spaces in which to perform their productive and reproductive labor. Environmental transformations are also disrupting riverine activities conventionally associated with men, such as fishing, as dwindling catches due to habitat destruction and toxic runoff are forcing fishermen into other vocations, or even to assume a larger share of household duties. Recurring cycles of violence further reconfigure the gendered dimensions of human-environment relations in a climate-changed world.

* * *

THE HISTORICAL ASSOCIATION of riverboat workers with bestiality aligns with a broader set of assumptions about the forms of masculinity intrinsic to this demanding occupation. Since the colonial period, when the river was fundamental to the circulation of goods and people, depictions of *bogas*

---

33 Gutiérrez Campo and Escobar Jiménez, "Territorio anfibio y despojo," 88.
34 Berman-Arévalo and Ojeda, "Ordinary Geographies."
35 Berman-Arévalo and Valdivia, "The Rhythms of 'Acostumbrarse.'"

have appeared in the writing of intellectuals and travelers, both foreign and domestic, who had experienced navigation along the waterway. These accounts, which persisted until the decline of the fluvial transport industry in the mid-1900s, consistently relegated *bogas* to the bottom of prevailing geo-racial hierarchies and ascribed to them a litany of pejorative qualifiers: animalistic, licentious, inebriate, itinerant, slothful, unreliable, obscene, adulterous, and irreverent, among others.[36] Some of these traits were said to be particular to boatmen, whereas others were attributed more widely to men from the lower Magdalena valley, especially those of African descent or mixed heritage. Though the figure of the *boga* has since dropped out of use, men now employed on the Magdalena's cargo vessels, like men laboring on ships and boats more generally, are widely assumed to embody many of the qualities once associated with the *bogas* of the past.

Feminist critiques of capitalism have frequently exposed the masculinist and often heterosexist logics undergirding the contemporary political-economic order.[37] In some accounts, fundamentally patriarchal and phallocentric modalities of power, such as penetration, domination, and expansion, are held responsible for the rapacious greed of market competition and the reckless destruction of capital accumulation, which ultimately inflict violence on women and nature alike.[38] Scholars of gender and infrastructure also argue "that the gendered rationalities of mainstream infrastructure planning rely overwhelmingly on masculine norms and values" and that infrastructural violence is borne disproportionately by women.[39] A key site for examining gender and infrastructure is the global shipping and logistics industry, which critical analysts have found saturated by toxic masculinity, heterosexual all-male homosociality, and patriarchal power.[40] Inspired by this line of inquiry, I am nevertheless keen to avoid reifying the male-female binary, essentializing gender roles, and equating the infrastructures of logistical capitalism with masculinity and masculinity with violence. Attentive to men's infrastructural lives, I

---

36 Nieto Villamizar and Riaño Pradilla, *Esclavos, negros libres y bogas*; Martínez Pinzón, "Tránsitos por el río Magdalena"; Lamus Canavate, "Esclavos, libres y bogas"; O'Bryen, "On the Shores of Politics."

37 Gibson-Graham, *The End of Capitalism*.

38 Gibson-Graham, *The End of Capitalism*.

39 Siemiatycki, Enright, and Valverde, "The Gendered Production," 298; Datta and Ahmed, "Intimate Infrastructures"; Truelove, "Gendered Infrastructure."

40 Chua, "Indurable Monstrosities"; Gambino, "Big Dick Energy"; Attewell, "The Lifelines of Empire"; Alimahomed-Wilson, "Men along the Shore."

approach masculinity less as a cohesive assemblage of norms, values, and logics and more through the heterogenous and divergent practices and performances of male personhood in the fluvial transport and logistics industry along the Magdalena River.[41] Focusing on two exclusively all-male groups—riverboat crews and the managers of shipping and logistics companies—alongside the vital work performed by women in an industry that presumes their absence not only advances understanding of the gendered dimensions of capitalism; it is also necessary for apprehending the power relations, regimes of difference, and interlocking hierarchies of gender, sexuality, race, class, and region endemic to the logistics industry.

Before boarding a commercial riverboat in the Caribbean port of Mamonal for a journey up the Magdalena River, I was burdened by my own assumptions about the kinds of men I would encounter. The images in my head were undoubtedly based on antiquated sailor stereotypes: crude, swashbuckling tough guys accustomed to hard work while on deck and hard drinking when on leave. I anticipated abundant swearing, copious off-color jokes, hyperbolic storytelling, and macho swagger. I presumed that I would be mocked for my lack of strength and endurance, and I braced myself for questions about my manhood. What I eventually encountered on the boat was notably different. Though my assumptions were not entirely misguided, the atmosphere was overwhelmingly one of discipline, respect, and humility. It was much closer to an orderly military regiment than a rowdy pirate ship. I considered the unusual fact of my presence—rarely is an outsider allowed onboard, especially one documenting their experiences and observations—and how it may have affected dynamics among the crew. But I had made it clear from the outset that I was sympathetic to their position and that I admired their expertise. Moreover, they would have had little reason to suspect that certain expressions of masculinity would be something to hide. On the contrary, the presence of an ethnographer frequently motivates people to exaggerate, not downplay, the qualities they believe are intrinsic to their own sense of personhood. Taken together, these factors made me relatively confident that I was not witnessing the crew on their best behavior, so to speak.

---

41 Gediminas Lesutis argues that among studies that focus on the gendered dynamics of infrastructure, "masculine forms of being gendered and how they intersect with infrastructure systems are not only bracketed but are also meshed with the violence of infrastructure." Lesutis, "Queering as (Un)Knowing," 399; see also Chowdhury, "The Social Life"; Fajardo, *Filipino Crosscurrents*.

All this came to a head when I became ill from drinking water treated by the onboard filtration system (see introduction). Though my fear of scorn made me slow to reveal my symptoms, the crew's responses eventually took me by surprise. Not once was I teased or criticized for having a fragile constitution or being unfit for riverboat life. Instead, expressions of concern and care flowed freely: oral rehydration salts, shared rations of fruit, advice on the health benefits of *sancocho de pescado* (fish stew), and frequent checks on my well-being. Even a crew member I had yet to meet extended his generosity, bringing me a package of supplies on his return from shore leave. My heightened sensitivity to contaminants and toxins in the water treatment system—ones that crew members were routinely exposed to—was seen not as a sign of weakness but rather ascribed to inherent differences between their bodies and mine. A racial ontology that separated us on biological grounds overshadowed any supposed hierarchy between varying degrees of masculinity. During the multiple days I spent abstaining from meals and sweating profusely, my illness was explained by the fact that I was a gringo from London, not an inferior grade of man.

At first, I felt guilty about the care and intimacy I was receiving onboard. Interpreting this as a manifestation of privilege, I appreciated but begrudged the compassion I received from people whose bodies were under far greater strain than mine. I tried to express this sentiment openly by declaring that I did not want or deserve special treatment, but they assured me they were treating me just as they would an infirm or injured fellow crew member. Stories circulated about a deckhand who once lost a finger in a winch, a pilot who had battled dysentery during a long shift at the helm, and an engineer who suffered from chronic migraines. Each of these comrades, I was told, was entitled to the same level of care that I felt so fortunate to receive. "We're a family," the captain explained, "and no one else is going to take care of us, so we have to care for ourselves and for each other."

This reference to kinship among crew members stuck with me long after I received a prescription of antibiotics and recovered my strength. Some riverboat workers are indeed related genealogically or by marriage, but the familial bonds the captain cited are forged by extensive periods of time spent together in close quarters under taxing conditions. This resonates with the work of feminist scholars who have long identified the fallacy of limiting the study of family and kinship to the domain of women and children.[42] Likewise, social reproduction theorists have linked kinship and work by showing how

---

42 Yanagisako, *Producing Culture and Capital*, 12.

feminized reproductive labor in the home is crucial to masculinized productive labor in the workplace.[43] Although reproductive labor is often associated
with caring practices (cooking, cleaning, and child-rearing), my onboard illness taught me that productive labor also depends on various forms of care.
But the captain's assertion that he and his crew had to fend for themselves
also recalls Black feminist theorizations of self-care under conditions of racism and patriarchy.[44] Depending on each other for sustenance and survival is
frequently how workers compensate for the degradation of their bodies on the
job and their devaluation in society at large.[45] The care I received onboard was
indeed a manifestation of racialized hierarchies, only not in the way I initially
assumed.

Beyond the body, the care practiced by crew members extends to the ropes,
cables, winches, engines, wires, propellers, hulls, tanks, and all the other material components of the towboat-and-barge convoy on which they live and
work. The productivity of their labor depends on these objects, and a malfunc-
tion or breakdown can easily delay the timing of a voyage and have negative
implications for job security, not to mention endanger the health and safety of
the crew members. Much of the work performed onboard commercial vessels
involves what Steven Jackson calls "material care," or the "sustained engagement with the well-being of things *as things* undertaken beyond and beneath
the instrumentalist relations usually held to govern our interactions with
objects."[46] Riverboat workers have pragmatic reasons for maintaining and repairing this complex sociotechnical system, but their caring relationship to
things also contains an ethical dimension. Proud enjoyment of a smoothly
running vessel or, conversely, emotional trauma from a navigation accident
both emanate from what Laura Bear calls the "sense of workmanship" or the
"ethics and affects of work," which "generate a duty of care to fellow-workers,
technologies, and the world."[47] Riverboat workers feel an obligation to care not
only for themselves and for each other, but also for the objects on which their
livelihood depends.

The diverse forms of material care practiced by riverboat crews on the
Magdalena are predominantly in the service of capital accumulation through

---

43 Federici, *Revolution at Point Zero.*
44 Lorde, *A Burst of Light.*
45 Hartman, "The Belly of the World."
46 Jackson, "Material Care," 428. See also Jackson, "Rethinking Repair"; Stokes and Coss-
    Corzo, "Doing the Work"; Coss-Corzo, "Patchwork."
47 Bear, "For Labour," 74.

resource extraction.[48] Fossil fuels belonging to Ecopetrol—Colombia's state-owned oil company—account for approximately 90 percent of the cargo transported along the artery. If workers stay healthy and engines run smoothly, oil flows and profits are made. However, if an accident among the crew or an equipment failure occurs, shipments are delayed and money is lost. The worst-case scenario is an oil spill, which could shut down the operations of a shipping line—even suspend all commercial transport along the river—for an indefinite period. This is why riverboat workers are especially careful when it comes to handling petroleum products, which they refer to rather unsentimentally as *producto*. A mistake while filling the tanks of the barges could discharge countless barrels of oil into the waterway, causing extensive damage and triggering regulatory sanctions. One deckhand I interviewed about such a scenario referred to the need to care not only for the product and for the equipment used to transport it, but ultimately for the river itself. In his speculative reflection, the river ceased to be an inert water body and became personified as a sick old man (*anciano enfermo*). Capitalist extractivism and environmental protection sit uncomfortably close in rivermen's practices of material care.[49]

Working twenty-one-day shifts punctuated by seven days of shore leave (closer to five days once travel is considered), crew members spend more time together than they do with their families and friends back home. In exceptional situations, such as during the COVID-19 pandemic, shifts may be extended indefinitely. Even under normal circumstances, the duration of time spent on-board in cramped spaces produces intensely strong ties between the men. The towboat, which is where workers spend nearly all their time, is 10 meters wide by 36 meters long and split across three levels. The lower deck, which is the largest, contains the engine room, the kitchen, the utility room, and the canteen. The middle deck, whose dimensions are smaller, houses cabins for senior crew members, a bathroom, and an office. On the upper deck, smaller still, is the wheelhouse, where the captain, helmsman, and pilots congregate, and the shared bunk room for junior crew members. The vessel is operated by a crew of eighteen, and they are not allowed to venture ashore except with the

---

48 I am indebted to Eloisa Berman-Arévalo and Diana Ojeda's analysis of gendered practices of care and their entanglement with war and extractivism in northern Colombia. Berman-Arévalo and Ojeda, "Ordinary Geographies."

49 Julia Corwin and Vinay Gidwani refer to the "double-sidedness to repair and maintenance work," whereby it both perpetuates socio-ecological catastrophe and points to "practices that renew the conditions of possibility for life." Corwin and Gidwani, "Repair Work as Care," 3.

captain's permission and only for tasks essential to the operation (disembarking for rest and relaxation is prohibited). Whether they like it or not, these eighteen men develop intimate homosocial relations, which range from the treatment of physical ailments and injuries to the provision of emotional support in times of need. I could certainly imagine these forms of male-male intimacy leaning toward the homoerotic, though I was never privy to anything of a sexual nature.[50]

Relationships among riverboat workers are not always so peaceful and caring. A veteran of the fluvial transport industry who had done his time at the helm as well as in management painted a more complex picture of the practices and performances of masculinity onboard. When asked whether there was ever conflict between the boatmen, Jorge said, "Yes, *navegantes* were always anticipating their next arrival in port and occasionally this led to arguments since everyone had their own reasons for wanting to stop in one town rather than another. One would say, 'We're going to sleep in Gamarra. I've got a girlfriend there.' The others would go drink beer. Sometimes they would end up in a fight." As it was unclear whom such fights were between, Jorge clarified: "Between them, the *navegantes*! Once we were on the towboat, and the engineer grabbed one of his comrades and stuck a kitchen knife in his gut, just like this [demonstrating with a swift hand motion], spilling his intestines. We had to catch them and push them back into his belly." The cause of these fights was always the same, Jorge said: "Fighting over beer, over women, whatever." I asked what happened to the guy who was stabbed. "We cared for him onboard for a while, but eventually it was clear we had to pick him up and take him to the hospital for treatment," Jorge recalled. "And the engineer went into hiding. He fled to Barranquilla because he was afraid the police were going to throw him in jail. But nothing ever happened because the other *compañero* [the stabbing victim] never reported it."

Melissa, a researcher accompanying me on this interview, looked at me in disbelief as she asked how they managed to resolve these disputes. "Just between the two of them," Jorge recalled. "Time passes, and then they meet again. One says, 'Fuck, you did so and so to me.' The other says, 'Man, forgive me. I love you so much. You are my brother [*mi hermano, mi broder*].' And that would put an end to it." Surprised by this resolution, Melissa remarked at the level of camaraderie between crew members. "Yeah, they might keep their distance

---

50 Here and throughout this chapter I am thinking with Deborah Cowen's provocative question: "What might a queer engagement with logistics space look like?" Cowen, *The Deadly Life of Logistics*, 222.

for a while, but they always resolve it between themselves. Usually, it's just a few punches. A group of *navegantes* are in a cantina, and a fight breaks out over something silly, like who is going to pay the bill. But they never stay angry for long." In Jorge's account, homosocial intimacy and caring practices among riverboat workers were entangled with the most stereotypical behaviors of men working on ships and boats (drinking, swearing, brawling, and philandering). The practices and performances of male personhood on the Magdalena's commercial riverboats are more complex than any simple binary would allow.

* * *

THE EVERYDAY LIFE of managers in the fluvial transport and logistics industry was more difficult to access, and yet my occasional visits to port terminals and corporate headquarters provided a glimpse of the gendered dimensions of these differently positioned worlds. One of the most notable encounters was with a port general manager whom everyone called Chico. A few years prior, Chico's employer, a commodity trading and logistics firm, decided to invest in riverfront land and build a fluvial port terminal—one of the biggest in Latin America. I was lucky to secure permission to visit the port and was offered a series of one-on-one meetings with its management team. Throughout these meetings, the response to many of my questions was essentially the same: "Pregúntale a Chico." Ask Chico.

The schedule of meetings I had been given by the company listed Chico's name last. This, combined with the frequent references to him throughout the day, created a feeling of suspense. It seemed that until I was face-to-face with Chico, I couldn't possibly understand the true story behind this unprecedented investment. He was recruited from another Latin American country shortly after the company had discovered the site, located its owner, and negotiated a price, and he had presided over the facility's construction and management ever since. Everyone else I met that day had joined the company later and had only heard stories. No one other than Chico, I surmised, had intimate knowledge of the company's decision to invest large sums of money in a scrubby patch of pasture in a notoriously violent location.

As 3 p.m. rolled around, and it was time for my most-anticipated appointment, I positioned myself facing the door of the glass-walled conference room to be ready as soon as Chico arrived. I nervously assembled and reassembled my notebook, pen, and audio recorder in an obsessive row in front of me on the table. I felt my heart rate accelerate each time an unknown person appeared, only to then drop again when it was not him. As I waited anxiously, though in sublimely air-conditioned comfort, I began to construct a mental image of the legendary figure I was about to meet. I pictured the quintessential businessman—imposing physique, commanding voice, sober demeanor—who would have little time to waste on banal pleasantries and no tolerance for flights of fancy. I imagined he would begin by grilling me on the reasons behind my interest in his business and then, if satisfied, move on to technical details of port operations and the logistics industry that I would likely struggle to follow.

After over an hour of waiting and idle chatter with the company's corporate social responsibility representative (who had sat through all my interviews), Chico finally arrived. A slight man with a tousled head of hair and a cheerful grin, Chico entered the room apologizing profusely for his lateness—he had been tied up in meetings with some *gente de Houston* (American oilmen, no doubt). And while I was prepared to meet someone self-evidently white and elite, his darker complexion and colloquial mannerisms made his racial and class position harder to read. His physical aspect was the first thing to make an impression on me, but as he continued to talk, I was also thrown slightly by his manner of speaking. Words slid liquidly out of Chico's mouth, often slurring into one another, as in the meandering chattiness of a happy drunk (although he had just been meeting with the American oilmen, I'm pretty sure he was sober). Chico frequently lowered his voice to nearly a whisper, as though sharing a juicy secret. His facial expressions also gave me pause. Whereas I expected someone with a severe, penetrating stare, Chico gazed breezily out the window with cool nonchalance. Though surprised by the man sitting before me, I now felt oddly relaxed, as though I was in the presence of a benevolent mystic.

As our conversation progressed, my initial impression of Chico aligned with the stories he told about his company. Less than two minutes had passed when he invited me to join him on a vision quest of sorts. "As you will see," he told me, "the enduring thing about our company is that every day we continue dreaming. Now that I'm out of meetings, if you have time, we can keep talking and the two of us can dream together!" He then began to reminisce about the early days of the project. "There were palm trees, there were buffalos," Chico recalled. "We took lots of photos of ourselves with the buffalos. People thought we were crazy. This area was more agricultural than industrial back then, so to see an investment like this one . . ." Chico trailed off, shaking his head in feigned disbelief. He then resumed: "They had still not seen the vision that we saw. We went back to the main office and made little circles, little drawings to show how all this would eventually look. What I saw then is what we see now: the navigability of the river, vessels going up and down, *chalupas* crossing from side to side, our operations here in the quay, the other shipping lines moving *producto* [oil] between the refinery and the coast. All that movement, it's like music. You hear the river swaying back and forth, flowing toward the sea. I can imagine a restaurant floating in the air where people come from the city for an outing and are given a 360-degree view of the river and the port. Someday all that and much more will come to pass."

I was mesmerized. Not only had Chico defied my expectations about the type of man I was going to meet that afternoon, but he had also quickly enveloped me in a dreamworld of buffalo selfies, musical waters, and floating restaurants. Replaying the audio recording of the conversation, I'm embarrassed by my inability to formulate a coherent question during the first pause in the narrative. I can imagine myself sitting there, mouth slightly open, at a loss for words. But Chico did not mind. He picked up right where he left off and continued to spin his web of illusion, only now at a larger scale.

"If you want to know the vision I have for the region, for the country," Chico offered, "it is important to realize that what you see here is not a port terminal." I felt perplexed as Chico conjured up an alternate reality with a subtle sleight of hand: "No, this is not a port terminal. This is a logistics hub, and we want the whole region to follow our lead. The idea is to bring the gateway of Colombia, which has traditionally been along the coast, upriver." In explaining what this would accomplish, Chico performed another magic trick: "And you also have to realize that what you see out there is not a river." I was again puzzled. "No, what you see out there is a fluvial expressway. And that fluvial expressway will give us the multimodal connectivity we need to be globally competitive." I began to feel stunned by the speed with which the world around me was shapeshifting, so it came as some relief when Chico slowed things down. "You may not see this happening in the next three years—it will probably take ten, maybe fifteen—but everything *will* change."

The rest of the interview, which lasted nearly two hours in total, continued in the same vein. Chico talked nonstop, barely pausing to breathe let alone allow me time to ask questions. He traveled freely across these logistical dreamworlds, jumping back and forth between past, present, and future, with occasional diversions into the nuts and bolts of multimodal transport and trade, which eventually gave way to more whimsical reflections on the port terminal in his charge. He peppered his stories with evocative metaphors (no one wanted this project to end up "like a stillborn child," he said at one point), and he made even ordinary statements sound aphoristic ("Lo que este mes decíamos, en el siguiente ya no es cierto"; what we've been saying this month, next month is no longer certain). At various points I sensed that our meeting was drawing to a close, only for Chico to then launch into another animated digression. When I finally did end the interview, thanking Chico for his time, he signed off with a characteristically sentimental recommendation: "You must come back sometime around dusk. The truth is that from here one sees the most beautiful sunsets. Reds, yellows . . . it's the most romantic view you can imagine. And at night, when the moon is full, it's the largest moon you will ever see."

Many of the meetings I attended during visits like these were with men who, unlike Chico, fit the stereotype of the corporate logistics manager. They were supremely confident, rational men asserting their gendered prowess, as Evelina Gambino observes among port developers, and they were prone to the macho banter that Charmaine Chua documents among ship builders.[51] Chua's analysis of the gendered and sexualized dynamics of logistical capitalism is instructive: "I want to suggest that these juvenile sexual metaphors [my ship is bigger than yours!] do more than reveal the performative masculinities embedded in corporate culture. These allusions to phallic imagery and sexual domination are linked to speculative desires about the continued well-being of the capitalist future, marking the extra-economic logics inherent in logistical fascination with infrastructural monstrosity and scale."[52] My interviews with similar figures operating along Colombia's Magdalena River confirm these analyses, and yet the story of Chico disrupts an easy association between stereotypical forms of corporate masculinity and infrastructures of logistical capitalism. Chico's fascination with infrastructural grandiosity was unmistakable, but he expressed his fascination through less typically masculinist logics and affects.

Chico's talent for flamboyantly beguiling performances must have contributed significantly to his professional success. Perhaps it has even been more important than his extensive knowledge of logistics or his prodigious managerial skills—although he may very well possess these. I would guess that he has risen to the top of his profession thanks to his ability to conjure enchanted dreamworlds around an otherwise uncharismatic site of logistical infrastructure and to envelop others (colleagues, investors, journalists, even ethnographers) within those dreamworlds. Chico clearly has a singular flair for showing that his company—and, by extension, logistical capitalism at large—is not a hardheaded business of flowcharts, big data, and time metrics but rather a

---

51 Gambino, "Big Dick Energy," 63–69; Chua, "Indurable Monstrosities."
52 Chua, "Indurable Monstrosities," 147.

softhearted one imbued with (even driven by) emotion, intuition, and inspiration. Like the riverboat workers who both confirm and complicate the typecast image of the crass, lecherous boatman, the forms of masculinity embodied by corporate logistics managers sometimes defy easy stereotypes.

* * *

IN MALE-DOMINATED PROFESSIONS like logistics, it is all too easy to assume that women are absent or irrelevant. This tendency exists within critical logistics studies and across the industry itself.[53] Following Jake Alimahomed-Wilson, the masculine character of logistics can be summarized as follows: "The global capitalist supply chain is controlled by white hegemonic masculinity. Affluent, corporate-elite, straight white men are structurally positioned as the managers and overseers of a vast global logistics labor force comprised primarily of working-class men of color."[54] Yet as Irene Peano argues, "the very assumption of logistics' masculine character can and should be put to the test for what it blinds us to."[55] In addition to the heterogenous and divergent practices and performances of male personhood in the fluvial transport and logistics industry, such assumptions blind us to the vital work performed by women in specifically gendered roles as well as to their reproductive labor on land and at home, which is a precondition for men's productive labor onboard. Both types of feminized labor are routinely neglected by critical analysts and go unacknowledged by most workers and managers, all of whom frequently reference the all-male homosociality of their business. This was surprising to me since, except for my journey on the riverboat, my time spent researching the social world of fluvial transport and logistics on the Magdalena River brought me into contact with roughly as many women as men.

My initial point of access—the first person I needed to contact to request permission for an interview or site visit—was almost always a woman. My initial approach to one company was through a generic email address I found on their website. Two minutes later, I received a response from Teresa, the director

<hr />

53 Peano, "Gendering Logistics," 15.
54 Alimahomed-Wilson, "Racialized Masculinities," 27.
55 Peano, "Gendering Logistics," 15. In an earlier intervention, Jacqueline Nassy Brown critiqued Paul Gilroy's emphasis on ships and sailors, arguing that "seafaring is too uniformly male to foster an understanding of women's agency in producing the black Atlantic." Rather than emphasizing "women's experience," Brown urges attention to "asymmetries of power called 'gender' [that] constitute and normalize masculinity and femininity as categories of difference." Brown, *Dropping Anchor, Setting Sail*, 55–56.

of corporate affairs for Latin America, who handled inquiries from the public and the media. After a few exchanges, Teresa put me in touch with Claudia, the company's corporate social responsibility manager, who invited me to her office in Bogotá. After our meeting, Claudia connected me with Lucia, another member of the corporate social responsibility team located on site at the port terminal. Lucia took over from there, arranging my visit and scheduling my interviews. She was the one to receive me at the company's office in the city center, and she and the receptionist (also a woman) outfitted me for my visit to the port and briefed me on protocol. Lucia then chauffeured me to the port terminal, gave me a personal tour of the installation, and accompanied me throughout my day of meetings. Not only was she friendly with each of the corporate managers I met, she also knew the rank-and-file workers in the terminal, from the security guards to the maintenance staff.

Lucia was much more than an informed tour guide, however, as she had in-depth knowledge of the company and of logistics more generally. Much of what I came to understand about the industry came from conversations with her during our drives or while waiting for a meeting to begin. We discussed everything from organizational hierarchies to local politics to commodity prices to legal systems, all of which were central to her company's ability to successfully conduct business along the Magdalena River. But Lucia was also the corporate social responsibility team's on-site point person and, as such, was responsible for a range of crucially important issues: from relations with adjacent communities to public information campaigns to job creation programs. She not only knew the company and its operations inside and out, she was also an expert on the social and political landscape of the local area. Lucia was on a first-name basis with the leaders of villages abutting the logistics hub; she knew how to navigate between local government agencies; and she knew the history of the armed conflict and how it continued to impact labor relations in the region. The more time I spent with her, the more I recognized the vital role Lucia played in the company: she was exceptionally skilled at mediating between the logistics hub and the outside world—me included.

Many of the other women I met in the fluvial transport and logistics industry performed similar functions. The head of security for one company—a man—informed me that nearly all the security guards employed on-site were women. Like Lucia, these women mediated between the terminal's inside and outside, although according to a different logic: they monitored who and what crossed the threshold and ensured that only the right kinds of circulation would be allowed. Women were also prevalent within the health, safety, and environment teams tasked with minimizing risks to workers or the environment. They, too, mediated along the boundary between logistical operations and the external forces and unexpected events that threaten to intrude (a traffic accident, a gas explosion, an oil spill). Sometimes the threat of disruption was located within riverboat crews—carelessness being an assumed quality of these men—and it was women who gave onboard health and safety trainings (one of the rare moments when the riverboat is not an all-male space). Many human resources teams were staffed primarily by women who controlled the onboarding and dismissal of personnel—again, managing who is selected to perform logistical work. One company's head of human resources was widely respected for her preternatural skills at handling negotiations with labor unions: "She's a sweet cookie, but a tough cookie. She's been spit on, called terrible names, and she remains cool as a cucumber. She's fair and follows all the rules. You can't break her," was how one executive described her. Throughout their multiple roles within the industry, women were often charged with mediating between the insides and outsides of logistics, performing the invisible, behind-the-scenes work necessary for logistical operations to run smoothly.

Cleaning and cooking are forms of feminized labor within the fluvial transport and logistics industry, as in Colombian society at large. The corporate offices and installations I visited were always staffed by a crew of *empleadas de servicio* (or *empleadas*, for short, to use the euphemistic name for women employed in domestic service). These women, usually dressed in white maid uniforms, were often visible throughout the workday, mopping floors or distributing coffee. Riverboats are spaces of exception to this rule, where cooking is done by a chef and his assistant (both men), and cleaning is the collective responsibility of the crew. However, on land, the *empleada* culture prevalent throughout Colombian society is alive and well. And like the distinction between (male) workers and (male) managers, domestic servants are differentiated from the women employed in other areas of the industry by physical characteristics: most would be classified as *morena* (brown) or *negra* (Black). These hierarchies of color and class are evident across the industry's workforce, in both feminized and masculinized roles.

After my journey on the riverboat, I often visited crew members on shore leave. These visits gave me a window into the home life of these men and were opportunities to meet members of their families. A captain I became especially close with would always come accompanied by some combination of his wife and children when we would meet. Knowing time with family is limited for riverboat workers, I was not surprised that they would choose to maximize that time by including their loved ones in our off-duty meetings. But there was something more significant about these events: they revealed the degree to which the strenuous nature of work on the river demanded that they seek the care and comfort of family when back on land. The wives or girlfriends I met rarely held jobs outside the home, and most dedicated themselves to caring for young children and elderly relatives, managing the household, and handling other domestic duties. A smoothly functioning logistics network is predicated on masculinized productive labor, which in turn is predicated on the reproductive labor of women (and other family members) at home. This phenomenon, which has been identified by numerous studies of the gender dimensions of capitalism, takes on a specific form in the fluvial transport and logistics industry. The seam between the inside and outside of logistics—which women employed within the industry are tasked with mediating—is both upheld and erased by other women's reproductive labor. That which is placed outside by assumptions about the all-male homosociality of the social world of logistics is itself constitutive of that social world. Without the feminized labor of women at home, logistics would cease to exist as a world of its own.

* * *

MASCULINITY OCCASIONALLY TAKES on political significance in the imagination of riverboat workers. The politics of masculinity they express, however, is different from that of corporate logistics managers fantasizing about big ships penetrating deep harbors or that of dockworkers resentful about the feminization of their jobs.[56] Some of the workers along the Magdalena River I came to know were critical of capitalist extractivism despite being fully embedded within it, and their critical perspectives were given a gendered inflection. Some spoke of the remarkable strength and endurance required to survive an exceptionally brutal occupation, and they reserved their greatest admiration for the *veteranos* (veterans) among their ranks. These were the true rivermen who had lasted the longest despite all manner of threats and dangers, many of which are intrinsic to work on towboat-and-barge convoys transporting petroleum products. But the use of a military honorific was not incidental, since these men would also have managed to survive the most violent years of the Colombian armed conflict, when those laboring along the river were often caught in the crossfire. Many *veteranos* told stories of being threatened or attacked and spoke proudly but with a tinge of disbelief that they were still alive. Here masculinity is equated not with the violence of war and extractivism but rather with the miracle of having survived their protracted entanglement.

---

56 Chua, "Indurable Monstrosities"; Alimahomed-Wilson, "Men along the Shore."

Masculinity in Colombia is deeply embedded in histories of warfare, such that dominant forms of male personhood are inseparable from the exercise of violence. Armed combatants, such as soldiers, paramilitaries, and guerrillas, have long been a key reference point for young men seeking to define and articulate their own masculine identity. This overflows into many areas of social life, especially the home in the form of domestic violence and violence against women. This is not unique to Colombia, of course, as the roots of male violence run deeper than the mid-twentieth century, when the current conflict officially began, and there are other important factors. But the centrality of violence to public culture for over half a century gives the man with a gun an especially prominent place in the popular imagination. Riverboat workers have occupied an unusual position relative to the armed conflict—surrounded by but not participating in the fighting—and this is reflected in their expressions of masculinity. For one, they have often been forced to declare their neutrality and to define themselves, if not in opposition to, at least as different from, those personally involved in the war. And like armed combatants, they are men who work with machines, though it is significant that these machines are not weapons. One riverboat worker joked that he and his comrades were "tougher than the guerrillas and the paramilitaries" since their hard labor was not mediated by the threat of violence and did not rely on guns. Boats and ships are often spaces where nonhegemonic forms of sociality emerge and flourish, and the masculinity onboard the Magdalena's commercial riverboats is another example.[57]

Riverboat workers also saw their masculinity as a source of pride in relation to managers and executives, who were occasionally derided as weak and effeminate. Regardless of their actual physical or emotional strength, those occupying higher positions within the industry were assumed to be office workers who sit at desks behind computers and make phone calls all day long. They were seen as unfit for the hard labor required of those working on the boat, especially the *marineros* (deckhands) and *maquinistas* (engineers), who are responsible for some of the more demanding tasks. Managers and executives are positioned differently within the hierarchical regimes of difference structuring the fluvial transport industry and Colombian society at large, and these inequalities were partly at stake. Focusing on superior and inferior forms of masculinity was a way of speaking about racialized and class hierarchies (by expressing them in gendered terms). This allowed those hierarchies to be criticized

---

57 Foucault, "Of Other Spaces."

more freely, since racialized differences are often coded in other language (region and accent, for example), and discussions of class conflict can be easily vilified for their association in Colombia with histories of war and violence. Gender, on the other hand, is a relatively palatable idiom in which to frame moral and political matters.

A more recent form of differentiation essential to the livelihoods of riverboat workers along the Magdalena is in relation to Venezuelan migrants and refugees. As the economic and humanitarian crisis in the neighboring country has intensified, pushing millions of Venezuelans to flee across the border into Colombia, many sectors have experienced an influx of laborers willing to work for lower wages than is customary, including within the fluvial transport and logistics industry. The shifting dynamics of the labor market have also coincided with the arrival of multinational logistics and commodity trading firms. This means more work, but it has also brought a heightened sense of insecurity for workers as the new employers are less committed to locally embedded moral economies upheld by the older shipping lines that have been operating along the river for decades. This insecurity manifests in questions about the inexperience of Venezuelan workers; even those with experience in fluvial transport and logistics are said to be less knowledgeable about the Magdalena River basin and its specific navigational challenges. But doubts about the suitability of these workers are also expressed in physical terms, with the bodily aptitude of Venezuelan *navegantes* said to be suspect relative to their Colombian counterparts. The former are not only accused of being weaker; their very masculinity is called into question through homophobic slang used to insult men who, regardless of their sexual orientation, possess gestures or attitudes considered more appropriate for women. For men working in a notoriously difficult profession under increasingly challenging conditions, logistics is a "terrain for struggles over and through gender" that is crosscut by interlocking hierarchies of race, class, region, and (in the context of international migration) nationality.[58]

---

58 Cowen, "Afterword," 107.

6

Navigating Racial Ecologies

There was no moon, the air was thick, and visibility was low. Through the impenetrable darkness, the banks of the river were indistinguishable from the expanse of water surrounding the boat. The silhouette of the occasional tree was barely perceptible on the horizon, but there were no buildings, roads, or other sources of illumination nearby. Dense cloud cover hung overhead, and rain had begun to streak the windows of the pilothouse. Fellow watercraft were nowhere to be seen.

We were heading upriver, against the current, on a relatively smooth reach, which meant we could navigate throughout the night. The captain stood alert at the helm, flanked by a young pilot, the three of us staring intently at what lay ahead. We did so in total darkness with the interior lights of the pilothouse switched off. The boat was fitted with electronic navigation equipment—echo sounder, radar detector, digital chart display, satellite tracker—but these instruments were either dormant or had their screens covered with aluminum foil. Mobile phones were stashed in pockets or lying face down on the table. The searchlight topping the control bridge was also inactive, reserved for emergency situations. The boat's white, green, and red navigation lights were on, as required by law, but they had no effect on visibility.

Without technologies of illumination or way finding, the captain and pilots relied on eyesight and intuition to navigate the river's meanders, eddies, sandbanks, and snags. There are no channel markers on the Magdalena River, as there are on many inland waterways. Struggling to identify discernable reference points, I remarked at their ability to maneuver confidently. "We have a few tricks," the pilot explained. "For example, we know the width of the river around here, so we keep a constant distance between the riverbank and the red light on our port side, and that tells us we're on course. Not too close, though, or we might run aground." This made sense, but I could barely make out land. "We know this river up and down. We know how to read its signs," said the captain. "And we know this boat." Navigation devices were used periodically, but they seemed more like adornments lending the boat an air of technical sophistication. In contrast, feel for the vessel and familiarity with the waterway were described as more trustworthy. But there was something about these navigation practices that exceeded their mere effectiveness.

Ethnographies of navigation have shown that intuitive knowledge and embodied skill are essential to the work of piloting vessels in challenging and changeable environments (figure 6.1).[1] Even as shipping technologies and logistical infrastructures have grown more complex, Ashley Carse points out, "feel" remains central to the global movement of ships and goods.[2] As in many other vocations, workers possessing such capabilities are often classified according to intersecting regimes of difference: for example, the association of masculinity with expertise is extreme in the shipping industry, but the divide between mental acumen and physical prowess is defined along lines of class,

---

1 There is an extensive literature on navigation across anthropology, geography, history, and related fields, and the knowledge and skill of navigators has been a rich site for theorizing how people learn to perform complex activities. For an overview of these discussions, see Carse, "The Feel of 13,000 Containers." For an influential discussion of piloting as a paradigmatic example of practical knowledge, see Scott, *Seeing Like a State*, 316–17. I am less concerned here with the question of how river captains and pilots on the Magdalena River acquire the ability to maneuver boats along the waterway, or with comparing their abilities to those found in other times and places, but rather with how their navigation practices reflect the social and spatial orders in which they are embedded and shed new light on how those orders are experienced and lived. For a particularly evocative analysis of how political and economic shifts shape the lives (and deaths) of river pilots, see Bear, "For Labour."

2 Carse, "The Feel of 13,000 Containers."

FIGURE 6.1. Helmsman navigating across the Bay of Cartagena by day.
Source: photograph by author.

race, and nation.[3] These classifications position workers within stratified social orders, and that positioning is not incidental to the knowledge systems
and practical skills themselves. In the case of riverboat workers on the Magdalena, the ways of knowing and doing that are essential for traversing the waterway bear traces of the hierarchies and taxonomies structuring Colombian
society and space. Techniques for navigating the social environment are often
intertwined with techniques for navigating the fluvial one.[4]

———

3 Carse, "The Feel of 13,000 Containers," 277–78; Dua, *Captured at Sea*; Khalili, *Sinews of War
   and Trade*.
4 Navigation has been a productive analytic beyond maritime and fluvial way finding, particularly in studies of migration and mobility. My understanding of navigation has been
   enriched substantially by Megan Ryburn's work on how Colombian migrants to Chile
   navigate violent borderland spaces. Ryburn's analysis is particularly helpful for bridging
   the gap between social and spatial approaches to navigation, and for highlighting the
   racialized and gendered barriers to mobility as well as the techniques for maneuvering
   within and around them. See Ryburn, "'I Don't Want You.'"

Chapter 2, on sociotechnical imaginaries and interventions in the domain of fluvial transport, highlighted the influence of geo-racial regimes that naturalize the superiority of the highland interior over the tropical coasts and the dominance of those with proximity to whiteness over those racialized as Black, Indigenous, or mixed race. The social and spatial order of the Magdalena basin reflects these enduring relations of inequality, as does the work of operating vessels and moving goods along the waterway—a vocation long associated with Blackness. Although this association has gradually weakened, and riverboat workers do not necessarily identify as Black or Afro-descendant, they nevertheless continue to negotiate a world organized around entrenched racial and regional hierarchies.[5] Accommodation, however, has not been their only response. Those whose lives and livelihoods depend on the river frequently enact forms of knowledge and skill that ensure their survival, defend their autonomy, or assert their humanity. Against this backdrop, the embodied aptitudes possessed by river captains and pilots take on new meaning. They are not only techniques for transporting vessels and cargo from port to port; they are also practices and performances of pursuing freedom from the structures and strictures governing their life and work.[6]

That these practices and performances take place on water is not insignificant. A rich scholarly tradition charts the oceanic itineraries of transatlantic slavery and the Middle Passage, the political and cultural imaginaries born of maritime crossings and connections, and the aqueous contours of African diasporic thought and practice.[7] Building on this tradition, yet wary of naturalizing the link between Blackness and the sea, Tiffany Lethabo King offers shoals—liminal, terraqueous spaces—as an analytic for thinking differently

---

5 My engagement with an occupational category and form of personhood that have long been associated with Blackness, but that have also undergone significant changes over time, follows Stuart Hall's work on the shifting cultural politics of identification under the sign *Black*. See Hall, "New Ethnicities." For a recent extension of these ideas to an analysis of subaltern spatial praxis that complicates prevailing racial taxonomies, see Chari, "The Ocean and the City." See also Simone, "Transcript."

6 Many parallels can be drawn with the case of enslaved pilots guiding ships in and out of ports in the Anglophone Americas. Dawson, "Enslaved Ship Pilots." See also Pérez Morales, *No Limits to Their Sway*.

7 For some key reference points, see Linebaugh and Rediker, *The Many-Headed Hydra*; Gilroy, *The Black Atlantic*; Glissant, *Poetics of Relation*; Smallwood, *Saltwater Slavery*; Brown, *Dropping Anchor, Setting Sail*; Brathwaite, *History of the Voice*; Dawson, *Undercurrents of Power*; Sharpe, *In the Wake*; Featherstone, "Maritime Labour"; Bolster, *Black Jacks*; Scott, *The Common Wind*.

about racial and spatial orders in the Americas.[8] Rivers, marshes, wetlands, swamps, and deltas have also been fundamental to the political and economic foundations, as well as the aesthetic and intellectual formations, of the Black Atlantic world.[9] These fluvial and estuarine environments have been conduits for enslaved workforces and plantation commodities, and remain sites where environmental racisms are plainly evident, but they have also been spaces of fugitivity, autonomy, creativity, and salvation. The racial ontologies and legacies of racism that have shaped the socio-ecological formations of coastal regions have only been made more perilous by the changing climate.[10] The Magdalena occupies a key place within a hemispheric history in which the work of navigating the complex ecology of waterways is entangled with the thorny raciality of the society through which they run.

There are, of course, practical explanations for why way-finding technologies are spurned. Charts are usually outdated, since submerged sandbanks, navigable channels, and water levels shift constantly, especially as fluctuations in weather patterns become more frequent and extreme. Moreover, satellite tracking systems give only general orientation, and losing the way is impossible on most stretches of the river. There are also obvious reasons to forgo illumination: in darkness, the eyes adjust better to the nocturnal environment, and the searchlight's high-powered beam compromises overall visibility. However, in a world structured by interlocking hierarchies of being and belonging, and along a waterway central to formations of colonial and racial capitalism in the Americas, alternative navigation techniques are more than just shared solutions to practical problems. They also enable river captains and pilots to exercise dominion over vessels and journeys, thwart the fungibility of their labor

---

8 King, *The Black Shoals*, 4–5. King argues that when an oceanic conceptual frame is naturalized, liquidity, fluidity, and flow become "totalizing metaphors" for Blackness. A corollary effect is that the hermeneutic frames of Black and Indigenous studies are sealed off from one another, with Blackness equated with the sea and Indigeneity with the land. As a liminal space between the terrestrial and the aquatic that impedes navigation and slows the movement of a vessel, the concept of the shoal opens analytical possibilities for thinking beyond the binaries of land/water and Indigenous/Black.

9 For fluvial and estuarine environments as spaces saturated with the history of race and racism throughout the Americas, see Johnson, *River of Dark Dreams*; Leal, *Landscapes of Freedom*; Nevius, "New Histories of Marronage"; Zeisler-Vralsted, "African Americans"; Oslender, *The Geographies of Social Movements*; Woods, *Development Drowned and Reborn*; Woods, *Development Arrested*; Wright, "The Morphology of Marronage"; Cecelski, *The Waterman's Song*.

10 Hardy, Milligan, and Heynen, "Racial Coastal Formation."

power, and assert the value of their personhood.[11] In facilitating the operations of the fluvial transport and logistics industry, these practices do not escape the grip of racial capitalism, but rather maneuver within its gaps and fissures.[12] What follows are reflections on the navigation practices deployed by riverboat workers, and their entanglement with the hierarchical regimes of difference structuring Colombian society and space.

* * *

IN 1801, THE renowned Prussian naturalist and explorer Alexander von Humboldt embarked on a journey up the Magdalena River. Quito was his destination, but he planned to pass through Bogotá to make the acquaintance of José Celestino Mutis, the Spanish priest who had led a royal botanical expedition and whose reputation was known throughout Europe. In Cartagena, Humboldt boarded a *champán*—the narrow boat with a shallow draft that the Spanish had copied from drawings of vessels on the inland waterways of southern China.[13] Made of hollowed trunks of the ceiba tree sealed with tar, these boats were roughly 20 meters long by 2 meters across. They were covered by a sturdy arched canopy lined with palm leaves, which sheltered the cargo. Each *champán* was manned by ten to twelve *bogas* who propelled the vessel with wooden poles. One was stationed at the bow, another at the stern, and the rest stood atop the canopy. Passengers sat either fore or aft, wedged between the cargo and the crew.

Throughout his forty-day journey upriver to Honda, from where he would ascend to Bogotá by mule, Humboldt recorded detailed observations of flora and fauna, of water flows and rock formations, of atmospheric conditions and cartographic coordinates (figure 6.2). But Humboldt's diaries reveal a parallel interest in the people of the river basin. Of the stretch from Mahates to

---

11 The wider significance of navigation technologies on the Magdalena also reflects the link between race and visibility, particularly in the domain of surveillance. See Browne, *Dark Matters*. From this perspective, techniques such as navigating at night without technological aids can be understood as tactics for maneuvering within racially regulated regimes of mobility.

12 In presenting what she calls the "meaningful struggle for freedom *in place*," Katherine McKittrick highlights the centrality of vessels: "Technologies of transportation, in this case the ship, while materially and ideologically enclosing black subjects—economic objects inside and often bound to the ship's walls—also contribute to the formation of an oppositional geography: the ship as a location of black subjectivity and human terror, black resistance, and in some cases, black possession." McKittrick, *Demonic Grounds*, x–xi.

13 This and the following specifications are found in Sanín, *Manual del Río Magdalena*, 145–46.

FIGURE 6.2. Sketch of the Magdalena River. Source: Alexander von Humboldt, *The Diary of Alexander von Humboldt, 1899-1904*, vol. 7ab, sheet 220. Staatsbibliothek Berlin.

Barranca Nueva, for example, Humboldt remarked, "a forest full of beautiful mimosas . . . singularly monstrous trunks of Bombax and Cavanillesia, a magnificent, picturesque mixture of majestic plant life. Halfway along, another wretched village. Shacks made of bamboo stalks inhabited by *zambos*. Nowhere in the world are there as many *zambos* because Indigenous women, tired of cold-hearted Indian men, lust after the *negros*, and since here so many *negros* (from el Chocó) have purchased their freedom from gold mining."[14] As Humboldt moved upriver, the botanical exuberance he encountered sparked reflections on its effect on the soul: this "vision of plenitude, the grandeur of form, the lack of clear vistas, the fearsome, impenetrable darkness caused by dense canopies of foliage arouse serious and gloomy emotions. This tropical region lacks the charming character of our German meadows, our Nordic countryside."[15] For Humboldt, these observations were united by the idea that nature and culture were inseparable.[16]

Humboldt's fascination with the human and nonhuman natures of the Magdalena River focused especially on the *bogas* he met during his voyage. Long passages of his diaries are dedicated to meticulous documentation of their rowing techniques, both individually and as a team. Humboldt greatly admired the boatmen's physique: their herculean strength, unparalleled athleticism, and exceptional lung capacity ("an anatomist," he reckoned, "should be able to differentiate the respiratory apparatus of a Magdalena River oarsmen from any other individual").[17] He also respected their toughness in the face of grueling and dangerous work: endless hours of rowing in suffocating heat; frequent tumbles into the swift current; the ever-present danger of attacks from snakes and caimans. Humboldt was equally fascinated, albeit perturbed, by the "barbaric, lewd, ululating and furious shouting, sometimes painful, sometimes jubilant, and at other times accompanied by blasphemy, with which these men try to ease their muscular exertion."[18] These practical skills and embodied aptitudes were, for Humboldt, adaptations to the environment in which the *bogas* lived and worked.

---

14 Humboldt, *Reise auf dem Rio Magdalena*, 67. All direct quotations from Humboldt that appear in English were translated by the author with help from Melissa Martínez. The original diaries in German were consulted, as was a Spanish translation. See Humboldt, *Alexander von Humboldt en Colombia*.

15 Humboldt, *Reise auf dem Rio Magdalena*, 74.

16 Zimmerer, "Humboldt and the History"; Zimmerer, "Humboldt's Nodes and Modes."

17 Humboldt, *Alexander von Humboldt en Colombia*, 14.

18 Humboldt, *Alexander von Humboldt en Colombia*, 13. See Ochoa Gautier, *Aurality*.

Humboldt also remarked extensively on the comportment of *bogas*, particularly in relation to their patrons and to the service they were hired to perform. "It is not that these men stir pity," he quipped, "since although badly paid . . . they are free men, insolent, indomitable, and boisterous."[19] In the early years of colonization, rowing was done by conscripted Indigenous and African boatmen, but throughout the seventeenth and eighteenth centuries the vocation was occupied primarily by people of African descent who had escaped slavery, purchased their freedom, or been born to mixed parentage (*mulatos* and *zambos*). Humboldt both praised and scorned the autonomy they possessed: "You have to pay them in advance at Mompox and allow them three days after the payment, on the pretext of having a shirt and trousers made for the trip. They spend those days drinking, and once they have spent all their money, one gathers some of their *bogas* (occasionally after 4 or 7 days of waiting). It would be better if the authorities intervened in boat work or if half the money was paid at Honda" upon completion of the journey.[20] The independence of *bogas* preoccupied Humboldt, partly because he was eager to reach his destination before falling prey to the river's menaces: "On 6 May we wanted to leave Mompox. All the oarsmen were assembled together. As soon as they realized we wanted to board the *champán*, they remembered that they still had not drunk away their advance wages. Eight of them set off and left us to spend the night in a brick hut a quarter mile from town. One of the most venomous and aggressive serpents, the Coral, appeared suddenly between our beds." With these observations, Humboldt acknowledged the unprecedented power *bogas* wielded, eventually reaching the paradoxical conclusion: "One is a slave to his oarsmen."[21]

Although often celebrated as the "second discoverer of the New World" and the "father of modern ecology," Humboldt was in dialogue with, even influenced by, a wide circle of scholars on both sides of the Atlantic who shared an interest in biogeography, or the study of the geographical distribution of life-forms according to environmental variables (such as elevation and temperature).[22] Humboldt's observations of the Magdalena basin's plant and

---

19 Humboldt, *Alexander von Humboldt en Colombia*, 13.
20 Humboldt, *Alexander von Humboldt en Colombia*, 15.
21 Humboldt, *Alexander von Humboldt en Colombia*, 15.
22 There is an extensive literature that could be summarized as Humboldt hagiography. For a recent example, see Wulf, *The Invention of Nature*. For efforts by historians to contextualize Humboldt's contributions, see Cañizares-Esguerra, *Nature, Empire, and Nation*; Thurner and Cañizares-Esguerra, "La invención de Humboldt."

animal communities were an early attempt to advance this burgeoning field of knowledge; so, too, were his descriptions of the human settlements along the riverbank and the anatomical structures of their inhabitants. As he traveled through present-day Colombia and Ecuador, Humboldt exchanged ideas with *ilustrados* from the Viceroyalty of New Granada, such as Francisco José de Caldas, who was also pursuing the geographical determinants of biological difference.[23] Within this intellectual milieu, Humboldt's stature and influence helped elevate biogeography as a framework for understanding Colombian society and space.

Following independence, a host of travelers, politicians, and naturalists set out to inventory the nascent nation's territory and population. Like Humboldt and Caldas, they shared a common interest in the link between environmental variation and human diversity. They did not, however, all agree on how to handle the ideologies inherited from the colonial past.[24] For example, Humboldt had held the conviction that all humans shared a common origin, and he was critical of Spanish colonialism, its racial and caste hierarchies, and its embrace of slavery.[25] This was partly what made his ideas attractive to the likes of Simón Bolívar, who saw in them a scientific justification for the republican cause. Following this strain of geographic thought, regional, not racial, typologies became the idiom through which the nation would be understood.[26] However, despite the increasing emphasis on environmental variables, like climate and topography, the racial hierarchies of colonial society remained implicit within a geographical order that asserted the dominance of the cool highland interior over the hot coastal lowlands.[27] These regional categories were explicitly racialized by some nineteenth-century intellectual and political leaders,

---

23 Caldas, *Del influjo del clima.*

24 For the invention of colonial legacy among political leaders in independent Colombia, see Castillo, *Crafting a Republic.*

25 Wade Davis celebrates Humboldt's "profound belief that no race was superior to another and that all humans shared a common origin. Just as plants adapt to various habitats, he wrote, people in different parts of the world take on certain traits of appearance, but they all belong to one great family of man. And no matter where or how men and women determine to live out their destinies, whatever the constraints of culture, as individuals, they 'all are alike designed for freedom.'" See Davis, *Magdalena*, 300.

26 Appelbaum, *Mapping the Country of Regions.*

27 Alfonso Múnera: "In Caldas's works, for example, the coastal provinces of New Granada, with their sweltering plains and their 'savages' and 'undisciplined' *negros* and *mulattos*, symbolize the image of the absence of progress and the impossibility of achieving it. The Andes, by contrast, seem to have been ideally created to produce a morally and intellec-

with Andean environments and inhabitants exalted for their whiteness and those of the Caribbean and Pacific coasts disparaged for their physical and cultural inferiority.[28]

Equating elevation with civilization was a leitmotif of nineteenth-century geographic thought in Colombia, and the Magdalena River played an important role within this tradition. Many of its key contributors traveled up or down the waterway in their quest to survey the country's human and natural resources: some saw it as the lynchpin of the nation's hopes for both economic and moral progress; others fixated on its ability to connect, even unify, Colombia's heterogenous provinces and populations. Running through these accounts were frequent discussions of *bogas*. Commentators partial to scientific racism and biological determinism depicted them as genetically predisposed for their vocation; those who believed that human nature was determined by climate, diet, and other environmental factors saw *bogas* as biologically and culturally adapted to the job. Either way, the Magdalena boatmen were beasts of burden suited to arduous work in harsh conditions, and their biological fitness was often explained by their mixed racial composition. Like *mestizaje* itself, which many nineteenth-century writers endorsed as the "unifying thread of Colombian nationality," *bogas* were needed if civilization and progress were to take hold despite the impediments of tropical nature.[29] In the words of the prominent late nineteenth-century intellectual Salvador Camacho Roldán: "As for the massive introduction of African settlers, considered by the writers of the ancient world to cause moral and intellectual degeneration, we can only say that without it the colonization of the sweltering valleys of our great rivers and of the unhealthy shores of our seas would have been impossible; that the mixture of European or Indigenous blood with African blood is the only one that has the power to resist the malarial influences of the floodplains and the deltas of our great commercial arteries."[30]

Like Humboldt, other nineteenth-century observers also recognized the autonomy *bogas* derived from their knowledge of the river, their skillful handling of boats, their control over the timing of journeys, and their indispensability to

---

tually superior individual." Múnera, *El Fracaso de la nación*, 54. See also Nieto Olarte, *Orden natural y orden social*; Rappaport, "Colombia and the Legal-Cultural Negotiation."

28 Samper, *Ensayo sobre las revoluciones políticas*. See also Arias Vanegas, *Nación y diferencia*.

29 Rappaport, "Colombia and the Legal-Cultural Negotiation," 9. See also Cadelo, "Race, Nature and History."

30 Restrepo Forero, "Trópicos, mestizaje y aclimatación," 384.

the circulation of passengers and goods.[31] And this recognition provoked re-peated invocations of the master-slave idiom Humboldt used to describe the topsy-turvy power relations onboard the *champán*.[32] This was cause for con-cern among criollo elite who deployed not only dehumanizing discourses and racial prejudices, which depicted *bogas* as unreliable, immoral, and animalistic, but also regulatory systems and disciplinary interventions, to shore up their control over the country's strategic transport corridor.[33] In response, *bogas* re-sorted to time-honored tactics, such as work stoppages and strikes, to assert their dominion over navigation.[34] This history lives on in the positioning of riverboat workers within the national imaginary, and in their techniques for navigating complex fluvial environments and unequal social and spatial orders.

* * *

AS THE TOWBOAT-AND-BARGE convoy continued upriver throughout the night, one technological device was regularly employed: the two-way radio. Mounted on the ceiling of the pilothouse, its handset dangling within easy reach, the radio was prized for its ability to facilitate communication with cap-tains and pilots of nearby watercraft. Its frequency was set to channel 16, the international standard for distress, urgency, and safety calls in both maritime and inland navigation, and once contact was made, conversations could con-tinue on other channels. The transmitter's use of VHF (very high frequency) radio waves restricted its range to line of sight, which was limited further by the river's meanders and bends. But this did not impede the device's ability to relay information between two vessels in close proximity: one that had just traversed a hazardous stretch and one that was about to do the same.

On its surface, the routine was straightforward enough. When a captain or pilot caught sight of an approaching convoy, he could summon his counter-part over the radio. Their communication would begin with a rapid exchange of identifying details (name of vessel, type of cargo, number of barges). The party instigating the call would then inquire about a specific reach; the party

---

31 Nieto Villamizar and Riaño Pradilla, *Esclavos, negros libres y bogas*, 237–38.

32 Nieto Villamizar and Riaño Pradilla, *Esclavos, negros libres y bogas*, 237–38.

33 For concerns about boatmen's dominion over navigation, see McGraw, *The Work of Rec-ognition*, 73. For discriminatory representations of *bogas*, see Villegas, "El valle del río Magdalena"; Martínez Pinzón, "Tránsitos por el río Magdalena"; Arias Vanegas, *Nación y diferencia*; O'Bryen, "On the Shores of Politics."

34 As McGraw notes, *bogas* "staged the country's first strike not just for better wages and working conditions but also for recognition as an honorable labor force." McGraw, *The Work of Recognition*, 10.

on the receiving end, having recently navigated that section, would then share a detailed report, focusing on the factors most critical to ensuring safe passage (position of the navigable channel, location of submerged hazards, current water levels and flow rates, amount of shipping traffic). Given the river's propensity to change, often dramatically, from day to day, even decades of practical experience and accumulated knowledge were not enough to predict what challenges lay ahead. The ability to solicit real-time information from other captains and pilots, and to trust the accuracy of that information, was essential to a successful voyage.

When I first overheard these exchanges, I was impressed by their grasp of the riverine environment; only later would I realize their social significance. On one occasion, after a particularly detailed description of a complicated section of the Middle Magdalena, I watched as the convoy that transmitted it passed us heading downstream. As the two pilots exchanged greetings, I noticed that the other vessel belonged to a rival shipping company. Until this point, I was accustomed to thinking about fluvial transport as an industry in which a small number of companies competed for limited contracts and slim profit margins in a high-risk environment. This had led to certain assumptions about relations between crews working for different employers. I knew many riverboat workers came from the same towns and had social ties, but I imagined those affinities were trumped by economic imperatives and market pressures. Instead, the importance of the two-way radio as a way-finding device revealed relations of solidarity and practices of mutuality among riverboat workers, regardless of their employer.

During a conversation with a captain on shore, I confessed surprise at the sharing of vital information outside the company. He responded with equal surprise that I would ever have assumed otherwise. "We're a brotherhood," the captain asserted. "There's no bad blood between any of us whatsoever. It doesn't matter if the shipping companies are fighting. We still collaborate." The boatswain sitting next to him nodded in agreement: "Sharing information and other forms of assistance are in everyone's best interest. We all look out for each other." In the words of a seasoned pilot, "We don't have any qualms about giving support to pilots from other firms; if we see a *navegante* from another company stuck on a stretch of river, we pull over, we leave him food, you understand? That's how it is, a brotherhood." Statements like these suggest that riverboat workers see themselves as an alliance bound by trade, but the use of the term brotherhood (*hermandad*) implied something more. In the world of fluvial transport, the relationship between men of shared parentage, commonly used to characterize professional associations, is more than metaphorical;

some riverboat workers are indeed from the same family. Moreover, the invocation of kinship and blood reflects the logics of biological fitness and genetic difference that once justified the position of riverboat workers within prevailing geo-racial regimes. This suggests that mutuality and solidarity are both effects of and responses to historically entrenched inequalities; likewise, the two-way radio mediates between workers whose common interests are tied to their shared position within hierarchical social and spatial orders.

On the occasion that people other than seasoned navigators were to overhear these exchanges, it is unlikely that they would know what to make of them. Official communications about the waterway tend to rely on a mileage marker system, with numbers increasing as one moves upstream. This Euclidean system is used occasionally in the course of everyday operations, but during radio communications between helmsmen it takes a backseat to idiosyncratic conventions of geo-referencing and place naming that are all but incomprehensible to everyone but the initiated. A veteran of the fluvial transport industry gave various examples of what he referred to as *el hablar del río* (river talk) or *la jeringonza* (the secret code) used by captains and pilots to communicate about the waterway:

> Upon setting off, one pilot says to another, "Hey, *tírame el agua*" [throw me the water], meaning, "toss me the map" or "give me the code." The other guy responds, "Okay, look, you get to Magangué and just above Retiro you veer to the left. Don't go to the right, since there's a big sandbank that's just formed. Stay left all the way until Barbosa, kilometer 269."

> "When you get to La Gloria, look out for the white lady's house [*la casa de la mona*], okay? From the white lady's house you jump over to the left."

> "Stick to the center until you get to the beach with the ducks [*la playa de los pisingos*], and from there you enter the branch of the iguanas [*el brazo de las iguanas*]."

> "Continue upriver on the right-hand side and when you get to the shallow water at the Black woman's red underpants [*las pantaletas rojas de la negra*] [laughter] you head over to the left." There was once a lady who hung her red underpants out to dry in that spot [more laughter], so we would say, "at the red underpants, you head left."[35]

---

35 For the category of *mona*, see Koopman, "Mona, Mona, Mona!" *Pisingo* is the common name for a local species of duck (*Dendrocygna autumnalis*), while iguanas are frequently

To make sense of such instructions, one must possess intimate knowledge of the local environment as well as proficiency in the taxonomic classifications used to identify its inhabitants. But most importantly, prior fluency in river talk is obligatory, since many of the landmarks are either highly generic (the beach with the ducks) or no longer exist (the red underpants); to make use of these toponyms, one must already know their assumed location. And one must be able both to receive and to give navigation advice. This informal cooperation is at least as important as any way-finding technology onboard—except for the two-way radio, of course, which is one of its preconditions.

When asked about the origins of these conventions, navigators tended to naturalize them as inherent to the job. However, if practices of way finding are always entangled with hierarchical regimes of difference, the implications of such practices can be inferred. For example, riverboat workers often referenced changes in the fluvial transport industry that threatened their job security. Companies recently entering the market were accused of recruiting pilots from outside the river basin (Venezuelans in particular) and paying them lower wages. These pilots were being trained on virtual simulator machines, I was told, which meant that they lacked the local knowledge needed to navigate safely and effectively (indeed, accidents caused by these pilots were frequently cited). "It used to take fifteen years, at least fifteen, for a guy to become a pilot," a captain told me, "but today they're turning out pilots in just four or five years." Referencing the shift from learning the knowledge and skills of navigation obtained from years of experience to being trained quickly with technological aids, the captain said, "They [pilots] are made in less time but they do not come out as good. There are already some that are failing." But more critically, perhaps, pilots recruited from elsewhere or trained on simulators were excluded from the assistance transmitted over the two-way radio—even if tuned into the right frequency, they would struggle to benefit from what they heard.

It is also significant that river talk is spoken by experienced captains and pilots but not by managers, except those few with a background in navigation. This means that one of the most vital navigational aids remains the inalienable property of the navigators themselves and cannot be easily appropriated, abstracted, or transferred. It is transmitted generationally between experienced

sighted throughout the Magdalena valley. None of these toponyms are recognized on maps or used outside the context of navigation.

navigators and recent recruits, but in general it is limited to communications onboard among trusted comrades. While the two-way radio enables captains and pilots to support one another in the difficult, even dangerous, work of navigation, the form and content of their communication protects their dominion over the vocation and thwarts the fungibility of their labor. The knowledge systems and practical skills used to maneuver vessels through the waterway are simultaneously techniques for navigating social and spatial orders in which riverboat workers feel obliged to assert the value of their expertise, even their personhood.

* * *

IN THE LYRICAL imagination of Candelario Obeso, the nineteenth-century forebear of *poesía negra* in Colombia, the demand for recognition, equality, and freedom among the racially subordinated is a recurring motif.[36] Obeso was born in 1849, just three years before the abolition of slavery, in the town of Mompox, which at the time was the Magdalena's preeminent river port. The son of a Black housemaid and a white lawyer, he attended university in Bogotá and spent much of his adult life among the Andean capital's lettered elite, both of which positioned him ambiguously within the geo-racial order of postemancipation Colombia.[37] Much of Obeso's work was dedicated to subverting the aesthetic and political norms of that order by using nonstandard orthography to create a poetic vernacular that celebrated the oral culture of the Afro-descendant *ribereños* of the lower Magdalena valley.[38] This is exemplified by Obeso's most famous poem, "Canció der boga ausente" (Song of the Absent Boatman), published in 1877, which exalted the language spoken by riverboat workers as they navigated the waterway (figure 6.3).[39]

Obeso's attention to the figure of the *boga* reflects the centrality of that figure to nineteenth-century political culture. As Rory O'Bryen observes, the Magdalena River "constituted the *mise-en-scène* for dramatic appropriations of republican discourse" and the "ritual dehumanisation of the *boga* . . . was central to literary contributions to the creation of a racist 'habitus' out of which elite

---

36 I am grateful to the anonymous reviewer of an earlier article in *Environment and Planning D: Society and Space* for the suggestion to engage more deeply with Candelario Obeso's work.

37 That said, like the subjects of his poetry, Obeso self-identified as *negro*.

38 Melgarejo, "The Production of a Multiple Consciousness," 99; Ochoa Gautier, *Aurality*, 108–9.

39 Obeso, *Cantos populares de mi tierra*, 25–26.

FIGURE 6.3. Commemorative stamp honoring Candelario Obeso. Source: Colección Filatélica, Banco de la República.

subjectivities were formed."[40] But *bogas* did not merely serve as foils for the construction of racial and national identities among lettered criollos from the Andean interior; like other Black and mixed-race commoners from the Caribbean coast, they were also instrumental in struggles for independence and in forging republican ideals, such as liberty, equality, and citizenship.[41] Extending this phenomenon to literary circles, Obeso's attention to the voices of the Magdalena's boatmen sought to democratize the poetics of nation-building by endowing popular orality from the margins with the status of the written word.[42]

The navigation practices of *bogas* were instrumental to Obeso's aesthetic and political project. Indeed, his homage to riverboat workers opens with a scene not unlike the one with which this chapter began:

> Qué trite que etá la noche,
> La noche qué trite etá;
> No hay en er cielo una etrella
> Remá, remá!

> How sad is this night,
> The night how sad it is;
> There is not a star in the sky
> Row the boat, row!

---

40 O'Bryen, "On the Shores of Politics," 465–66.
41 McGraw, *The Work of Recognition*; Helg, *Liberty and Equality*. See also Sanders, *Contentious Republicans*.
42 O'Bryen, "On the Shores of Politics," 468.

Here the reference to nocturnal navigation alludes to something other than the *boga*'s intuitive knowledge of the river: like the "absent boatman" of the poem's title, the starless night evokes nostalgia for a time when the dominion of *bogas* went unchallenged.[43] The poem was written in the 1870s as steam-powered vessels (*vapores*) began to supersede traditional watercraft (such as the *champán*), and alliances between business interests and public officials were implementing measures designed to make the labor of *bogas* obsolete.[44] The imperative to promote steam navigation had been in force since the early days of the republic, and for many intellectual and political leaders this imperative contained modernizing and civilizing impulses, both of which were predicated on the *boga*'s absence—and not only from the transportation business but also from the body politic.[45] Yet the poem enjoins boatmen to keep on rowing ("Remá, remá!"). The subsequent stanzas cite other embodied skills that were also under threat: the knack for catching fish ("Con ácte se saca er peje"), the ability to bend iron ("Con ácte se abranda el jierro"), the power to tame serpents ("Se roma la mapaná"). And the final lines return to the trope of loss ("No hai má, no hai má!") before again entreating boatmen to resist their prescribed disappearance ("Bogá, bogá!").

Scholars have acknowledged Obeso's contributions to the archive of African diasporic poetics and politics, identifying in his work common themes such as the yearning for home, double consciousness, the valorization of vernacular orality, and the demand for recognition.[46] Some have even traced intercultural exchanges between Afro-Colombian thinkers like Obeso and intellectual and creative luminaries from elsewhere in Latin America, the Caribbean, and the United States.[47] But Obeso's writing suggests something beyond the shared epistemology of Black thought spanning geographical and linguistic divides: namely, the centrality of riverine environments to the cultural and political imagination of the African diaspora in the Americas. From Richard Wright's

---

43 My reading here is indebted to Rory O'Bryen's analysis of the poem's "reflective" nostalgia. See also Jaúregui, "Candelario Obeso."

44 Posada-Carbó, "Bongos, champanes y vapores"; Solano, *Puertos, sociedad y conflictos.*

45 Martínez Pinzón, "Tránsitos por el río Magdalena," 31–32; O'Bryen, "On the Shores of Politics," 466; McGraw, *The Work of Recognition.*

46 Jackson, *Black Writers in Latin America*; Prescott, *Candelario Obeso*; Melgarejo, "The Production of a Multiple Consciousness"; Maglia, "Candelario Obeso"; McGraw, *The Work of Recognition.*

47 Prescott, "We, Too, Are America"; Flórez Bolívar, "Un diálogo diaspórico"; Múnera, "Manuel Zapata."

stories about the 1927 Mississippi floods to Langston Hughes's "The Negro Speaks of Rivers" to Toni Morrison's *Sula*, riverscapes are more than scenic backdrops for the literary examination of racial orders of being and belonging: they are intrinsic to those orders and to efforts to transcend them.[48] Obeso's poems dwell on the river and the *ribereños* living and working along it because of their centrality to the struggle for equality and freedom.

Paul Gilroy alludes to this phenomenon when he urges attention to the elements of the "black Atlantic archive that relate to the history of liquid modernity, fluvial thinking, riparian thinking, pelagic thinking, abyssal thinking, fluministic thinking."[49] The interstitial space between land and water, Gilroy proposes, is a "standpoint from which certain creative, imaginative, and ethical possibilities begin to force themselves into consciousness."[50] This proposition builds on Gilroy's long-standing interest in the aqueous, though mostly oceanic, contours of the Atlantic world's political formations and cultural sensibilities, and it resonates with the work of renowned Colombian sociologist Orlando Fals Borda.[51] Writing in the 1970s, Fals Borda advanced the concept of *cultura anfibia* (amphibian culture) to encapsulate the distinctive social-environmental practices, beliefs, and relations among *ribereño* communities of the lower Magdalena valley.[52] *Bogas* were Fals Borda's paradigmatic

---

48 These are merely a few examples, and others would be better placed to expand on this point. For the three specific works cited above, see Gooch, "Death by the Riverside"; Gooch, "'Shall We Gather at the River?'"; Miller, "Justice, Lynching, and American Riverscapes." For more recent writing in this vein, see Coates, *The Water Dancer*.

49 Gilroy and Shatz, "The Absurdities of Race." Gilroy has not yet elaborated in print on his highly suggestive concept of "fluvial thinking."

50 Gilroy and Shatz, "The Absurdities of Race."

51 "At the shoreline and on the quayside, land-based sovereignty confronted the unruly force of rivers and oceans as well as the distinctive habits, peregrinations and insubordinate mentalities of those who worked upon the waters." Gilroy, "'Where Every Breeze Speaks,'" 9. This line of thinking converges with recent work by Kevin Dawson, historian of African-Atlantic culture, who argues that African-descendant societies "wove terrestrial and aquatic experiences into amphibious lives, interlacing spiritual and secular beliefs, economies, social structures, and political institutions—their very way of life—around relationships with water." Dawson, *Undercurrents of Power*, 11.

52 According to Fals Borda, *cultura anfibia* refers to the "complex of behaviors, beliefs, and practices related to the management of the natural environment, technology (productive forces), and the norms of agriculture, fishing, and hunting that prevail in the communities of the *depresión momposina*." Fals Borda, *Historia doble de la Costa*, 21B. For other uses of his work, see Gutiérrez Campo and Escobar Jiménez, "Territorio anfibio y despojo." Fals Borda may be the only social scientist to have conducted interviews with former *bogas*.

example, and his inspiration was none other than Candelario Obeso. Reflecting on his methodology, Fals Borda notes that he "builds on the thought of this great poet to illustrate the Black Colombian culture [*cultura negra colombiana*] that begins to take shape among the *bogas* of the river in the seventeenth century. . . . Obeso, native of Mompox, was the first Black writer to offer literary articulation of the forms of expression, key concerns, and class interests of his race, not only in Colombia but in the Americas."[53] While this assessment of Obeso's originality may overreach, the tradition of thought it indexes parallels Gilroy's notion of "fluvial thinking" in focusing on riverine environments as privileged sites for understanding the ordering of society and space through the political ontology of race.

* * *

WHEN I FIRST entered the pilothouse, my eyes were immediately drawn to a crack in one of the windows (figure 6.4). Its spiderweb shape led me to assume it was caused by a gunshot, so I decided not to ask questions right away. But when the topic arose a few days later, I learned that the damage was from a rock, not a bullet. I was told of an incident in which people from a riverside community had attempted to blockade cargo transport. Commercial riverboats had been using a minor branch of the waterway ever since seasonal fluctuations had rendered the main stem unnavigable, and the appearance of large-boat traffic along the alternate route was unwelcome. A group armed with sticks and stones assembled along the riverbank and proceeded to harass vessels floating past. The primary shipping channel remained obstructed indefinitely, which made the temporary bypass a choke point for the fluvial transport industry, increasing the blockade's leverage. Shipping companies were left to choose between appealing to local authorities and negotiating with their adversaries. A combination of these strategies eventually led to an agreement, which established regulations on boat traffic as well as compensation for the accusing parties.

In conversations with riverboat workers and others knowledgeable about the industry, I heard differing interpretations of the underlying dynamics fueling this dispute. One began with the observation that many river communities feel excluded from the benefits of fluvial transport and trade, and that commercial vessels ranging outside their customary domain are seen as transgressors. This explanation highlighted the sharp inequalities separating river

53 Fals Borda, *Historia doble de la Costa*, 48B–49B.

FIGURE 6.4. Damage incurred during hostile encounter with riverside community. Source: photograph by author.

towns and villages from the regional capitals of Barranquilla and Cartagena, where many shipping companies are based, and from the cities of the highland interior. From this angle, boats straying beyond the main shipping channel appeared as manifestations of urban elites profiting illegitimately by transporting cargo along waterways they did not have permission to use. This generated anger among some, while others sensed an economic opportunity to be seized by force. Blockades of fluvial transport, as well as occasional attacks on passing vessels, were the result.

A second interpretation also explained this as a dispute over resources and boundaries, only with the economic interests and power relations shifted. According to this version, the people assembled at the blockade were recruited and paid by large landowners who saw this branch of the river as an extension of their private property and the use of it by commercial riverboats as trespassing. The perceived violation was not merely symbolic, since these property owners were said to be concerned about the material effects of increased boat traffic on their land: erosion caused by the wake of passing vessels; barges ramming into riverbanks; propellers churning through shallow sandbars. Here the conflict was between two regimes of accumulation—one based on land, the other on water; one invested in establishing boundaries, the other in the ability to traverse them—and the blockade was a struggle between equally powerful and propertied actors over the legitimate use of fluvial space.

On hearing these interpretations, I was less concerned about which was true—indeed, both could have been—but rather in how riverboat crews understood such conflicts as well as their own place within them. The majority felt trapped between positions that did not encompass their interests or concerns. If those throwing stones at the pilothouse were marginalized, disaffected *ribereños*, riverboat workers could not exactly endorse their actions—rocks were being thrown at them, after all—but nor could they condemn them. Most crew members themselves identified as *ribereños* and hailed from nearby towns and villages that had languished despite their strategic position along the waterway. Notwithstanding their own success at securing livelihoods within the fluvial transport industry, these workers sympathized with the many others lacking comparable opportunities. If instead the blockades were orchestrated by large landowners, riverboat workers were less likely to sympathize. But their position did not align comfortably with that of the shipping companies either. Although employed by these companies, they were not blind to the divides between workers, managers, and owners. Rather than automatic expressions of solidarity, they felt ensnared by a struggle between divergent factions, none of which they identified with in any straightforward way.

The liminal position riverboat workers occupied within this dispute reflects the complexity of the social and spatial order in which they were embedded. The geo-racial regimes governing the infrastructural environments of the Magdalena basin may be organized around the presumed superiority of the Andean highlands over the Caribbean coast and the dominance of those with proximity to whiteness over those racialized as Black, Indigenous, or mixed race.[54] And these entrenched inequalities may be manifest within the fluvial transport and logistics industry, usually to the detriment of captains, pilots, deckhands, mechanics, and other crew members. But from outside the industry, and especially for those with a grievance, riverboat workers are often associated with power and privilege, even seen as complicit with the operations of racial capitalism, extractive regimes of accumulation, and the political and economic elite. Disputes like the one described above reveal no simple binary between structures of inequality and subjects who mobilize techniques

---

54 Agudelo, "Analizar a Colombia."

for surviving within them. Even so, for riverboat workers forced to maneuver through hostile environments like a blockade, navigation requires the negotiation of local and regional power structures and forms of racial, regional, and economic hierarchy. With projectiles whizzing past their heads, their very existence again depends on it.

* * *

THE SIGNIFICANCE OF rivers, canals, swamps, deltas, and other waterscapes to the cultural and political imagination of the Black Atlantic reflects their dual history, both as conduits for the expansion of racial capitalism and as spaces of autonomy, mobility, and flight.[55] The Lower Magdalena has exemplified this dynamic, serving as an infrastructure for racialized regimes of accumulation as well as a channel for the circulation of ideas and practices of freedom seeking. In the colonial period, the river connected the commercial hubs of Cartagena and Mompox via the Canal del Dique, while facilitating the transport of valuable commodities and enslaved workers throughout the Viceroyalty of New Granada. The waterway's integral relationship to circuits of power, exchange, and information also enabled adjacent lands to become strategic sites for the establishment of *palenques*, or maroon settlements. One of the earliest communities of *cimarrones*, or escaped slaves, was located in the vicinity of Barranca de Malambo, a river port that housed customs offices and warehouses, which allowed the settlement to torment colonial authorities by organizing attacks on passing vessels and threatening the flow of cargo—blockades not unlike the ones occasionally staged today.[56] Proximity to the river also enabled logics and tactics of resistance to be shared with other *palenques* throughout the region.

The ecology of the lower Magdalena valley proved important to the pursuit of freedom from racial subjugation and to the establishment of spaces of Black sovereignty and survival, with the river's treacherous conditions playing an early role.[57] Legend has it that Benkos Biohó, the maroon leader who remains a symbol of Afro-Colombian identity and struggle, first escaped bondage when the boat transporting him and other enslaved Africans up the Magdalena ran

---

55 In a contribution to the blog of the African American Intellectual History Society, Tyler Parry makes a similar point, though limited to the history of the United States. Parry, "The Role of Water." For a review of literature on the historical relationship between Britain's vast canal network and transatlantic slavery, see Matthews, "Canals and Transatlantic Slavery."
56 Navarrete, "Los cimarrones."
57 For the linkages between self-emancipation and ecology, see Connell, "Maroon Ecology."

aground and sank.[58] Biohó would later go on to establish the maroon community of San Basilio de Palenque, and this community worked to convey many others to freedom. Although San Basilio de Palenque was in the forested hills outside Cartagena, many subsequent maroon settlements found refuge in the Lower Magdalena's marshy lowlands, meandering branches, forested backwaters, and mangrove swamps. These territories were difficult to access, prone to periodic flooding, and exposed to menacing wildlife, among other perils, which shielded them from retribution by colonial authorities.[59] Throughout the tropical lowlands of the Caribbean coast, environments the Spanish colonizers found unappealing, even threatening, could be used by *cimarrones* as means of protection, and the river and its tributaries functioned as liquid routes of escape.[60]

The independence achieved by these settlements, however, was never complete or secure. *Palenques* were the target of numerous military campaigns, they were under constant pressure to engage with colonial society at large, and migration both in and out threatened their wider political objectives.[61] Far from isolated pockets of sovereignty, *palenques* occupied an in-between position, which often forced compromises between autonomy and dependence.[62] These compromises were magnified for settlements located in the floodplains and marshlands of the lower Magdalena valley due to the importance of these areas, especially the waterway itself, to regimes of accumulation based on agriculture, livestock, and shipping. In this respect, *palenqueros* were not unlike the much larger population of free people of African descent, who represented the majority throughout the Colombian Caribbean well before emancipation in 1852.[63] The *bogas* of the Magdalena River belonged mainly to the latter group, and they too had an ambivalent relation to the wider market economy

58 This account of Biohó's attempted escape is undocumented. Ali, "Benkos Biohó." For the contemporary symbolism attached to Benkos Biohó, see Cunin, *Identidades a flor de piel*, 100.

59 For other examples from elsewhere in the Americas, see Nevius, *City of Refuge*; Wright, "The Morphology of Marronage." For the territorial biases of the literature on *marronage* and the useful concept of oceanic literacy in the context of fugitivity, see Dunnavant, "Have Confidence in the Sea."

60 Castaño, "Palenques y Cimarronaje," 78.

61 Navarrete, "Palenques."

62 Zavala Guillen, "Afro-Latin American Geographies." For deeper analysis of the tensions between freedom and unfreedom in the Pacific Coast region, see Leal, *Landscapes of Freedom*; Barragán, "Commerce in Children."

63 McGraw, *The Work of Recognition*, 17.

and the dominant social order. Their vocation aligned them with the shipping industry and with commercial interests more generally, and yet their collective resistance to merchant capital and state power combined with their intimate relationship to local hydrography afforded them control over multiple aspects of their work.[64] As in the history of *cimarronaje* (*marronage*, i.e., being a maroon), fluvial environments offered boatmen opportunities for self-determination even as those opportunities were constrained by the waterway's centrality to formations of colonial and racial capitalism.

The cultural and political imagination of riverboat workers today reflects this history. Although the artery may no longer represent a path to liberation, as it did for some of the formerly enslaved, *navegantes* nevertheless understand it as a semiautonomous space that enables degrees of freedom from problems plaguing their lives onshore. A common thread running through interviews with riverboat workers was the lack of economic opportunities for people like them. In contrast, the river—or the fluvial transport industry—was said to offer pathways for social mobility that were otherwise scarce. When pressed further, the more forthright among them alluded to a discriminatory, hierarchical, and rigid social order in which skin tone, education, accent, family connections, and regional affiliation strictly determine life chances and future possibilities (some referenced stereotypes that depict Black and mixed-race *costeños* as lacking a work ethic, even impeding economic development, whereas white *antioqueños* are praised for their entrepreneurial spirit and contribution to the greater good). For riverboat workers, occupying a famously demanding vocation in an industry that undergirds the national economy undermines these tropes. Others referenced feelings of exclusion when discussing the river or the riverboat as "our space," which implied a contrast with other spatial categories—the nation, the city, the office—in which they did not feel a sense of belonging and entitlement.

These perspectives initially sounded Pollyannaish since work in the fluvial transport industry is difficult and demanding. According to a 2018 agreement between management and workers of one shipping company, salaries range from around $8 per day for the cook's assistant to around $28 per day for captains with expertise in pilotage. Most workers are on short-term contracts, and they circulate through twenty-one-day shifts followed by seven days of shore leave without holidays (some companies grant workers a few days off for either Christmas or Easter but not both). There is no specific regula-

----

64 McGraw, *The Work of Recognition*, 77.

tory framework that governs working conditions in the sector (though basic labor laws apply), which not only opens a space for informal hiring and training but also for unsafe practices. Workers have frequently made demands on their employers for greater guarantees and safeguards, some of which have been granted, but levels of transparency and formalization are still relatively low. Trade union representation has also been fraught, partly due to the ambiguous relationship between the fluvial transport and oil industries, which leaves riverboat workers without clear pathways for collective bargaining and legal support. And the social order of the boat is not egalitarian, with a strict hierarchy of rank and pay, nor is it worlds apart from its terrestrial analog, since the embodied characteristics facilitating advancement sometimes mirror those of Colombian society at large.[65] Despite its intrinsic connection to extractive and exploitative regimes of accumulation, life on the river was spoken of as freer and fairer than the one *navegantes* were accustomed to back on land.

These substantive concerns notwithstanding, even the most politically militant riverboat workers emphasized the positive aspects of their jobs and their gratitude toward their employer. An experienced mechanic I will call Edgar, who is known for his union organizing and outspoken opinions, put it this way during a private conversation:

> Well, the truth is I have a lot to thank the company for. I definitely should not be ungrateful, because I have worked here for sixteen years. These are sixteen years in which I have seen people in the head office come and go, but we [crew members] have stayed. I have good memories, and I have nothing bad to say about the company. On the contrary, I am grateful. Even when competitors arrived on the scene and tried to recruit personnel from other firms . . . one day they invited me to come work for them, to put in an application, and I said, "No, I'm happy here," and thank God I still am. This is a good company.

On other occasions, Edgar had gone out of his way to explain some of the unsavory aspects of his industry, so I had no reason to suspect he was now sugarcoating things. Instead, during our conversation he spoke at length about how the company had recruited him at an early age and promoted him steadily

---

65 An important argument in the literature on maritime labor is that ships have been spaces for the development of social relations and political imaginaries that were far more egalitarian and democratic than their land-based counterparts. See Linebaugh and Rediker, *The Many-Headed Hydra*.

through the ranks. "They reward hard work," he added, "and they treat us with respect and dignity." In other conversations, Edgar had made similar points about working on the river versus on land. Since mechanics accompany vessels needing repairs or maintenance, Edgar frequently found himself assigned to the shipyard—an assignment he regarded as constraining, whereas navigating the river he "felt free." When I asked for clarification, Edgar responded that he felt free from the stresses and iniquities of everyday life, but also free to realize his potential and ambitions. Similar sentiments were expressed by his colleagues, many of whom used the idiom of freedom to explain their fondness for working on the water. Whether in relation to their employers or to riverboat work more generally, *navegantes* emphasized that their vocation allowed them opportunities, even liberties, that would simply not have been available to them otherwise. Never did they express a desire to subvert or upend the fluvial transport industry—instead, they saw it as providing them a space in which to secure their ontological standing within (or despite) prevailing taxonomies and hierarchies.

The independence valued by riverboat workers stems in part from their mobility, and this mobility is enabled by the reproductive labor of others, mainly women, back on land and at home, who are decidedly immobile. Again, Candelario Obeso's "Song of the Absent Boatman" is prescient. Assuming the voice of the *boga*, the poem bemoans the "*negra* of my soul" who forgets about "her beloved *zambo*" as he toils away on the water. In Jason McGraw's reading, this lament for failed domesticity expresses two things: an appeal for familial solidarity in the pursuit of autonomy and equality and a rejection of racist invectives that depicted *bogas* as innately unfaithful. But McGraw notes that references like these throughout Obeso's work also "shifted the onus to women of color, whose subordination in the poems forms a precondition for masculine independence."[66] Not much has changed in this regard: life on the river continues to free *navegantes* from the everyday injustices of a notoriously unequal social order, but it also relieves them of domestic duties, such as raising children, caring for elderly relatives, and managing the household. Some riverboat workers discussed this as "women's stuff" (*cosas de mujeres*) while others lamented their absence from family life. A lifelong *marinero* (deckhand) I'll call Rodolfo provided a particularly poignant example of the latter: "The year I began working in navigation was 1985, and in those days there were no mobile phones.

---

66 McGraw, *The Work of Recognition*, 119. McGraw also notes that boatmen's autonomy from wage servitude depended on provision grounds, fishing, and market sales, often done by women (78).

Communication was difficult. On one of my first voyages I had to leave my missus with a big belly. A cousin was the one to tell me: the woman just gave birth to a boy! I was able to visit every two, three months because back then leave was only forty-eight hours, and so whenever I showed up my son was afraid of me. . . . I missed seeing my kids grow up." Another seasoned veteran recounted a similar story spread across two generations:

> The only thing I don't like [about this job] is that one leaves home in a solitary state. The children are raised all alone, the wife remains alone. So when I get there . . . to spend time with my wife and my daughters, sometimes it feels like it's not enough, as if I was running out of time to dedicate to one or the other. So that creates conflict. What I don't like is that one has to neglect the home a lot. I experienced this growing up with a father who was a *navegante*. The authority in my house was our mother. Thank God she was a grounded lady. She always gave us good advice. She raised us well. She taught us to be good people—not with money but good people, people who were taught to do things the right way. I used to say, "But when's Dad coming home?" It always took him forever, and then he'd stay for two days. "Where's Dad?" "No, he's already gone." I understand now that being a *navegante* means sacrificing being with one's family.

Regardless of whether riverboat workers celebrate or regret being absented from the roles and responsibilities of domestic life, most valued their mobility as well as the ability to return to somewhere that feels like home when granted shore leave. The taxing nature of the job makes these periods of leave essential to the physical and psychological well-being of riverboat workers—they truly could not survive without them. Like the freedom to escape the burdens of life on land, having a stable and comfortable place to rest and recuperate between shifts is predicated on the reproductive labor of women (and other family members). The pursuit of autonomy and dignity among mobile riverboat workers depends on gender roles and kinship relations that have forms of inequality and immobility embedded within them.

* * *

IT WAS MIDAFTERNOON, and a trio of *marineros* was taking a break. They seemed in a jolly mood, so I climbed down from the upper deck to see if I could join their animated conversation. Perhaps nudged by my presence, their light-hearted banter quickly gave way to a more serious discussion of the river, and our position just inches above the waterline provided an ideal vantage point.

One of the three, a deckhand I'll call Jesús, took it upon himself to explain some of the ways experienced *navegantes* read the waterway. He began by showing me how to interpret signs—shadows on the surface of the water, seams between faster and slower currents, the movement of floating debris—that help discern channel depth and submerged hazards. This information was crucial for helmsmen, but deckhands often served as lookouts and communicated directly with the pilothouse when they saw something notable on the horizon. Jesús then jumped scale from the boat's immediate vicinity to the watershed: "It's raining in the mountains," he reported, gesturing to the clear skies above our heads for dramatic effect. "You know how I know this? By looking at the water." Jesús explained further: "All those sticks, branches, and other crap floating on the surface—that's being washed into the river upstream. And you see the color of the water? It's brown, dirty, full of sediment. That also tells us rain is falling, causing the slopes to carry mud into the streams that feed the river." Knowledge like this was vital for Jesús and his coworkers, since a fuller river meant less of the backbreaking work required of deckhands when their convoy was forced to maneuver through shallow water.

Similar lessons were offered by other crew members. Many of them pertained to factors like rainfall and sedimentation, both of which influenced the depth of the shipping channel and had a major impact on the success of the journey. However, variations in water levels could also be caused by releases from hydroelectric dams sited on upstream tributaries. This was harder to detect by looking at the river's surface, but *navegantes* (especially captains) kept abreast of the operations of energy companies in order to estimate their effect on navigation. Experienced navigators also knew how to glean useful information by observing the activities of fishermen. A cluster of *canoas* suggested shallow water, partly because that is where the fishing is usually good and partly because they are required by law to know the location of the shipping channel and avoid it. Another factor to take into account was runoff and sewage outflow from cities and towns within the watershed. This was less relevant to water levels than to water quality, which mattered since the boat's drinking water was siphoned directly from the river and then treated by an onboard filtration system. The mechanics were the ones responsible for this system and for ensuring the availability of potable water, so they were well aware of points where harmful effluent was more likely.

Taken together, these tactics for reading the river amount to a synoptic form of hydrographical knowledge that enables riverboat workers to comprehend the subtleties of specific stretches of water while simultaneously grasping the river basin as a whole. The ability to jump from their immediate environs to the entire watershed derives from an ecological imagination that can visualize connections among a complex set of factors, including rainfall, sediment, depth, flow, and runoff, across multiple scales. Either by intuition or by necessity, they have developed the ability to think holistically about the river, not as a discrete object but rather as a part of an interconnected web of relations between living and nonliving entities, human and more-than-human processes, and aqueous and terrestrial spaces. This comprehensive understanding of the river's place within a wider social and environmental order endows *navegantes* with the capacity to read and respond to hydrological changes in real time.

The knowledge and skills that enable riverboat workers to recognize, even anticipate, fluctuations in the river are becoming even more crucial as climate change radically reconfigures the hydrological cycle. Since the early 2000s, studies conducted by scientific bodies in Colombia have warned of the likely effects of global warming on the Magdalena River basin.[67] Their models predict amplified seasonality, rising temperatures, worsening droughts, and greater sedimentation—all of which would alter the timing and volume of water in the river as well as the behavior and shape of the shipping channel.[68] This would present significant navigational challenges, which would fall squarely on the shoulders of captains and their crews. These studies also forecast heightened uncertainty and unpredictability, which would present their own problems for *navegantes* reliant on decades of accumulated experience. As historical patterns of rainfall and sedimentation can no longer be trusted, the ability of boatmen to continuously monitor the waterway as they navigate along it becomes even more indispensable.

The ecological upheavals on the horizon will adversely affect riverboat workers, given how dependent they are on stable hydrological conditions, and this is compounded by the concentration of climate-related risks in the areas where they live and work. The tropical lowlands of northern Colombia have been hit hard recently by extreme episodes of flooding and prolonged periods of drought, both of which scientists attribute to anthropogenic factors, and this pattern is predicted to continue.[69] Although the devastation caused by these extreme weather events has been exacerbated by deforestation and the draining of wetlands for ranching, mining, and agriculture, the activities most responsible are

67 IDEAM-Cormagdalena, "Estudio ambiental."

68 Restrepo and Escobar, "Sediment Load Trends"; IDEAM et al., "Tercera comunicación nacional"; Alifu et al., "Enhancement of River Flooding."

69 Rodríguez Becerra, *¿Para dónde va el río Magdalena?*, 20; Restrepo Ángel, *Los sedimentos del río Magdalena*, 1.

ones the Magdalena River boatmen know well—the extraction and combustion of fossil fuels. The fluvial transport and oil industries have long been tightly entwined, with petroleum products accounting for over 90 percent of the cargo currently shipped along the waterway. This means that riverboat workers are exposed to the localized effects of planetary transformations that they themselves have a hand in producing. Put another way, their labor sustains a regime of accumulation that directly threatens their lives and livelihoods: a paradox one might say is representative of a large swath of humanity.

This paradox was especially present during my journey, since it happened to coincide with the largest oil spill in Colombian history. Just three weeks before, a well operated by state-owned Ecopetrol began discharging crude oil into a tributary of the Sogamoso River, which flows into the Magdalena. It took nearly a month for cleanup crews to contain the seepage, and not before 550 barrels of oil were released into the waterways, causing immense damage to flora and fauna and to the people living and working nearby. On the boat the disaster was a regular topic of conversation, especially when the television in the galley flashed images of fish floating belly-up, birds with blackened plumage, and a lifeless jaguar pulled from a contaminated stream.[70] Crew members responded uniformly with disgust and indignation, and as we neared the juncture where the Sogamoso and the Magdalena meet they were on alert for signs of the spill, such as oil slicks or unusually dark water. Those I spoke to about the disaster sounded personally violated, which was not surprising given how closely they identified with the river. But they were also clearly disturbed by the fact that the company responsible was their employer's biggest client, and that they were on their way to the Ecopetrol refinery in Barrancabermeja to load their barges with the same substance that was currently causing widespread suffering. In struggling to adjust to the hydrological fluctuations of a climate-altered world, riverboat workers also struggled to reconcile their relationship to an extractive economy that had provided them valued opportunities and liberties, and that was responsible for radically disrupting the environment they call home.

* * *

THE VACILLATIONS OF the waterway are not the only uncertainty riverboat workers must navigate; they must also maneuver within the continually shifting regimes of difference structuring Colombian society and space. The most obvious example is the disappearance of the explicitly racialized connotations

---

70 Minuto30 Colombia, "Fotos."

once attached to the vocation itself, which intersects with the ascendance of the official mythologies of *mestizaje*, racial democracy, and multiculturalism.[71] These wider trends have not only reconfigured the cultural politics of race in Colombia (recognizing Black communities as an ethnic group, for example) but have also ushered in the illusion of a postracial social formation.[72] When matters of race and racism do occasionally become visible as such in contemporary public and political discourse, as with recent mobilizations around police brutality, they tend to refer to Afro-descendant and Indigenous populations or to get explained as anomalies—rarely are they understood to reflect the salience of racialization in Colombia at large. This phenomenon extends to the case of the Magdalena River, where debates that were once framed in racial terms are now often devoid of explicitly racial content. The racially infused taxonomies and hierarchies that were common to the social and spatial order of the river basin at earlier moments are rarely recognized, even by critical voices advocating for equality and justice.

At the heart of these shifts is the historical process through which regional typologies have been supplanting racial taxonomies since the early nineteenth century. Regionalism, not racism, remains the dominant framework through which inequalities in Colombia are routinely explained and addressed. However, spatially organized hierarchies, like their racially structured counterparts, are neither fixed nor static—they may be deep-rooted and enduring, but they also face regular challenges and undergo frequent mutations. For example, in the decade since negotiations with the FARC began and the Colombian state inaugurated what was imagined as a phase of postconflict development, or peace building, the problem of geographical (or regional) inequality has been foregrounded. Multiple initiatives have sought to close the massive wealth gap between rural and urban areas, as well as between lowland and highland regions. In this historical conjuncture, the Magdalena River has been thrust back into the limelight: proponents of an infrastructural approach to development and security espouse the waterway's potential to unify a fragmented nation and to bring peace and prosperity to the marginalized and excluded. With these shifts, the coded racism embedded within ideologies of regional superiority have had to accommodate the valorization of places and peoples that have long been subjected to discrimination and relegation. As the waterway comes to signify the political and economic future rather than the past,

71 Restrepo, "Talks and Disputes."
72 Restrepo, "Ethnicization of Blackness"; Paschel, *Becoming Black Political Subjects.*

ribereño communities, including riverboat workers, are forced to contend with new logics of inclusion and exclusion.

Geo-racial regimes can be unstable and slippery terrain: those maneuvering within them can all too easily lose their footing or find themselves disoriented. Navigation techniques are as necessary for shifting social orders as they are for unstable environmental conditions. Riverboat workers are sensitive to how both fluctuations directly impact their lives and livelihoods, and they use a range of techniques to read and respond to changes in the hydrological system and the social order alike. In both cases, they rely on synoptic knowledge that is attuned both to local specifics and to general patterns. Like their ability to visualize the river as an ecosystem, their knowledge of the geo-racial regimes structuring Colombian society and space partly stems from the mobility inherent to their work. As they move along the river from port to port, constantly crossing boundaries of all sorts, the continually shifting racial ecologies in which they are embedded come into sharper relief.

Afterword

Two adjacent screens display a stream of moving images, some from Colombia, others from Germany: free-flowing rivers, traditional fisherfolk, and forested slopes alternate with gargantuan dams, expansive reservoirs, and engineered spillways (figure A.1). The contrast, though visually stark, is underscored by the artist's whispered voice-over, in both Spanish and English, denouncing the defacement of waterways by capitalist extraction, recognizing the insepa-rability of human and more-than-human flourishing, and affirming ancestral and Indigenous understandings of the natural world. Interspersed with these aquatic and infrastructural scenes is jarringly dissimilar footage of political demonstrations in Berlin. Here the camera focuses on both the movement of protesters and orchestrated attempts by security forces to control their circulation. The voice-over connects the dots between choked waterways and policed politics: "The dam is a siege on nature as security is a siege on society."[1]

This video installation, titled *Spaniards Named Her Magdalena, but Natives Call Her Yuma*, is by the multimedia artist Carolina Caycedo. The solo exhibi-tion in which the installation appeared, *Land of Friends*, borrowed its title from one of the Indigenous names for the waterway, which itself featured promi-nently in many of the works on display.[2] The footage from Colombia was re-

1 Carolina Caycedo, *Spaniards Named Her Magdalena, But Natives Call Her Yuma*, 2013, two-channel HD video installation (color, sound), 27 min; see http://carolinacaycedo.com /spaniards-named-her-magdalena-but-natives-call-her-yuma-2013. Translation by author from the Spanish.
2 *Carolina Caycedo: Land of Friends*, Baltic Centre for Contemporary Art, Gateshead, UK, May 28, 2022–January 29, 2023.

FIGURE A.1. Carolina Caycedo, *Spaniards Named Her Magdalena, but Natives Call Her Yuma*, 2013.

corded mainly on the upper reaches of the Magdalena River near the site of the El Quimbo hydroelectric dam. The destruction of ecosystems and dispossession of communities associated with El Quimbo's construction have been central to Caycedo's wider body of work, in particular the project titled *Be Dammed* (or *Represa Represión* in Spanish), which includes performance, text, photography, video, textiles, and drawing. Encompassing over a decade of studio and field-based practice, begun in 2013, her project examines the violence of large-scale extractive infrastructures alongside strategies of resistance on waterways, not only in Colombia but also in Brazil, Sweden, Spain, the United States, and elsewhere.

"Rivers are the veins of the planet," Caycedo writes, and in her work she advocates for the recognition of agency of the more-than-human world and its protection.[3] An ontological politics that dissolves the boundary between water

3 Carolina Caycedo, *Be Dammed*, 2013–ongoing, http://carolinacaycedo.com/be-dammed -ongoing-project; quote from homepage. See also Acevedo-Yates, "Embodied Spiritual Fieldwork."

bodies and human bodies runs through Caycedo's art, such as in the photocollage *Multiple Clitoris* (2016), in which she printed onto a cascading cotton banner images of the Iguazú Falls that sexualize the river, as her title indicates.[4] The series of works to which that piece belongs, *Water Portraits*, is polemical, as one curator points out: it "invite[s] the viewer to reflect on the fluidity of bodies of water, which resist the phallogocentric logic of extraction."[5] Rooted in ecofeminism, Caycedo sees patriarchy and extractivism as conjoined: "Health, knowledge, labor, and, ultimately, life have been historically extracted from women's bodies in the same way fossil fuels, genetic codes, and energy have been extracted from the land, from plants and animals, from rivers."[6] Caycedo's *My Feminine Lineage of Environmental Struggle* (2019) comprises a frieze of portraits of women activists: mostly women of color whom she identifies both as burdened disproportionally by ecological damage and as the vanguard of the environmental movement.[7]

Yet the association of racialized and gendered violence with ecological injury has hardly been restricted to works of art. In Colombia, the transitional justice process underway since 2016 has begun to resonate with Caycedo's project. Here, too, the category of victimhood has been expanded to include nature. In recent years, the National Center of Historical Memory has commissioned researchers to examine the environmental effects of the armed conflict, and the Truth Commission has solicited testimonies on behalf of wounded forests and animals. Meanwhile, the Special Jurisdiction for Peace (JEP), which was established to prosecute crimes committed during the conflict, has acknowledged nature as a "silent victim" (*víctima silenciosa*), and the judiciary has recognized

---

4 Carolina Caycedo, *Multiple Clitoris*, 2016, photocollage printed on cotton canvas, 150×1000 cm, Instituto de Visión, Colombia/New York, http://carolinacaycedo.com/water-portraits-2016.

5 Barbican Centre, "RE/SISTERS."

6 Quoted in Bury, "Water Portraits."

7 Carolina Caycedo, *My Feminine Lineage of Environmental Struggle*, 2019, printed canvas banner, 165×635 cm. "Young women are leading environmentalism today because it is precisely women and the feminized body, the feminine body, who feel the worst impacts of extractivism across the world. It's the Indigenous woman, it's the Black woman, it's the mestiza and brown woman, it's the transgender woman, who take the worst part of these processes of destruction. And it's precisely our economies of care, or the territory of life, that become the most important tool in counteracting these destructive processes." MCA Chicago, "*Carolina Caycedo*."

the environment as a "subject of rights" (*sujeto de derechos*).[8] While such moves have been controversial and their implications remain uncertain, pressure is mounting to address the suffering inflicted on beings other than human. Most of the attention has been paid thus far to water bodies, notably rivers, with the Constitutional Court first granting legal personhood to the Atrato River in northwestern Colombia in 2016, followed by several others, including the Magdalena in 2019.[9] Though indicative of wider trends, these arteries have become test cases for definitions of violence, victimhood, and justice that encompass the more-than-human world.

Recognizing nature as victim has the effect of unsettling conventional understandings of the armed conflict—and not only by questioning anthropocentrism but also by focusing on water. Although accounts of violence and displacement in Colombia consistently conjure fights over land, property, and territory, water bodies such as wetlands, swamps, and rivers have seen their share of warfare and bloodshed.[10] A 2018 exhibition in Bogotá, however, provoked a public dialogue that mapped the conflict beyond the terrestrial.[11] Some of its displays drew attention to the victimization of watery nature itself—wetland drainage, toxic effluent—while others highlighted the centrality of water in interhuman conflict—fishers and farmers being denied access to water resources, waterways serving as conduits for armed groups and illegal activities. In their analysis of the exhibition, Sofía González-Ayala and Alejandro Camargo argued that foregrounding water lays the "foundation for a more comprehensive discussion about the implications of deeming non-human beings . . . victims of the armed conflict and subjects of reparations for whom non-repetition should also be guaranteed."[12]

The transitional justice process has also begun to confront the multiple hierarchies of difference structuring violence in Colombia, thereby challenging dominant explanations that privilege economic inequality. As Leyner Palacios,

---

8 Comisión de la Verdad, "La naturaleza." For the JEP declaration, see Unidad de Investigación y Acusación, Comunicado 009.

9 Sentence T-622 of 2016 was the first, granting legal status to the Atrato River. The others were added in 2019. For the Magdalena sentence, see Juzgado Primero Penal del Circuito con Funciones de Conocimiento, Neiva, Huila, October 24, 2019, Sentence no. 071.

10 González-Ayala and Camargo, "Voices of Water and Violence," 184; Gutiérrez Campo and Escobar Jiménez, "Territorio anfibio y despojo." For an analysis of the centrality of land-based property to the conflict as well as attempts to move beyond it, see Morris, "Speculative Fields."

11 González-Ayala and Camargo, "Voices of Water and Violence," 186.

12 González-Ayala and Camargo, "Voices of Water and Violence," 201.

an Afro-Colombian leader from Chocó and survivor of the brutal 2002 Bojayá massacre, put it succinctly, "The Colombian armed conflict was racist." In a 2022 interview with a Spanish news agency, Palacios summarized a recent congress on structural racism organized by Colombia's Truth Commission by elaborating on the racial logics impacting the conflict plaguing the country since the mid-twentieth century: "The massacres, the murders, the displacements, the multiple violations of women, the practices of marking the bodies, the human beings, and the contempt with which they acted in some cases with an extraordinarily inhuman level of cruelty show us that there were traces of racism embedded in the conscience of those who acted."[13] Palacios's comments attracted media attention, but they were not breaking news. For decades, social movement activists and community organizers, like himself, had been doggedly denouncing the uneven distribution of violence and displacement along racial and regional lines.[14] As far back as 2009, the Constitutional Court had issued a ruling requiring the state to take demographic differences into account when protecting the constitutional rights of the displaced population.[15] That Palacios on this occasion was speaking as one of eleven acting members of the Truth Commission lent gravity to his indictment.

Among the topics of discussion at the congress was a report titled "Racism, Patriarchy, and Armed Conflict," which had been submitted to the Truth Commission in 2021 by researchers from a prestigious university in Cali. Palacios's comments to the media corresponded to one of the report's headline messages: "the black, Afro-descendant, *raizal* and *palenquera* population has . . . suffered the greatest proportion of violent acts related to the armed conflict," especially forced displacement.[16] The report made critical contributions to transitional justice in Colombia, not least by foregrounding an intersectional

---

13 Análisis Urbano, "'El conflicto colombiano fue racista.'" The Bojayá massacre took place in 2002 when the FARC bombed a church in the department of Chocó, claiming the lives of 119 inhabitants of the town.

14 Cárdenas, "'Thanks to My Forced Displacement.'"

15 Auto 005 of 2009. For constitutional jurisprudence relating to the Afro-Colombian population, see Paschel, *Becoming Black Political Subjects*.

16 The *raizales* are an Afro-Caribbean ethnic group from the archipelago of San Andrés, Providencia, and Santa Catalina in Colombia. The *palenquera* community is made up of the descendants of the enslaved who, through acts of resistance and freedom, took refuge beginning in the sixteenth century in the territories of northern coastal lowlands called *palenques*. Universidad ICESI and Centro de Estudios Afrodiaspóricos, "Racismo, patriarcado y conflicto armado," 7. The report cited 39 percent of the victims of the conflict in the country as Afro-descendant and 9.7 percent as Indigenous.

approach in which racism and patriarchy were intrinsic to the conflict.[17] Citing the research of one of its contributors, Aurora Vergara-Figueroa, the report also advanced the concept of deracination (*destierro*) to emphasize the systematic use of violence to sever deep-rooted ties between Afro-Colombian communities and the land.[18] The report joined an upsurge of popular mobilization challenging public institutions and civil society to confront the interlocking hierarchies structuring the armed conflict, as well as Colombian society more broadly.[19]

In my conversations with riverboat workers, the racial dimensions of the armed conflict rarely surfaced. I initially took this to reflect the narrow scope of discourse on race in Colombia, which rarely engages with the implicit workings of racial hierarchies unless they are blatantly expressed. But the more I discussed histories of violence with these men, the more I came to appreciate their awkward position within the conceptual and institutional frameworks through which the conflict has been understood. Neither victims nor victimizers, they fail to conform to the conventional image of either group. Nor can they be identified with the other category used to imagine and govern the conflict's impact on lives and livelihood: mobile by profession, they can hardly be counted among the internally displaced population (*los desplazados*). Moreover, their racial identity eludes categories like *Afro-desplazado*, the term by which the intersection of race and violence has primarily been framed.[20] As Roosbelinda Cárdenas shows, this category, because it excludes the violence of structural racism, anti-Blackness, and institutionalized white (and *mestizo*) supremacy, effaces victims the state does not recognize as Black or displaced. For example, the deckhand who joked about his dark skin preventing him from passing as gringo (chapter 4) also reported having been held hostage by the ELN. He was traumatized by prolonged exposure to warfare (*quedé "psicosiao"*

---

17 The process of transitional justice in Colombia has been underway since 2005 and has ramped up significantly since the 2016 peace accord. For an overview of key dimensions of this process, see Sánchez and Rudling, *Reparations in Colombia*.

18 Vergara-Figueroa, *Afrodescendant Resistance*. In dialogue with Afro Colombian social movements and their organizing around the concept of territory (*territorio*), this approach became especially important for conceptualizing and operationalizing demands for reparations, which in Colombia have historically been linked to the restitution of property in the form of collective land titles.

19 Protests foregrounding structural racism and violence (including police brutality) have been on the rise in Colombia.

20 Cárdenas, "'Thanks to My Forced Displacement.'"

de tanto plomo), he disclosed, but was never considered a victim either by the state or in society at large.[21]

The experience of riverboat workers also jars with the cultural and legal framing of the victimization of nature. Though impacted by the armed conflict, their own victimhood has mostly gone unrecognized. Nor are they accorded the state-mandated forms of support and protection accompanying such recognition, as is seen in the movement to designate rivers as subjects of rights. And since nonhuman entities are unable to speak for themselves, a new figure of environmental stewardship has emerged—guardians (*guardianes*)—who can advocate on their behalf.[22] However, crew members who have spent their lives working along the Magdalena are predictably excluded from representing its interests, despite their intimate connection to the river and extensive knowledge of its hydrology and ecology. Given their close association with the oil industry, riverboat workers are more likely assumed to be too complicit with extractivism and violating the river's rights rather than as capable of defending them.

Herein lies the complexity of confronting racialized violence and redressing ecological injury. Both initiatives are welcome and overdue, and a central argument of this book is that they are intrinsically linked, yet the realities of riverboat life and labor that have been this book's focus expose some of their limitations and contradictions. Rivers can sometimes be elevated to the status of rights-bearing subject while the suffering of those who live and work along them continues to be overlooked; water bodies can be recognized as deserving of protection while certain human bodies are still presumed to have a high tolerance for abuse. While the correlation of human and more-than-human justice is a step forward, the conferral of personhood on rivers while some humans are denied this enfranchisement demonstrates the stubbornness of entrenched hierarchies. This problematic, though somewhat dispiriting, can open new theoretical and practical possibilities for imagining planetary futures beyond the entanglement of race and nature.

---

21 *Quedé psicosiao* is a colloquial expression derived from the word for *psychosis* that refers to anxiety and fear following exposure to violent or otherwise traumatic events.

22 Cagüeñas, Galindo Orrego, and Rasmussen, "El Atrato y sus guardianes."

Bibliography

Acevedo-Yates, Carla. "Embodied Spiritual Fieldwork: Dismantling Western Perspectives through Affective Exchanges (Trabajo de campo espiritual desde el cuerpo: Desmantelando las perspectivas occidentales por medio de intercambios afectivos)." In *Carolina Caycedo: From the Bottom of the River*, edited by Carla Acevedo-Yates, 23–49. Chicago: Museum of Contemporary Art Chicago, 2020.

Afanador-Llach, María José. "Una república colosal: La unión de Colombia, el acceso al Pacífico y la utopía del comercio global, 1819–1830." *Anuario Colombiano de Historia Social y de la Cultura* 45, no. 2 (2018): 35–63.

Agudelo, Ángela Lucía. "Analizar a Colombia, percibir a los 'costeños': Región y raza entre 1900 y 1950." *Anuario de Historia Regional y de las Fronteras* 18, no. 2 (2013): 471–91.

Ali, Omar H. "Benkos Biohó: African Maroon Leadership in New Grenada." In *Atlantic Biographies: Individuals and Peoples in the Atlantic World*, 263–94. Leiden: Brill, 2014.

Alifu, Haireti, Yukiko Hirabayashi, Yukiko Imada, and Hideo Shiogama. "Enhancement of River Flooding Due to Global Warming." *Scientific Reports* 12, no. 1 (2022): 2–7.

Alimahomed-Wilson, Jake. "Men along the Shore: Working-Class Masculinities in Crisis." *Norma: Nordic Journal for Masculinity Studies* 6, no. 1 (2011): 22–44.

Alimahomed-Wilson, Jake. "Racialized Masculinities and Global Logistics Labor." In *Gendering Logistics: Feminist Approaches for the Analysis of Supply-Chain Capitalism*, edited by Carlotta Benvegnù, Niccolò Cuppini, Mattia Frapporti, Evelina Gambino, Floriano Milesi, Irene Peano, and Maurilio Pirone, 27–43. Bologna: University of Bologna, 2021.

Alimahomed-Wilson, Jake. "Unfree Shipping: The Racialisation of Logistics Labour." *Work Organisation, Labour and Globalisation* 13, no. 1 (2019): 96–113.

Alimonda, Héctor. "La colonialidad de la naturaleza: Una aproximación a la Ecología Política Latinoamericana." In *La naturaleza colonizada: Ecología política y minería en América Latina*, 21–58. Buenos Aires: CLACSO, 2011.

Alvear Sanín, José. *Manual del Río Magdalena*. Bogotá: Cormagdalena, 2005.

Análisis Urbano. "'El conflicto colombiano fue racista,' dice la Comisión de la Verdad." 2022. https://analisisurbano.org/el-conflicto-colombiano-fue-racista-dice-la-comision-de-la-verdad/198422/.

Anim-Addo, Anyaa, William Hasty, and Kimberley Peters. "The Mobilities of Ships and Shipped Mobilities." *Mobilities* 9, no. 3 (2014): 337–49.

Appel, Hannah. *The Licit Life of Capitalism: US Oil in Equatorial Guinea*. Durham, NC: Duke University Press, 2019.

Appel, Hannah, Nikhil Anand, and Akhil Gupta. "Introduction: Temporality, Politics, and the Promise of Infrastructure." In *The Promise of Infrastructure*, edited by Nikhil Anand, Akhil Gupta, and Hannah Appel, 1–38. Durham, NC: Duke University Press, 2018.

Appelbaum, Nancy P. *Mapping the Country of Regions: The Chorographic Commission of Nineteenth-Century Colombia*. Chapel Hill: University of North Carolina Press, 2016.

Appelbaum, Nancy P. *Muddied Waters: Race, Region, and Local History in Colombia, 1846–1948*. Durham, NC: Duke University Press, 2003.

Appelbaum, Nancy. "Whitening the Region: Caucano Mediation and 'Antioqueño Colonization' in Nineteenth-Century Colombia." *Hispanic American Historical Review* 79, no. 4 (1999): 631–67.

Arango Echeverri, Manuel. "Los conocimientos de embarque en el río Magdalena: Desde el periodo colonial hasta 1886." *La Timonera* 22 (2014): 70–78.

Arendt, Hannah. *The Origins of Totalitarianism*. New York: Meridian, 1958.

Arias, Julio, and Eduardo Restrepo. "Historizando raza: Propuestas conceptuales y metodológicas." *Crítica y emancipación* 2, no. 3 (2010): 45–64.

Arias Vanegas, Julio. *Nación y diferencia en el siglo XIX colombiano: Orden nacional, racialismo y taxonomías poblacionales*. Bogotá: Universidad de los Andes, 2007.

Arnold, David. *The Problem of Nature: Environment and Culture in Historical Perspective*. Oxford: Blackwell, 1996.

Asher, Kiran. *Black and Green: Afro-Colombians, Development, and Nature in the Pacific Lowlands*. Durham, NC: Duke University Press, 2009.

Asher, Kiran. "Fragmented Forests, Fractured Lives: Ethno-territorial Struggles and Development in the Pacific Lowlands of Colombia." *Antipode* 52, no. 4 (2020): 949–70.

Attewell, Wesley. "The Lifelines of Empire: Logistics as Infrastructural Power in Occupied South Vietnam." *American Quarterly* 72, no. 4 (2020): 909–35.

Ballantine, Amory. "The River Mouth Speaks: Water Quality as Storyteller in Decolonization of the Port of Tacoma." *Water History* 9, no. 1 (2017): 45–66.

Ballestero, Andrea. *A Future History of Water*. Durham, NC: Duke University Press, 2019.

Ballvé, Teo. *The Frontier Effect: State Formation and Violence in Colombia*. Ithaca, NY: Cornell University Press, 2020.

Barbary, Olivier, and Fernando Urrea, eds. *Gente negra en Colombia: Dinámicas sociopolíticas en Cali y el Pacífico*. Medellín: Editorial Lealon, 2004.

Barbican Centre. "RE/SISTERS: A Lens on Gender and Ecology." London, October 5, 2023–January 14, 2024. Exhibition brochure.

Barragán, Yesenia. "Commerce in Children: Slavery, Gradual Emancipation, and the Free Womb Trade in Colombia." *Americas* 78, no. 2 (2021): 229–57.

Bassi, Ernesto. *An Aqueous Territory: Sailor Geographies and New Granada's Transimperial Greater Caribbean World*. Durham, NC: Duke University Press, 2016.

Bear, Laura. "For Labour: Ajeet's Accident and the Ethics of Technological Fixes in Time." *Journal of the Royal Anthropological Institute* 20, no. S1 (2014): 71–88.

Bear, Laura. *Navigating Austerity: Currents of Debt along a South Asian River*. Stanford, CA: Stanford University Press, 2015.

Bell Lemus, Gustavo A. "El Canal del Dique 1810–1840: El viacrucis de Cartagena." *Boletín Cultural y Bibliográfico* 26, no. 21 (1989): 15–23.

Beltrán, William Mauricio, and Ivón Natalia Cuervo. "Pentecostalismo en contextos rurales de violencia: El caso de El Garzal, sur de Bolívar, Colombia." *Revista Colombiana de Antropología* 52, no. 1 (2016): 139–68.

Benjamin, Ruha, ed. *Captivating Technology: Race, Carceral Technoscience, and Liberatory Imagination in Everyday Life*. Durham, NC: Duke University Press, 2019.

Benjamin, Ruha. "Catching Our Breath: Critical Race STS and the Carceral Imagination." *Engaging Science, Technology, and Society* 2 (2016): 145–56.

Benjamin, Ruha. "Introduction: Discriminatory Design, Liberating Imagination." In *Captivating Technology: Race, Carceral Technoscience, and Liberatory Imagination in Everyday Life*, edited by Ruha Benjamin, 1–22. Duke, NC: Duke University Press, 2019.

Berman-Arévalo, Eloisa. "El 'fracaso ruinoso' de la reforma agraria en clave de negridad: Comunidades afrocampesinas y reconocimiento liberal en Montes de María, Colombia." *Memorias* 15, no. 37 (2019): 117–49.

Berman-Arévalo, Eloisa. "Geografías negras del arroz en el Caribe Colombiano: Tongueo y cuerpo territorio 'en las grietas' de la modernización agrícola." *Latin American and Caribbean Ethnic Studies* 18, no. 3 (2023): 437–55.

Berman-Arévalo, Eloisa. "Mapping Violent Land Orders: Armed Conflict, Moral Economies, and the Trajectories of Land Occupation and Dispossession in the Colombian Caribbean." *Journal of Peasant Studies* 48, no. 2 (2021): 349–67.

Berman-Arévalo, Eloisa, and Diana Ojeda. "Ordinary Geographies: Care, Violence, and Agrarian Extractivism in 'Post-conflict' Colombia." *Antipode* 52, no. 6 (2020): 1583–1602.

Berman-Arévalo, Eloisa, and Gabriela Valdivia. "The Rhythms of 'Acostumbrarse': Noticing Quiet Hydro-politics in Colombia's Caribbean Coast." *Environment and Planning D: Society and Space* 40, no. 5 (2022): 843–61.

Bledsoe, Adam, and Willie Jamaal Wright. "The Pluralities of Black Geographies." *Antipode* 51, no. 2 (2019): 419–37.

Bocarejo Suescún, Diana. "Gobernanza del agua: Pensar desde las fluctuaciones, los enmarañamientos y políticas del día a día." *Revista de Estudios Sociales* 63 (2018): 111–18.

Bocarejo Suescún, Diana. "Lo público de la Historia pública en Colombia: Reflexiones desde el Río de la Patria y sus pobladores ribereños." *Historia Crítica* 68 (2018): 67–91.

Boelens, Rutgerd, Arturo Escobar, Karen Bakker, Lena Hommes, Erik Swyngedouw, Barbara Hogenboom, Edward H. Huijbens, et al. "Riverhood: Political Ecologies of Socionature Commoning and Translocal Struggles for Water Justice." *Journal of Peasant Studies* 50, no. 3 (2022): 1125–56.

Boelens, Rutgerd, Juliana Forigua-Sandoval, Bibiana Duarte-Abadía, and Juan Carlos Gutiérrez-Camargo. "River Lives, River Movements: Fisher Communities Mobilizing Local and Official Rules in Defense of the Magdalena River." *Journal of Legal Pluralism and Unofficial Law* 53, no. 3 (2021): 458–76.

Bolster, W. Jeffrey. *Black Jacks: African American Seamen in the Age of Sail*. Cambridge, MA: Harvard University Press, 1997.

Bonil-Gómez, Katherine. "Free People of African Descent and Jurisdictional Politics in Eighteenth-Century New Granada: The *Bogas* of the Magdalena River." *Journal of Iberian and Latin American Studies* 24, no. 2 (2018): 183–94.

Bonilla, Yarimar. "Unsettling Sovereignty." *Cultural Anthropology* 32, no. 3 (2017): 330–39.

Booth, Kate. "Critical Insurance Studies: Some Geographic Directions." *Progress in Human Geography* 45, no. 5 (2021): 1295–1310.

Bourke, Joanna. *Loving Animals: On Bestiality, Zoophilia and Post-Human Love*. London: Reaktion, 2020.

Brahinsky, Rachel, Jade Sasser, and Laura-Anne Minkoff-Zern. "Race, Space, and Nature: An Introduction and Critique." *Antipode* 46, no. 5 (2014): 1135–52.

Brathwaite, Edward Kamau. *History of the Voice: The Development of Nation Language in Anglophone Caribbean Poetry*. London: New Beacon, 1984.

Brooks, Iolanthe, and Asha Best. "Prison Fixes and Flows: Carceral Mobilities and Their Critical Logistics." *Environment and Planning D: Society and Space* 39 (2021): 459–76.

Brown, Jacqueline Nassy. *Dropping Anchor, Setting Sail: Geographies of Race in Black Liverpool*. Princeton, NJ: Princeton University Press, 2005.

Browne, Simone. *Dark Matters: On the Surveillance of Blackness*. Durham, NC: Duke University Press, 2015.

Buchanan, Thomas C. *Black Life on the Mississippi: Slaves, Free Blacks, and the Western Steamboat World*. Chapel Hill: University of North Carolina Press, 2007.

Bury, Louis. "Water Portraits: Carolina Caycedo Interviewed by Louis Bury." BOMB *Magazine*, June 12, 2020. https://bombmagazine.org/articles/water-portraits-carolina-caycedo-interviewed/.

Cadelo, Andrea. "Race, Nature and History in *Ensayo sobre las revoluciones políticas* and *El Español de Ambos Mundos*." *Bulletin of Latin American Research* 38, no. 2 (2019): 136–49.

Cagüeñas, Diego, María Isabel Galindo Orrego, and Sabina Rasmussen. "El Atrato y sus guardianes: Imaginación ecopolítica para hilar nuevos derechos." *Revista Colombiana de Antropología* 56, no. 2 (2020): 169–96.

Caldas, Francisco José de. *Del influjo del clima sobre los seres organizados, por Francisco José de Caldas, individuo meritorio de la Expedición Botánica de Santafé de Bogotá y encargado del Observatorio Astronómico de esta capital*. Bogotá: Universidad Nacional de Colombia, Biblioteca Virtual Colombiana, 1966.

Camacho, Juana. "Acumulación tóxica y despojo agroalimentario en La Mojana, Caribe colombiano." *Revista Colombiana de Antropología* 53, no. 1 (2017): 123–50.

Camargo, Alejandro. "Land Born of Water: Property, Stasis, and Motion in the Floodplains of Northern Colombia." *Geoforum* 131 (2022): 223–31.

Camargo, Alejandro. "Stagnation: Waterflows and the Politics of Stranded Matter in La Mojana, Colombia." In *Delta Life: Exploring Dynamic Environments Where Rivers Meet the Sea*, edited by Franz Krause and Mark Harris, 83–101. New York: Berghahn, 2021.

Camargo, Alejandro. "Una tierra bondadosa: Progreso y recursos naturales en la región del río San Jorge, siglo XX." *Historia Crítica*, no. 37 (2009): 170–91.

Camargo, Alejandro, and Luisa Cortesi. "Flooding Water and Society." *Wiley Interdisciplinary Reviews: Water* 6, no. 5 (2019): 1–9.

Camargo, Alejandro, and Diana Ojeda. "Ambivalent Desires: State Formation and Dispossession in the Face of Climate Crisis." *Political Geography* 60 (2017): 57–65.

Camargo, Alejandro, and Simón Uribe. "Infraestructuras: Poder, espacio, etnografía." *Revista Colombiana de Antropología* 58, no. 2 (2022): 9–24.

Cañizares-Esguerra, Jorge. "How Derivative Was Humboldt? Microcosmic Nature Narratives in Early Modern Spanish America and the (Other) Origins of Humboldt's Ecological Sensibilities." In *Colonial Botany: Science, Commerce, and Politics in the Early Modern World*, edited by Londa Schiebinger and Claudia Swan, 148–65. Philadelphia: University of Pennsylvania Press, 2005.

Cañizares-Esguerra, Jorge. *Nature, Empire, and Nation: Explorations of the History of Science in the Iberian World*. Stanford, CA: Stanford University Press, 2006.

Cañizares-Esguerra, Jorge. "New World, New Stars: Patriotic Astrology and the Invention of Indian and Creole Bodies in Colonial Spanish America, 1600–1650." *American Historical Review* 104, no. 1 (1999): 33–68.

Carby, Hazel V. *Imperial Intimacies: A Tale of Two Islands*. London: Verso, 2019.

Cárdenas, Roosbelinda. "'Thanks to My Forced Displacement': Blackness and the Politics of Colombia's War Victims." *Latin American and Caribbean Ethnic Studies* 13, no. 1 (2018): 72–93.

Carse, Ashley. "The Ecobiopolitics of Environmental Mitigation: Remaking Fish Habitat through the Savannah Harbor Expansion Project." *Social Studies of Science* 51, no. 4 (2021): 512–37.

Carse, Ashley. "The Feel of 13,000 Containers: How Pilots Learn to Navigate Changing Logistical Environments." *Ethnos* 88, no. 2 (2020): 264–87.

Carse, Ashley. "Keyword: Infrastructure—How a Humble French Engineering Term Shaped the Modern World." In *Infrastructures and Social Complexity: A Companion*, edited by Penny Harvey, Casper Bruun Jensen, and Atsuro Morita, 27–39. London: Routledge, 2017.

Carse, Ashley. "Nature as Infrastructure: Making and Managing the Panama Canal Watershed." *Social Studies of Science* 42, no. 4 (2012): 539–63.

Carse, Ashley, and Joshua A. Lewis. "New Horizons for Dredging Research: The Ecology and Politics of Harbor Deepening in the Southeastern United States." *Wiley Interdisciplinary Reviews: Water* 7, no. 6 (2020): 1–16.

Carse, Ashley, and Joshua A. Lewis. "Toward a Political Ecology of Infrastructure Standards: Or, How to Think about Ships, Waterways, Sediment, and Communities Together." *Environment and Planning A* 49, no. 1 (2017): 9–28.

Carse, Ashley, Townsend Middleton, Jason Cons, Jatin Dua, Gabriela Valdivia, and Elizabeth Cullen Dunn. "Chokepoints: Anthropologies of the Constricted Contemporary." *Ethnos* 88, no. 2 (2023): 193–203.

Castaño, Alen. "Palenques y Cimarronaje: Procesos de resistencia al sistema colonial esclavista en el Caribe Sabanero (siglos XVI, XVII y XVIII)." *Revista CS* 16 (2015): 61–86.

Castillo, Lina del. *Crafting a Republic for the World: Scientific, Geographic, and Historiographic Inventions of Colombia*. Lincoln: University of Nebraska Press, 2018.

Cecelski, David S. *The Waterman's Song: Slavery and Freedom in Maritime North Carolina*. Chapel Hill: University of North Carolina Press, 2001.

Césaire, Aimé. *Discourse on Colonialism*. New York: Monthly Review Press, 2000.

Chalfin, Brenda. "Recasting Maritime Governance in Ghana: The Neo-developmental State and the Port of Tema." *Journal of Modern African Studies* 48, no. 4 (2010): 573–98.

Chao, Sophie, Karin Bolender, and Eben Kirksey, eds. *The Promise of Multispecies Justice*. Durham, NC: Duke University Press, 2022.

Chari, Sharad. "Critical Geographies of Racial and Spatial Control." *Geography Compass* 2, no. 6 (2008): 1907–21.

Chari, Sharad. "The Ocean and the City: Spatial Forgeries of Racial Capitalism." *Environment and Planning D: Society and Space* 39, no. 6 (2021): 1026–42.

Chari, Sharad. "State Racism and Biopolitical Struggle: The Evasive Commons in Twentieth-Century Durban, South Africa." *Radical History Review* 108 (2010): 73–90.

Chari, Sharad. "Three Moments of Stuart Hall in South Africa: Postcolonial-Postsocialist Marxisms of the Future." *Critical Sociology* 43, no. 6 (2017): 831–45.

Chowdhury, Romit. "The Social Life of Transport Infrastructures: Masculinities and Everyday Mobilities in Kolkata." *Urban Studies* 58, no. 1 (2021): 73–89.

Chua, Charmaine. "Indurable Monstrosities: Megaships, Megaports, and Transpacific Infrastructures of Violence." In *FutureLand: Stories from the Global Supply Chain*. London: Centre for Research Architecture, Goldsmiths University of London, 2019.

Chua, Charmaine. "Logistics." In *The SAGE Handbook of Marxism*, edited by Beverley Skeggs, Sara Farris, Alberto Toscano, and Svenja Bromberg, 1442–60. London: Sage, 2021.

Chua, Charmaine, Martin Danyluk, Deborah Cowen, and Laleh Khalili. "Introduction: Turbulent Circulation: Building a Critical Engagement with Logistics." *Environment and Planning D: Society and Space* 36, no. 4 (2018): 617–29.

Coates, Ta-Nehisi. *The Water Dancer*. London: Penguin, 2019.

Comisión de la Verdad. "La naturaleza: Una víctima silenciosa del conflicto armado." October 8, 2019. https://web.comisiondelaverdad.co/actualidad/noticias/la-naturaleza-una-victima-silenciada-del-conflicto-armado.

Connell, Robert. "Maroon Ecology: Land, Sovereignty, and Environmental Justice." *Journal of Latin American and Caribbean Anthropology* 25, no. 2 (2020): 218–35.

Coronil, Fernando. *The Magical State: Nature, Money, and Modernity in Venezuela*. Chicago: University of Chicago Press, 1997.

Corredor, Luz Rocío, and Luis Carlos Díaz Barragán. "Navegabilidad del río Magdalena y competitividad de la logística del transporte en Colombia." *Questionar Investigación Específica* 6, no. 1 (2018): 67–78.

Corwin, Julia E., and Vinay Gidwani. "Repair Work as Care: On Maintaining the Planet in the Capitalocene." *Antipode*, October 18, 2021, 1–20.

Coss-Corzo, Alejandro De. "Patchwork: Repair Labor and the Logic of Infrastructure Adaptation in Mexico City." *Environment and Planning D: Society and Space* 39, no. 2 (2021): 237–53.

Cowen, Deborah. "Afterword." In *Gendering Logistics: Feminist Approaches for the Analysis of Supply-Chain Capitalism*, edited by Carlotta Benvegnù, Niccolò Cuppini, Mattia Frapporti, Evelina Gambino, Floriano Milesi, Irene Peano, and Maurilio Pirone, 105–14. Bologna: University of Bologna, 2021.

Cowen, Deborah. *The Deadly Life of Logistics: Mapping Violence in Global Trade*. Minneapolis: University of Minnesota Press, 2014.

Cowen, Deborah. "Following the Infrastructures of Empire: Notes on Cities, Settler Colonialism, and Method." *Urban Geography* 41, no. 4 (2020): 469–86.

Cowen, Deborah. "A Geography of Logistics: Market Authority and the Security of Supply Chains." *Annals of the Association of American Geographers* 100, no. 3 (2010): 600–620.

Cowen, Deborah. "Infrastructures of Empire and Resistance." *Verso* (blog), January 25, 2017. https://www.versobooks.com/en-gb/blogs/news/3067-infrastructures-of-empire-and-resistance.

Cronon, William. *Uncommon Ground: Rethinking the Human Place in Nature.* New York: W. W. Norton, 1996.

Cross, Jamie. "Detachment as a Corporate Ethic: Materializing CSR in the Diamond Supply Chain from Hard Rock to Diamond Ring." *Focaal—Journal of Global and Historical Anthropology*, no. 60 (2011): 34–46.

Cunin, Elisabeth. *Identidades a flor de piel.* Bogotá: IFEA-ICANH-Uniandes-Observatorio del Caribe Colombiano, 2003.

da Cunha, Dilip. *The Invention of Rivers: Alexander's Eye and Ganga's Descent.* Philadelphia: University of Pennsylvania Press, 2018.

Darwin, Charles. *The Descent of Man, and Selection in Relation to Sex.* Princeton, NJ: Princeton University Press, 1981.

Datta, Ayona, and Nabeela Ahmed. "Intimate Infrastructures: The Rubrics of Gendered Safety and Urban Violence in Kerala, India." *Geoforum* 110 (2020): 67–76.

Davies, Archie. "The Coloniality of Infrastructure: Engineering, Landscape and Modernity in Recife." *Environment and Planning D: Society and Space* 39, no. 4 (2021): 740–57.

Davis, Wade. *Magdalena: River of Dreams.* London: Bodley Head, 2020.

Dawson, Kevin. "Enslaved Ship Pilots: Challenging Notions of Race and Slavery along the Peripheries of the Revolutionary Atlantic World." In *Atlantic Biographies: Individuals and Peoples in the Atlantic World*, 143–72. Leiden: Brill, 2014.

Dawson, Kevin. *Undercurrents of Power: Aquatic Culture in the African Diaspora.* Philadelphia: University of Pennsylvania Press, 2020.

Deavila Pertuz, Orlando, and Andrea Guerrero Mosquera. "La imagen de las personas racializadas y la construcción del sujeto negro: El racismo y la agencia través de la mirada de los viajeros en el siglo XIX colombiano." *Anuario de Historia Regional y de las Fronteras* 26, no. 2 (2021): 287–315.

Delvalle Quevedo, Rocío. "El proyecto de Recuperación de la Navegabilidad del Río Magdalena como generador de conflictos ambientales en la llanura inundable del río Magdalena." Master's thesis, Universidad Nacional de Colombia, 2017.

Derickson, Kate Driscoll. "Urban Geography II: Urban Geography in the Age of Ferguson." *Progress in Human Geography* 41, no. 2 (2017): 230–44.

Díaz Ángel, Sebastián, Santiago Muñoz Arbeláez, and Mauricio Nieto Olarte. *Ensamblando la nación: Cartografía y política en la historia de Colombia.* Bogotá: Ediciones Uniandes, 2010.

Doshi, Sapana, and Malini Ranganathan. "Towards a Critical Geography of Corruption and Power in Late Capitalism." *Progress in Human Geography* 43, no. 3 (2019): 436–57.

Dua, Jatin. *Captured at Sea: Piracy and Protection in the Indian Ocean.* Oakland: University of California Press, 2019.

Duarte, Carlos, Óscar David Andrade Becerra, Alen Castaño, Lina Díaz, Isabel Giraldo Quijano, Bárbara Lacoste, Hernán Camilo Montenegro Lancheros, Martiza Tangarife, and Daniella Trujillo Ospina. *Entre paramilitares y guerrillas: La desposesión territorial en los Montes de María. Dinámicas históricas y territoriales del conflicto político, social y armado 1958-2016*. Cali: Universidad Javeriana-Cali, 2019.

Du Bois, W. E. B. "The Negro and the Warsaw Ghetto." *Jewish Life*, May 1952.

Du Bois, W. E. B. *The Souls of Black Folk*. Oxford: Oxford University Press, 2007.

Dunnavant, Justin P. "Have Confidence in the Sea: Maritime Maroons and Fugitive Geographies." *Antipode* 53, no. 3 (2021): 884–905.

DW Pía Castro. "Las mujeres de Puerto Boyacá toman las riendas." YouTube, July 26, 2019. https://www.youtube.com/watch?v=J6oUHjbAfts.

Easterling, Keller. *Extrastatecraft: The Power of Infrastructure Space*. London: Verso, 2014.

Easterling, Keller. "The New Orgman: Logistics as an Organising Principle of Contemporary Cities." In *The Cybercities Reader*, edited by Stephen Graham, 179–84. London: Routledge, 2003.

Echandía Castilla, Camilo. *Dos décadas de escalamiento del conflicto armado en Colombia, 1986-2006*. Bogotá: Universidad Externado, 2006.

El Heraldo. "Santos anuncia inversión de $2.5 billones para río Magdalena." May 4, 2014. https://www.elheraldo.co/nacional/santos-anuncia-inversion-de-25-billones-para-rio -magdalena-151398.

Escobar, Arturo. *Otro posible es posible: Caminando hacia las transiciones desde Abya Yala/Afro/ Latino-América*. Bogotá: Ediciones Desde Abajo, 2018.

Escobar, Arturo. *Pluriversal Politics: The Real and the Possible*. Durham, NC: Duke University Press, 2020.

Escobar, Arturo. "Worlds and Knowledges Otherwise: The Latin American Modernity/ Coloniality Research Program." *Cultural Studies* 21, no. 2–3 (2007): 179–210.

Eski, Yarin. *Policing, Port Security and Crime Control: An Ethnography of the Port Securityscape*. London: Routledge, 2016.

Estrada, Valentín. *Análisis del Proyecto de Recuperación del río Magdalena-Odebrecht*. Coalición Regional por la Transparencia y la Participación, 2017.

Fajardo, Kale Bantigue. *Filipino Crosscurrents: Oceanographies of Seafaring, Masculinities, and Globalization*. Minneapolis: University of Minnesota Press, 2011.

Fals Borda, Orlando. *Historia doble de la Costa: Mompox y Loba*. Bogotá: Carlos Valencia Editores, 1979.

Fanon, Frantz. *Black Skin, White Masks*. London: Pluto, 1986.

Fanon, Frantz. *The Wretched of the Earth*. New York: Grove, 2004.

Fawcett, Louise, and Eduardo Posada-Carbo. "Arabs and Jews in the Development of the Colombian Caribbean, 1850-1950." *Immigrants and Minorities* 16, no. 1-2 (1997): 57-79.

Featherstone, David. "Maritime Labour, Transnational Political Trajectories and Decolonization from Below: The Opposition to the 1935 British Shipping Assistance Act." *Global Networks* 19, no. 4 (2019): 539-62.

Federici, Silvia. *Revolution at Point Zero: Housework, Reproduction, and Feminist Struggle*. Oakland, CA: PM Press, 2012.

Ferdinand, Malcom. *Decolonial Ecology: Thinking from the Caribbean World*. Cambridge: Polity Press, 2022.

Ferro Medina, Germán. "El río Magdalena: Territorio y cultura en movimiento." *Boletín Cultural y Bibliográfico* 47, no. 84 (2013): 4–35.

Flórez Bolívar, Francisco Javier. "Celebrando y redefiniendo el mestizaje: Raza y nación durante la República Liberal, Colombia, 1930–1946." *Memorias: Revista digital de historia y arqueología desde el Caribe colombiano* 15, no. 37 (2019): 93–116.

Flórez Bolívar, Francisco Javier. "Un diálogo diaspórico: El lugar del Harlem Renaissance en el pensamiento racial e intelectual afrocolombiano (1920–1948)." *Historia Crítica*, no. 55 (2015): 101–24.

Foucault, Michel. "Of Other Spaces: Utopias and Heterotopias." *Architecture/Mouvement/Continuité*, October 1984, 1–9.

Foucault, Michel. *Security, Territory, Population: Lectures at the Collège de France, 1977–1978*. Edited by Michel Senellart. New York: Palgrave Macmillan, 2007.

Fullwiley, Duana. *The Enculturated Gene: Sickle Cell Health Politics and Biological Difference in West Africa*. Princeton, NJ: Princeton University Press, 2011.

Gambino, Evelina. "Big Dick Energy at the End of the World: Technopolitics for a Global Hustle." In *Gendering Logistics: Feminist Approaches for the Analysis of Supply-Chain Capitalism*, edited by Carlotta Benvegnù, Niccolò Cuppini, Mattia Frapporti, Evelina Gambino, Floriano Milesi, Irene Peano, and Maurilio Pirone, 61–74. Bologna: University of Bologna, 2021.

Gambino, Evelina. "The Georgian Logistics Revolution: Questioning Seamlessness across the New Silk Road." *Work Organisation, Labour and Globalisation* 13, no. 1 (2019): 190–206.

Gandy, Matthew. *The Fabric of Space: Water, Modernity, and the Urban Imagination*. Cambridge, MA: MIT Press, 2014.

García Becerra, Andrea. "Mujeres: Pesca artesanal y río Magdalena." *Hoy en la Javeriana* 55, no. 1318 (2016): 4–5.

Gibson-Graham, J. K. *The End of Capitalism (As We Knew It): A Feminist Critique of Political Economy*. Cambridge: Blackwell, 1996.

Gill, Lesley. *A Century of Violence in a Red City: Popular Struggle, Counterinsurgency, and Human Rights in Colombia*. Durham, NC: Duke University Press, 2016.

Gilmore, Robert Louis, and John Parker Harrison. "Juan Bernardo Elbers and the Introduction of Steam Navigation on the Magdalena River." *Hispanic American Historical Review* 28, no. 3 (1948): 335–59.

Gilmore, Ruth Wilson. "Fatal Couplings of Power and Difference: Notes on Racism and Geography." *Professional Geographer* 54, no. 1 (2002): 15–24.

Gilroy, Paul. *The Black Atlantic: Modernity and Double Consciousness*. London: Verso, 1993.

Gilroy, Paul. "'Where Every Breeze Speaks of Courage and Liberty': Offshore Humanism and Marine Xenology, or, Racism and the Problem of Critique at Sea Level." *Antipode* 50, no. 1 (2018): 3–22.

Gilroy, Paul, and Adam Shatz. "The Absurdities of Race." *LRB Podcast*, August 18, 2020.

Glissant, Édouard. *Poetics of Relation*. Ann Arbor: University of Michigan Press, 1997.

Gómez-Barris, Macarena. *The Extractive Zone: Social Ecologies and Decolonial Perspectives*. Durham, NC: Duke University Press, 2017.

Gómez Picón, Rafael. *Magdalena, río de Colombia: Interpretación geográfica, histórica y social-económica de la gran arteria colombiana desde su descubrimiento hasta nuestros días.* 6th ed. Bogotá: Instituto Colombiano de Cultura, 1973.

González-Ayala, Sofía N., and Alejandro Camargo. "Voices of Water and Violence: Exhibition Making and the Blue Humanities for Transitional Justice." *Curator: The Museum Journal* 64, no. 1 (2021): 183–204.

González G., Fernán E., Diego Quiroga, Támara Ospina-Posse, Andrés Felipe Aponte G., Víctor A. Barrera R., and Eduardo Porras M. *Territorio y conflicto en la Costa Caribe.* Bogotá: Ediciones Antropos, 2014.

Gooch, Catherine D. "Death by the Riverside: Richard Wright's Black Pastoral and the Mississippi Flood of 1927." *ISLE: Interdisciplinary Studies in Literature and Environment* 28, no. 4 (winter 2021): 1614–36.

Gooch, Catherine D. "'Shall We Gather at the River?' The Folklore and Trauma of Toni Morrison's Landscape in *Sula.*" *Comparative American Studies* 18, no. 1 (2021): 92–108.

Graham, Stephen. "FlowCity: Networked Mobilities and the Contemporary Metropolis." *Journal of Urban Technology* 9, no. 1 (2002): 1–20.

Grove, Richard H. *Green Imperialism: Colonial Expansion, Tropical Island Edens and the Origins of Environmentalism, 1600–1860.* Cambridge: Cambridge University Press, 1996.

Guerra, Adriano. "El imaginario oficial: Revolución y formalidad: La visión de los navegantes del Río Magdalena con respecto a los levantamientos revolucionarios en Colombia en abril de 1948." *Historia Caribe* 4, no. 11 (2006): 145–65.

Gutiérrez Campo, Rubén, and Kelly Escobar Jiménez. "Territorio anfibio y despojo en una zona de humedales protegida del Caribe colombiano." *Revista de Estudios Sociales* 76 (2021): 75–92.

Guyer, Jane I. *Legacies, Logics, Logistics: Essays in the Anthropology of the Platform Economy.* Chicago: University of Chicago Press, 2016.

Hall, Stuart. "New Ethnicities." In *Stuart Hall: Critical Dialogues in Cultural Studies,* edited by David Morley and Kuan-Hsing Chen, 441–49. London: Routledge, 1996.

Hall, Stuart. "Race, Articulation and Societies Structured in Dominance." In *Sociological Theories: Race and Colonialism,* 305–45. Paris: UNESCO, 1980.

Hall, Stuart, Chas Critcher, Tony Jefferson, John Clarke, and Brian Roberts. *Policing the Crisis: Mugging, the State, and Law and Order.* Basingstoke, UK: Palgrave Macmillan, 2013.

Haraway, Donna J. *Primate Visions: Gender, Race, and Nature in the World of Modern Science.* New York: Routledge, 1989.

Haraway, Donna. *Simians, Cyborgs, and Women: The Reinvention of Nature.* London: Free Association, 1991.

Haraway, Donna. "Situated Knowledges: The Science Question in Feminism and the Privilege of Partial Perspective." *Feminist Studies* 14, no. 3 (1988): 575–99.

Harding, Sandra G. *Whose Science? Whose Knowledge? Thinking from Women's Lives.* Ithaca, NY: Cornell University Press, 1991.

Hardy, R. Dean, Richard A. Milligan, and Nik Heynen. "Racial Coastal Formation: The Environmental Injustice of Colorblind Adaptation Planning for Sea-Level Rise." *Geoforum* 87 (2017): 62–72.

Harney, Stefano, and Fred Moten. *The Undercommons: Fugitive Planning and Black Study*. New York: Minor Compositions, 2013.

Hart, Gillian. *Disabling Globalization: Places of Power in Post-apartheid South Africa*. Berkeley: University of California Press, 2002.

Hartigan, John. *Care of the Species: Races of Corn and the Science of Plant Biodiversity*. Minneapolis: University of Minnesota Press, 2017.

Hartman, Saidiya. "The Belly of the World: A Note on Black Women's Labors." *Souls* 18, no. 1 (2016): 166–73.

Hartman, Saidiya. *Lose Your Mother: A Journey along the Atlantic Slave Route*. London: Farrar, Straus and Giroux, 2007.

Hawthorne, Camilla. "Black Matters Are Spatial Matters: Black Geographies for the Twenty-First Century." *Geography Compass* 13, no. 11 (2019): 1–13.

Helg, Aline. *Liberty and Equality in Caribbean Colombia, 1770–1835*. Chapel Hill: University of North Carolina Press, 2004.

Helmreich, Stefan. "How to Hide an Island." In *New Geographies 8: Island*, edited by Daniel Daou and Pablo Pérez-Ramos, 82–87. Cambridge, MA: Harvard University Press, 2017.

Hepworth, Kate. "Enacting Logistical Geographies." *Environment and Planning D: Society and Space* 32, no. 6 (2014): 1120–34.

Hering Torres, Max S. "Purity of Blood: Problems of Interpretation." In *Race and Blood in the Iberian World*, edited by Max S. Hering Torres, María Elena Martínez, and David Nirenberg, 11–38. Zurich: LIT Verlag GmbH, 2013.

Herrera Ángel, Marta Clemencia. "'Chimilas' y 'Españoles': El manejo político de los estereotipos raciales en la sociedad neogranadina del siglo XVIII." *Memoria y Sociedad* 7, no. 13 (2002): 5–24.

Herzog, Tamar. "Beyond Race: Exclusion in Early Modern Spain and Spanish America." In *Race and Blood in the Iberian World*, edited by Max S. Hering Torres, María Elena Martínez, and David Nirenberg, 151–67. Zurich: LIT Verlag GmbH, 2013.

Hetherington, Kregg. "Surveying the Future Perfect: Anthropology, Development and the Promise of Infrastructure." In *Infrastructures and Social Complexity: A Companion*, edited by Penny Harvey, Casper Bruun Jensen, and Atsuro Morita, 40–50. London: Routledge, 2017.

Heynen, Nik. "Urban Political Ecology II: The Abolitionist Century." *Progress in Human Geography* 40, no. 6 (2016): 839–45.

Heynen, Nik, Maria Kaika, and Erik Swyngedouw. *In the Nature of Cities: Urban Political Ecology and the Politics of Urban Metabolism*. London: Routledge, 2006.

Hori, Kazuaki, and Yoshiki Saito. "Classification, Architecture, and Evolution of Large-River Deltas." In *Large Rivers: Geomorphology and Management*, 75–96. Chichester, UK: John Wiley and Sons, 2007.

Horna, Hernán. "Transportation Modernization and Entrepreneurship in Nineteenth Century Colombia." *Journal of Latin American Studies* 14, no. 1 (1982): 33–53.

Hosbey, Justin, Hilda Lloréns, and J. T. Roane. "Global Black Ecologies." *Environment and Society* 13, no. 1 (2022): 1–10.

Humboldt, Alexander von. *Alexander von Humboldt en Colombia: Extractos de sus diarios*. Bogotá: Flota Mercante Grancolombiana, 1982.

Humboldt, Alexander von. *Reise auf dem Rio Magdalena durch die Anden und Mexico*. Berlin: Akademie-Verlag, 1986.

Huntington, Ellsworth. *The Character of Races as Influenced by Physical Environment, Natural Selection and Historical Development*. London: Charles Scribner, 1924.

Huntington, Ellsworth. *Civilization and Climate*. New Haven, CT: Yale University Press, 1915.

Huntington, Ellsworth. "Geography and Natural Selection." *Annals of the Association of American Geographers* 14, no. 1 (1924): 1–16.

IDEAM-Cormagdalena. "Estudio ambiental de la Cuenca Magdalena–Cauca y elementos para su ordenamiento territorial." Bogotá, 2001.

IDEAM, PNUD, MADS, DNP, and Cancillería. "Tercera comunicación nacional de Colombia a la convención marco de las Naciones Unidas sobre cambio climático (CMNUCC)." Bogotá, 2017.

Jackson, Richard L. *Black Writers in Latin America*. Albuquerque: University of New Mexico Press, 1979.

Jackson, Steven J. "Material Care." In *Debates in the Digital Humanities 2019*, edited by Matthew K. Gold and Lauren F. Klein, 427–30. Minneapolis: University of Minnesota Press, 2019.

Jackson, Steven J. "Rethinking Repair." In *Media Technologies: Essays on Communication, Materiality, and Society*, edited by Tarleton Gillespie, Pablo J. Boczkowski, and Kirsten A. Foot, 221–40. Cambridge, MA: MIT Press, 2014.

Jackson, Zakiyyah Iman. *Becoming Human: Matter and Meaning in an Antiblack World*. New York: New York University Press, 2020.

Jaffe, Rivke. *Concrete Jungles: Urban Pollution and the Politics of Difference in the Caribbean*. Oxford: Oxford University Press, 2016.

James, C. L. R. *Mariners, Renegades and Castaways: The Story of Herman Melville and the World We Live In*. Hanover, NH: University Press of New England, 2001.

James, Preston E. "The Transportation Problem of Highland Colombia." *Journal of Geography* 22, no. 9 (1923): 346–54.

Jaramillo, Pablo. "Mining Leftovers: Making Futures on the Margins of Capitalism." *Cultural Anthropology* 35, no. 1 (2020): 48–73.

Jaramillo, Pablo. "Sites, Funds and Spheres of Exchange in a Clean Development Mechanism Project." *Journal of Cultural Economy* 11, no. 4 (2018): 277–90.

Jasanoff, Sheila. "Future Imperfect: Science, Technology, and the Imaginations of Modernity." In *Dreamscapes of Modernity: Sociotechnical Imaginaries and the Fabrication of Power*, edited by Sheila Jasanoff and Sang-Hyun Kim, 1–33. Chicago: University of Chicago Press, 2015.

Jaúregui, Carlos. "Candelario Obeso: Entre la espada del romanticismo y la pared del proyecto nacional." *Revista Iberoamericana* 65, no. 188–89 (1999): 567–90.

Jazeel, Tariq. *Sacred Modernity: Nature, Environment and the Postcolonial Geographies of Sri Lankan Nationhood*. Liverpool: Liverpool University Press, 2013.

Jensen, Robert G. "Memorial: Preston Everett James, 1899–1986." *Journal of Geography* 85, no. 6 (1986): 273–74.

Jiménez Ortega, Muriel. "Las violencias y el río Magdalena en la segunda mitad del siglo XX." Posted by Banrepcultural, YouTube, June 30, 2021. https://www.youtube.com/watch?v=jsexdrFpA6k.

Jobson, Ryan Cecil. "Public Thinker: Yarimar Bonilla on Decolonizing Decolonization." Public Books, May 27, 2020. https://www.publicbooks.org/public-thinker-yarimar-bonilla -on-decolonizing-decolonization/.

Johnson, Walter. *River of Dark Dreams: Slavery and Empire in the Cotton Kingdom*. Cambridge, MA: Harvard University Press, 2017.

Jones, Donna V. *The Racial Discourses of Life Philosophy: Négritude, Vitalism, and Modernity*. New York: Columbia University Press, 2010.

"Julius Berger (Building Contractor)—Julius Berger (Bauunternehmer)." Second Wiki, November 26, 2020. https://second.wiki/wiki/julius_berger_bauunternehmer.

Kahn, Jeffrey S. *Islands of Sovereignty: Haitian Migration and the Borders of Empire*. Chicago: University of Chicago Press, 2018.

Keighren, Innes M. "History and Philosophy of Geography III: The Haunted, the Reviled, and the Plural." *Progress in Human Geography* 44, no. 1 (2020): 160–67.

Kelley, Robin D. G. "A Poetics of Anticolonialism." In *Discourse on Colonialism* by Aimé Césaire, translated by Joan Pinkham, 7–28. New York: Monthly Review Press, 2000.

Kelley, Robin D. G. *Race Rebels: Culture, Politics, and the Black Working Class*. New York: Free Press, 1996.

Khalili, Laleh. *Sinews of War and Trade: Shipping and Capitalism in the Arabian Peninsula*. London: Verso, 2020.

King, Tiffany Lethabo. *The Black Shoals: Offshore Formations of Black and Native Studies*. Durham, NC: Duke University Press, 2019.

Kobayashi, Audrey. "The Dialectic of Race and the Discipline of Geography." *Annals of the Association of American Geographers* 104, no. 6 (2014): 1101–15.

Koopman, Sara. "Mona, Mona, Mona! Tropicality and the Imaginative Geographies of Whiteness in Colombia." *Journal of Latin American Geography* 20, no. 1 (2021): 49–78.

Lamus Canavate, Doris. "'Aquí no hay negros': Develando la presencia de población afrodescendiente en Santander, Colombia." *Reflexión Política* 16, no. 31 (2014): 114–31.

Lamus Canavate, Doris. "Esclavos, libres y bogas en Santander, Colombia." *Reflexión Política* 16, no. 32 (2014): 98–110.

Lara, Juan De. *Inland Shift: Race, Space, and Capital in Southern California*. Oakland: University of California Press, 2018.

Lázaro, Julián Andrés. "Los medios impresos como recurso para la difusión del nacionalsocialismo: Sobre boletines y magazines nazis circulando en el Caribe colombiano, 1935–1939." *Memorias: Revista Digital de Arqueología e Historia desde el Caribe*, no. 33 (2017): 62–87.

Leal, Claudia. *Landscapes of Freedom: Building a Postemancipation Society in the Rainforests of Western Colombia*. Tucson: University of Arizona Press, 2018.

Leal, Claudia. "Usos del concepto 'raza' en Colombia." In *Debates sobre ciudadanía y políticas raciales en las Américas Negras*, edited by Claudia Mosquera Rosero-Labbé, Agustín Laó-Montes, and César A. Rodríguez Garavito, 389–438. Bogotá: Universidad del Valle, Universidad Nacional de Colombia, 2010.

LeCavalier, Jesse. *The Rule of Logistics: Walmart and the Architecture of Fulfillment*. Minneapolis: University of Minnesota Press, 2016.

Leivestad, Hege Høyer, and Johanna Markkula. "Inside Container Economies." *Focaal—Journal of Global and Historical Anthropology*, no. 89 (2021): 1–11.

Le Menager, Stephanie. "Floating Capital: The Trouble with Whiteness on Twain's Mississippi." *ELH* 71, no. 2 (2004): 405–31.

Lesutis, Gediminas. "Queering as (Un)Knowing: Ambiguities of Sociality and Infrastructure." *Progress in Human Geography* 47, no. 3 (2023): 392–408.

Linebaugh, Peter, and Marcus Rediker. *The Many-Headed Hydra: The Hidden History of the Revolutionary Atlantic*. London: Verso, 2012.

Livingstone, David N. "Race, Space and Moral Climatology: Notes toward a Genealogy." *Journal of Historical Geography* 28, no. 2 (2002): 159–80.

Lobo-Guerrero, Luis. "Lloyd's and the Moral Economy of Insuring against Piracy." *Journal of Cultural Economy* 5, no. 1 (2012): 67–83.

Lobo-Guerrero, Luis. "Los seguros marítimos y la movilidad como biopolítica de seguridad." *Política y Sociedad* 49, no. 3 (2012): 533–47.

Lorde, Audre. *A Burst of Light: And Other Essays*. Mineola, NY: Dover, 2017.

Lowe, Lisa. *The Intimacies of Four Continents*. Durham, NC: Duke University Press, 2015.

Maglia, Graciela. "Candelario Obeso a la luz del debate contemporáneo." *Revista de Estudios Colombianos*, no. 47 (2016): 43–48.

Maldonado Rozo, Ricardo. "Canal del Dique, un gran cementerio de la violencia paramilitar en Colombia." *Eje 21*, November 30, 2021. https://www.eje21.com.co/2021/11/canal-del-dique-un-gran-cementerio-de-la-violencia-paramilitar-en-colombia/.

Márquez Calle, Germán. *El hábitat del hombre caimán y otros estudios sobre ecología y sociedad en el Caribe*. San Andrés: Universidad Nacional de Colombia, Sede Caribe, 2008.

Márquez Calle, Germán. "Un río difícil: El Magdalena: Historial ambiental, navegabilidad y desarrollo." *Memorias*, no. 28 (2016): 29–60.

Martínez Martín, Abel Fernándo. "Trópico y raza: Miguel Jiménez López y la inmigración japonesa en Colombia, 1920–1929." *Historia y Sociedad*, no. 32 (2017): 103–38.

Martínez Pinzón, Felipe. "Tránsitos por el río Magdalena: El boga, el blanco y las contradicciones del liberalismo colombiano de mediados del siglo XIX." *Estudios de Literatura Colombiana*, no. 29 (2011): 17–41.

Mascarenhas, Michael. "White Space and Dark Matter: Prying Open the Black Box of STS." *Science, Technology, & Human Values* 43, no. 2 (2018): 151–70.

Matthews, Jodie. "Canals and Transatlantic Slavery: A Preliminary Literature Review." Cheshire, UK: Canal and River Trust, 2020.

Mbembe, Achille. *Critique of Black Reason*. Translated by Laurent Dubois. Durham, NC: Duke University Press, 2017.

Mbembe, Achille. "Futures of Life and Futures of Reason." *Public Culture* 33, no. 1 (2021): 11–33.

MCA Chicago. "*Carolina Caycedo: From the Bottom of the River* Audio Experience." 2020. https://mcachicago.org/publications/audio/2020/carolina-caycedo-from-the-bottom-of-the-river-virtual-gallery.

McCarthy, Jesse, and Adam Shatz. "Blind Spots." *The LRB Podcast*, April 28, 2021. https://www.lrb.co.uk/podcasts-and-videos/podcasts/the-lrb-podcast/blind-spots.

McGraw, Jason. "Purificar la nación: Eugenesia, higiene y renovación moral-racial de la periferia del Caribe colombiano, 1900–1930." In *Historias de raza y nación en América Latina*, edited by Claudia Leal and Carl Henrik Langebaek, 313–34. Bogotá: Universidad de los Andes, 2010.

McGraw, Jason. *The Work of Recognition: Caribbean Colombia and the Postemancipation Struggle for Citizenship*. Chapel Hill: University of North Carolina Press, 2014.

M'charek, Amade. "Curious about Race: Generous Methods and Modes of Knowing in Practice." *Social Studies of Science* 53, no. 6 (2023): 826–49.

McKittrick, Katherine. *Dear Science and Other Stories*. Durham, NC: Duke University Press, 2021.

McKittrick, Katherine. *Demonic Grounds: Black Women and the Cartographies of Struggle*. Minneapolis: University of Minnesota Press, 2006.

McKittrick, Katherine. "Plantation Futures." *Small Axe: A Caribbean Journal of Criticism* 17, no. 3 (2013): 1–15.

McKittrick, Katherine, ed. *Sylvia Wynter: On Being Human as Praxis*. Durham, NC: Duke University Press, 2015.

McKittrick, Katherine, and Clyde Woods, eds. *Black Geographies and the Politics of Place*. Cambridge, MA: South End Press, 2007.

McLaughlin, Rosanna. "Sondra Perry: Typhoon Coming On." *Frieze*, March 28, 2018. https://www.frieze.com/article/sondra-perry-typhoon-coming-2018-review.

Meehan, Katie, Mabel Denzin Gergan, Sharlene Mollett, and Laura Pulido. "Unsettling Race, Nature, and Environment in Geography." *Annals of the American Association of Geographers* 113, no. 7 (2023): 1535–42.

Meisel Roca, Adolfo. "Volando sobre la ruta de los vapores: Los comienzos de Scadta, 1919–1930." *Revista Credencial*, March 2014.

Mejía Moreno, Catalina. "'Nos están matando' (We Are Being Killed)." *Journal of Architectural Education* 74, no. 2 (2020): 315–18.

Melgarejo, María del Pilar. "The Production of a Multiple Consciousness: Candelario Obeso and Linton Kwesi Johnson." *Afro-Hispanic Review* 32, no. 1 (2013): 99–114.

Melville, Herman. *Benito Cereno*. Adelaide: University of Adelaide Library, 2016.

Melville, Herman. *Moby-Dick*. London: Penguin, 2003.

Mezzadra, Sandro, and Brett Neilson. *The Politics of Operations: Excavating Contemporary Capitalism*. Durham, NC: Duke University Press, 2019.

Mignolo, Walter D., and Catherine E. Walsh. *On Decoloniality: Concepts, Analytics, Praxis*. Durham, NC: Duke University Press, 2018.

Millán Valencia, Alejandro. "El modelo matemático que se usa para encontrar cuerpos de desaparecidos en los ríos de Colombia." BBC Mundo, July 13, 2022. https://www.bbc.com/mundo/noticias-61864463.

Miller, W. Jason. "Justice, Lynching, and American Riverscapes: Finding Reassurance in Langston Hughes's 'The Negro Speaks of Rivers.'" *Langston Hughes Review* 18 (Spring 2004): 24–37.

Ministerio de Transporte. Resolución 3666 de 1998: Por se establecen las cuantías mínimas que deberán cubrir las pólizas de seguros relacionadas en el Artículo 28 del Decreto 3112 de 1997. 1998.

Minuto30 Colombia. "Fotos: El impresionante panorama que deja el derrame de petroleo en Barrancabermeja." Minuto30.com, March 24, 2018. https://www.minuto30.com/fotos-el-impresionante-panorama-que-deja-el-derrame-de-petroleo-en-barrancabermeja/595312/.

Mitchell, Timothy. *Carbon Democracy: Political Power in the Age of Oil*. London: Verso, 2011.

Mol, Annemarie. "Ontological Politics: A Word and Some Questions." *Sociological Review* 47, no. S1 (1999): 74–89.

Molesworth, Helen, ed. *Kerry James Marshall: Mastry*. New York: Skira Rizzoli, 2016.

Moore, Donald S., Jake Kosek, and Anand Pandian, eds. *Race, Nature, and the Politics of Difference*. Durham, NC: Duke University Press, 2003.

Moore, Jason W. *Capitalism in the Web of Life: Ecology and the Accumulation of Capital*. London: Verso, 2015.

Mora Angueira, Hernando. "Compendio histórico del río Magdalena." *Boletín de la Sociedad Geográfica de Colombia* 6, no. 2-3 (1939): 1-9.

Morales, Jorge. "Mestizaje, malicia indígena y viveza en la construcción del carácter nacional." *Revista de Estudios Sociales*, no. 1 (1998): 39-43.

Moreno Sarmiento, Christian, and Edgar Zamora Aviles. "Acumulación capitalista y nueva espacialidad en el Magdalena Medio." *Ciencia Política*, no. 13 (2012): 6-39.

Morris, Meghan L. "Speculative Fields: Property in the Shadow of Post-conflict Colombia." *Cultural Anthropology* 34, no. 4 (2019): 580-606.

Muir, Sarah, and Akhil Gupta. "Rethinking the Anthropology of Corruption: An Introduction to Supplement 18." *Current Anthropology* 59, no. S18 (2018): S4-S15.

Mukerji, Chandra. *Impossible Engineering: Technology and Territoriality on the Canal du Midi*. Princeton, NJ: Princeton University Press, 2009.

Múnera, Alfonso. *El Fracaso de la nación: Región, clase y raza en el Caribe Colombiano (1717-1821)*. Bogotá: El Áncora Editores, 1998.

Múnera, Alfonso. *Fronteras imaginadas: La construcción de las razas y de la geografía en el siglo XIX colombiano*. Bogotá: Planeta, 2005.

Múnera, Alfonso. "Manuel Zapata y la nación inclusiva." In *Por los senderos de sus ancestros: Textos escogidos, 1940-2000*, edited by Alfonso Múnera, 11-43. Bogotá: Ministerio de Cultura, República de Colombia, 2010.

Museo del río Magdalena. "Sabiendas y subiendas: Tejer, lanzar y pescar. Entre Cóngolos y Atarrayas." Museo del río Magdalena, Honda, Tolima. YouTube, July 2, 2020. https://youtu.be/7NxAV83QmAM.

Navarrete, María Cristina. "Los cimarrones de la provincia de Cartagena de Indias en el siglo XVII: Relaciones, diferencias y políticas de las autoridades." *Revue Interdisciplinaire de Travaux sur les Amériques*, no. 5 (2012).

Navarrete, María Cristina. "Palenques: Maroons and *Castas* in Colombia's Caribbean Regions." In *Orality, Identity, and Resistance in Palenque (Colombia): An Interdisciplinary Approach*, edited by Armin Schwegler, Bryan Kirschen, and Graciela Maglia, 269-96. Amsterdam: John Benjamins, 2017.

Neimanis, Astrida. *Bodies of Water: Posthuman Feminist Phenomenology*. London: Bloomsbury, 2017.

Nevius, Marcus P. *City of Refuge: Slavery and Petit Marronage in the Great Dismal Swamp, 1763–1856*. Atlanta: University of Georgia Press, 2020.

Nevius, Marcus P. "New Histories of Marronage in the Anglo-Atlantic World and Early North America." *History Compass* 18, no. 5 (2020): 1–14.

Nichols, Theodore E. "The Rise of Barranquilla." *Hispanic American Historical Review* 34, no. 2 (1954): 158–74.

Nieto, Patricia. *Los escogidos*. Bogotá: Sílaba Editores, 2012.

Nieto Olarte, Mauricio. *Orden natural y orden social: Ciencia y política en el semanario del Nuevo Reino de Granada*. Bogotá: Universidad de los Andes, 2008.

Nieto Villamizar, María Camila, and María Riaño Pradilla. *Esclavos, negros libres y bogas en la literatura del siglo XIX*. Bogotá: Universidad de los Andes, 2011.

Nishime, Leilani, and Kim D. Hester Williams. "Introduction: Why Racial Ecologies?" In *Racial Ecologies*, edited by Leilani Nishime and Kim D. Hester Williams, 3–15. Seattle: University of Washington Press, 2018.

Noticias NCC. "Mujeres luchan por la conservación del río Magdalena." Noticiero Científico y Cultural Iberoamericano, 2019. https://noticiasncc.com/ciencia/destacada-ciencia/07/15/mujeres-luchan-conservacion-magdalena/.

Núñez Navarro, Rafael. "Evaluación de la conducta sexual zoofílica en la zona este de la ciudad de Barranquilla." Universidad Industrial de Santander, Universidad del Magdalena, 1995.

Obeso, Candelario. *Cantos populares de mi tierra*. Edited by Javier Ortiz Cassiani. Bogotá: Fundación Gilberto Alzate Avendaño, 2009.

O'Bryen, Rory. "On the Shores of Politics: Popular Republicanism and the Magdalena River in Candelario Obeso's *Cantos populares de mi tierra*." *Bulletin of Latin American Research* 37, no. 4 (2017): 464–78.

O'Bryen, Rory. "Untangling the Mangrove: Slow Violence and the Environmentalism of the Poor in the Colombian Caribbean." In *Liquid Ecologies in Latin American and Caribbean Art*, edited by Lisa Blackmore and Liliana Gómez, 73–88. New York: Routledge, 2022.

Ochoa Gautier, Ana María. *Aurality: Listening and Knowledge in Nineteenth-Century Colombia*. Durham, NC: Duke University Press, 2014.

ONU Mujeres. *Mujeres que cuidan la naturaleza: Relatos de defensoras del ambiente en Colombia*. Bogotá: La Imprenta Editores S.A., 2019.

Ortega, Francisco A. "Precarious Time, Morality, and the Republic: New Granada, 1818–1853." *Contributions to the History of Concepts* 11, no. 2 (2016): 85–109.

Oslender, Ulrich. *The Geographies of Social Movements: Afro-Colombian Mobilization and the Aquatic Space*. Durham, NC: Duke University Press, 2016.

Parish, Erin. "Burning and Rebuilding Bridges: Forensic Infrastructures in War and Its Aftermath." *Journal of Latin American and Caribbean Anthropology* 24, no. 1 (2019): 127–44.

Parrinello, Giacomo, and G. Mathias Kondolf. "The Social Life of Sediment." *Water History* 13, no. 1 (2021): 1–12.

Parry, Tyler. "The Role of Water in African American History." Black Perspectives, May 4, 2018. https://www.aaihs.org/the-role-of-water-in-african-american-history/.

Paschel, Tianna S. *Becoming Black Political Subjects: Movements and Ethno-racial Rights in Colombia and Brazil*. Princeton, NJ: Princeton University Press, 2016.

Peano, Irene. "Gendering Logistics: Subjectivities, Biopolitics and Extraction in Supply Chains." In *Gendering Logistics: Feminist Approaches for the Analysis of Supply-Chain Capitalism*, edited by Carlotta Benvegnù, Niccolò Cuppini, Mattia Frapporti, Evelina Gambino, Floriano Milesi, Irene Peano, and Maurilio Pirone, 15–26. Bologna: University of Bologna, 2021.

Peet, Richard. "The Social Origins of Environmental Determinism." *Annals of the Association of American Geographers* 75, no. 3 (1985): 309–33.

Peñas Galindo, David Ernesto. *Los bogas de Mompox: Historia del zambaje*. Bogotá: Tercer Mundo Editores, 1988.

Pérez Morales, Edgardo. *La obra de Dios y el trabajo del hombre: Percepción y transformación de la naturaleza en el virreinato del Nuevo Reino de Granada*. Medellín: Universidad Nacional de Colombia Sede Medellín, 2011.

Pérez Morales, Edgardo. *No Limits to Their Sway: Cartagena's Privateers and the Masterless Caribbean in the Age of Revolutions*. Nashville, TN: Vanderbilt University Press, 2018.

Peters, Kimberley, and Jennifer Turner. "Carceral Mobilities: A Manifesto for Mobilities, an Agenda for Carceral Studies." In *Carceral Mobilities: Interrogating Movement in Incarceration*, edited by Jennifer Turner and Kimberley Peters, 1–13. London: Routledge, 2017.

Posada-Carbó, Eduardo. "Bongos, champanes y vapores en la navegación fluvial colombiana del siglo XIX." *Boletín Cultural y Bibliográfico* 26, no. 21 (1989): 2–13.

Posada-Carbó, Eduardo. *The Colombian Caribbean: A Regional History, 1870–1950*. Oxford: Oxford University Press, 1996.

Prescott, Laurence E. *Candelario Obeso y la iniciación de la poesía negra en Colombia*. Bogotá: Instituto Caro y Cuervo, 1985.

Prescott, Laurence E. "We, Too, Are America: Langston Hughes in Colombia." *Langston Hughes Review* 20 (Fall 2006): 34–46.

Presidencia de la República. Decreto 1295 de 1994: Por el cual se determina la organización y administración del Sistema General de Riesgos Profesionales. 1994.

Presidencia de la República. Decreto 776 de 1987: Por el cual se modifica la tabla de evaluación de incapacidades resultantes de accidentes de trabajo, contenida en el artículo 209 del Código Sustantivo del Trabajo. 1987.

"Preston E. James Receives NCGE Distinguished Service Award." *Journal of Geography* 64, no. 3 (1965): 127.

Pritchard, Sara B. *Confluence: The Nature of Technology and the Remaking of the Rhône*. Cambridge, MA: Harvard University Press, 2011.

Puar, Jasbir K. *The Right to Maim: Debility, Capacity, Disability*. Durham, NC: Duke University Press, 2017.

Pulido, Laura, and Juan De Lara. "Reimagining 'Justice' in Environmental Justice: Radical Ecologies, Decolonial Thought, and the Black Radical Tradition." *Environment and Planning E: Nature and Space* 1, no. 1–2 (2018): 76–98.

Quijano, Aníbal. "Coloniality and Modernity/Rationality." *Cultural Studies* 21, no. 2–3 (2007): 168–78.

Quijano, Aníbal. "Coloniality of Power, Eurocentrism, and Latin America." *Nepantla: Views from South* 1, no. 3 (2000): 533–80.

Quijano, Aníbal. "Questioning 'Race.'" *Socialism and Democracy* 21, no. 1 (2007): 45–53.

Rademacher, Anne. *Reigning the River: Urban Ecologies and Political Transformation in Kathmandu.* Durham, NC: Duke University Press, 2011.

Raffles, Hugh. *In Amazonia: A Natural History.* Princeton, NJ: Princeton University Press, 2002.

Raffles, Hugh. *Insectopedia.* New York: Pantheon, 2011.

Randle, Sayd. "Missing Power: Nostalgia and Disillusionment among Southern California Water Engineers." *Critique of Anthropology* 41, no. 3 (2021): 267–83.

Ranganathan, Malini. "Caste, Racialization, and the Making of Environmental Unfreedoms in Urban India." *Ethnic and Racial Studies* 45, no. 2 (2021): 257–77.

Ranganathan, Malini. "The Racial Ecologies of Urban Wetlands." *International Journal of Urban and Regional Research* 46, no. 4 (2022): 721–24.

Rappaport, Joanne. "Colombia and the Legal-Cultural Negotiation of Racial Categories." In *Oxford Research Encyclopedia of Latin American History.* Oxford: Oxford University Press, 2020. https://doi.org/10.1093/acrefore/9780199366439.013.532.

Ratzel, Friedrich. "Lebensraum: A Biogeographical Study." *Journal of Historical Geography* 61 (2018): 59–80.

Repetto, Elena, Myriam Bautista, Oscar David Barrera, and Holman Sierra Suárez. *Los árabes en Colombia.* Bogotá: Ministeria de Cultura, 2011.

Restrepo Ángel, Juan Darío, ed. *Los sedimentos del río Magdalena: Reflejo de la crisis ambiental.* Medellín: Universidad EAFIT, 2005.

Restrepo, Eduardo. "Ethnicization of Blackness in Colombia: Toward De-racializing Theoretical and Political Imagination." *Cultural Studies* 18, no. 5 (2004): 698–715.

Restrepo, Eduardo. "'Negros indolentes' en las plumas de corógrafos: Raza y progreso en el occidente de la Nueva Granada de mediados del siglo XIX." *Nómadas* 26 (2007): 28–43.

Restrepo, Eduardo. "Talks and Disputes of Racism in Colombia after Multiculturalism." *Cultural Studies* 32, no. 3 (2018): 460–76.

Restrepo, Juan Darío, and Heber Alejandro Escobar. "Sediment Load Trends in the Magdalena River Basin (1980–2010): Anthropogenic and Climate-Induced Causes." *Geomorphology* 302 (2018): 76–91.

Restrepo Forero, Olga. "Trópicos, mestizaje y aclimatación: 'Leyes naturales y hechos científicos' en el discurso darwinista colombiano." In *Darwinismo, biología y sociedad*, edited by Rosaura Ruiz Gutiérrez, Miguel Ángel Puig-Samper Mulero, and Graciela Zamudio Varela, 377–98. Mexico City: Universidad Nacional Autonoma de Mexico, 2014.

Rhenals Doria, Ana Milena, and Francisco Javier Flórez Bolívar. "Escogiendo entre los extranjeros 'indeseables': Afro-antillanos, sirio-libaneses, raza e inmigración en Colombia, 1880–1937." *Anuario Colombiano de Historia Social y de la Cultura* 40, no. 1 (2013): 243–71.

Roberts, Elizabeth F. S. "What Gets Inside: Violent Entanglements and Toxic Boundaries in Mexico City." *Cultural Anthropology* 32, no. 4 (2017): 592–619.

Robinson, Cedric J. *Black Marxism: The Making of the Black Radical Tradition.* Chapel Hill: University of North Carolina Press, 2000.

Robinson, Cedric J. *Forgeries of Memory and Meaning: Blacks and the Regimes of Race in American Theater and Film before World War II*. Chapel Hill: University of North Carolina Press, 2012.

Rodney, Walter. *A History of the Guyanese Working People, 1881–1905*. Baltimore: Johns Hopkins University Press, 1981.

Rodríguez Becerra, Manuel, ed. *¿Para dónde va el río Magdalena? Riesgos sociales, ambientales y económicos del proyecto de navegabilidad*. Bogotá: Friedrich-Ebert-Stiftung en Colombia (Fescol), 2015.

Roediger, David R. *The Wages of Whiteness: Race and the Making of the American Working Class*. London: Verso, 2007.

Roediger, David R., and Elizabeth D. Esch. *The Production of Difference: Race and the Management of Labor in U.S. History*. Oxford: Oxford University Press, 2012.

Rofel, Lisa, and Sylvia J. Yanagisako. *Fabricating Transnational Capitalism: A Collaborative Ethnography of Italian-Chinese Global Fashion*. Durham, NC: Duke University Press, 2019.

Roldán, Mary. *Blood and Fire: La Violencia in Antioquia, Colombia, 1946–1953*. Durham, NC: Duke University Press, 2002.

Rosa, Jonathan, and Vanessa Díaz. "Raciontologies: Rethinking Anthropological Accounts of Institutional Racism and Enactments of White Supremacy in the United States." *American Anthropologist* 122, no. 1 (2020): 120–32.

Rothenberg, Janell. "Ports Matter: Supply Chain Logics and the Sociocultural Context of Infrastructure in Port Studies." *Mobility in History* 8, no. 1 (2017): 115–22.

Rushton, Alan, Phil Croucher, and Peter Baker. *The Handbook of Logistics and Distribution Management: Understanding the Supply Chain*. London: Kogan Page, 2014.

Rutas del Conflicto. "El silencio del río grande." Accessed July 12, 2023. https://rutasdelconflicto.com/rios-vida-muerte/especial/rio-magdalena/el-silencio-rio.html.

Rutas del Conflicto. "Las mujeres y el río." Accessed July 12, 2023. https://rutasdelconflicto.com/rios-vida-muerte/especial/rio-magdalena/mujeres-rio.html.

Ryburn, Megan. "'I Don't Want You in My Country': Migrants Navigating Borderland Violences between Colombia and Chile." *Annals of the American Association of Geographers* 112, no. 5 (2022): 1424–40.

Sabayu C. Gil, Ismael. "¿Qué es malicia indígena?" *Memoria Indígena*, 2018.

Sáez, Aitor. "El pueblo que adopta cadáveres: 'Bajaban por el río entre 20 y 25 cuerpos cada semana.'" *El Confidencial*, June 28, 2018. https://www.elconfidencial.com/mundo/2018-06-28/colombia-asesinatos-narco-paramilitares-berrio_1585136/.

Safford, Frank. "Foreign and National Enterprise in Nineteenth-Century Colombia." *Business History Review* 39, no. 4 (1965): 503–26.

Salama, Jordan. "Inside the Local Movement to Recover Colombia's River Turtles." *Smithsonian Magazine*, November 15, 2021. https://www.smithsonianmag.com/science-nature/inside-the-local-movement-to-recover-colombias-river-turtles-180978887/.

Salvatore, Ricardo Donato. *Disciplinary Conquest: U.S. Scholars in South America, 1900–1945*. Durham, NC: Duke University Press, 2018.

Samper, José María. *Ensayo sobre las revoluciones políticas y la condición social de las Repúblicas Colombianas (hispano-americanas)*. Bogotá: Universidad Nacional de Colombia, 1861.

Sánchez, Nelson Camilo, and Adriana Rudling. *Reparations in Colombia: Where to? Mapping the Colombian Landscape of Reparations for Victims of the Internal Armed Conflict*. Belfast: Queens University Belfast, 2019.

Sanders, James E. *Contentious Republicans: Popular Politics, Race, and Class in Nineteenth-Century Colombia*. Durham, NC: Duke University Press, 2004.

Schouten, Peer, Finn Stepputat, and Jan Bachmann. "States of Circulation: Logistics off the Beaten Path." *Environment and Planning D: Society and Space* 37, no. 5 (2019): 779–93.

Schwartz-Marín, Ernesto, and Peter Wade. "Explaining the Visible and the Invisible: Public Knowledge of Genetics, Ancestry, Physical Appearance and Race in Colombia." *Social Studies of Science* 45, no. 6 (2015): 886–906.

Scott, James C. *Seeing Like a State: How Certain Schemes to Improve the Human Condition Have Failed*. New Haven, CT: Yale University Press, 1998.

Scott, Julius S. *The Common Wind: Afro-American Currents in the Age of the Haitian Revolution*. London: Verso, 2018.

Semana. "Cobra vida el río Magdalena." May 23, 2015. https://www.semana.com/la-rehabilitacion-del-rio-magdalena/428893-3/.

Semana. "Fallo de tutela reconoce al río Magdalena como nuevo sujeto de derechos." October 25, 2019. https://www.semana.com/medio-ambiente/articulo/declaran-al-rio-magdalena-sujeto-de-derechos/47279/.

Semana. "'Recuperar el río es una bendición para el país.'" October 23, 2015. https://www.semana.com/especial-infraestructura-2015entrevista-con-el-presidente-de-navelena/447304-3/.

Senu, Amaha. "Stowaways, Seafarers and Ship Security in Insecure Ports." *MARE Report*, 2018: 12–15.

Serrano López, Adriana María, and Daniel Eduardo Hernández Chitiva. *Del Río Grande de la Magdalena y la 'producción' del territorio caribeño: Análisis de las tensiones políticas, económicas y sociales entre Cartagena de Indias, Barranquilla y Santafé de Bogotá durante la primera mitad del siglo XX*. Bogotá: Editorial Universidad del Rosario, 2015.

Sharpe, Christina. *In the Wake: On Blackness and Being*. Durham, NC: Duke University Press, 2016.

Siemiatycki, Matti, Theresa Enright, and Mariana Valverde. "The Gendered Production of Infrastructure." *Progress in Human Geography* 44, no. 2 (2020): 297–314.

Silva Fajardo, Germán. *Champanes, vapores y remolcadores: Historia de la navegación y la ingeniería fluvial Colombiana*. Bogotá: Academia Colombiana de Historia de la Ingeniería y las Obras Públicas, 2009.

Silver, Jonathan. "Corridor Urbanism." In *Global Urbanism: Knowledge, Power and the City*, edited by Michele Lancione and Colin McFarlane, 251–58. New York: Routledge, 2021.

Simone, AbdouMaliq. "Transcript: Blackness and the Urban," October 1, 2021. In *Black Urbanisms Podcast Series*, podcast. https://www.ucl.ac.uk/urban-lab/publications/2021/oct/black-urbanisms-podcast-series.

Simone, AbdouMaliq. "Urbanity and Generic Blackness." *Theory, Culture and Society* 33, no. 7–8 (2016): 183–203.

Smallwood, Stephanie. *Saltwater Slavery: A Middle Passage from Africa to American Diaspora*. Cambridge, MA: Harvard University Press, 2007.

Smith, Neil. *American Empire: Roosevelt's Geographer and the Prelude to Globalization*. Berkeley: University of California Press, 2004.

Solano, Sergio Paolo. *Puertos, sociedad y conflictos en el Caribe colombiano, 1850-1930.* Cartagena: Observatorio del Caribe Colombiano, Universidad de Cartagena, 2003.

Sourdis Nájera, Adelaida. "Los judíos sefardíes en Barranquilla: El caso de Jacob y Ernesto Cortissoz." *Boletín Cultural y Bibliográfico* 35, no. 49 (1998): 31-47.

Steiner, Claudia. *Imaginación y poder: El encuentro del interior con la costa en Urabá, 1900-1960.* Medellín: Editorial Universidad de Antioquia, 2000.

Stepan, Nancy Leys. *"The Hour of Eugenics": Race, Gender, and Nation in Latin America.* Ithaca, NY: Cornell University Press, 1991.

Stepan, Nancy Leys. *Picturing Tropical Nature.* London: Reaktion, 2001.

Stokes, Kathleen, and Alejandro De Coss-Corzo. "Doing the Work: Locating Labour in Infrastructural Geography." *Progress in Human Geography* 47, no. 3 (2023): 427-46.

Strauss, Kendra. "Labour Geography III: Precarity, Racial Capitalisms and Infrastructure." *Progress in Human Geography* 44, no. 6 (2020): 1212-24.

Taussig, Michael. *Palma Africana.* Chicago: University of Chicago Press, 2018.

Thomas, Deborah A. *Political Life in the Wake of the Plantation.* Durham, NC: Duke University Press, 2019.

Thomas, Deborah A. "Time and the Otherwise: Plantations, Garrisons and Being Human in the Caribbean." *Anthropological Theory* 16, no. 2-3 (2016): 177-200.

Thurner, Mark, and Jorge Cañizares-Esguerra. "La invención de Humboldt y la destrucción de las pirámides de La Condamine." *Procesos: Revista Ecuatoriana de Historia*, no. 51 (2020): 201-4.

Toscano, Alberto, and Jeff Kinkle. *Cartographies of the Absolute.* Alresford, UK: Zero, 2015.

Truelove, Yaffa. "Gendered Infrastructure and Liminal Space in Delhi's Unauthorized Colonies." *Environment and Planning D: Society and Space* 39, no. 6 (2021): 1009-25.

Tsing, Anna Lowenhaupt. *Friction: An Ethnography of Global Connection.* Princeton, NJ: Princeton University Press, 2005.

Tsing, Anna Lowenhaupt. *The Mushroom at the End of the World: On the Possibility of Life in Capitalist Ruins.* Princeton, NJ: Princeton University Press, 2015.

Twain, Mark. *Life on the Mississippi.* London: Penguin, 1984.

Unidad de Investigación y Acusación. Comunicado 009. June 5, 2019. https://www.jep.gov .co/SiteAssets/Paginas/UIA/sala-de-prensa/Comunicado%20UIA%20-%20009.pdf.

Universidad ICESI and Centro de Estudios Afrodiaspóricos. "Racismo, patriarcado y conflicto armado: Informe a la Comisión para el Esclarecimiento de la Verdad, la Convivencia y la No Repetición." Cali, 2021.

Uribe, Simón. "Suspensión: Espacio, tiempo y política en la historia interminable de un proyecto de infraestructura en el piedemonte Andino-Amazónico colombiano." *Antípoda: Revista de Antropología y Arqueología*, no. 42 (2021): 205-29.

Uribe, Simón, Silvia Otero-Bahamón, and Isabel Peñaranda. "Hacer el estado: Carreteras, conflicto y órdenes locales en los territorios de las FARC." *Revista de Estudios Sociales* 75 (2021): 87-100.

Vanegas Beltrán, Muriel. "Elementos para identificar el Caribe colombiano como una región histórica." *Cuadernos del Caribe* 16, no. 1 (2013): 95-105.

VerdadAbierta.com. "'A su hermano lo lanzaron vivo a los cocodrilos': Desmovilizados." November 17, 2011. https://verdadabierta.com/a-su-hermano-lo-lanzaron-vivo-a-los -cocodrilos-desmovilizados/.

Vergara-Figueroa, Aurora. *Afrodescendant Resistance to Deracination in Colombia: Massacre at Bellavista-Bojayá-Chocó*. London: Palgrave Macmillan, 2018.

Villegas, Álvaro. "El valle del río Magdalena en los discursos letrados de la segunda mitad del siglo XIX: Territorio, enfermedad y trabajo." *Folios*, no. 39 (2014): 149–59.

Villegas Vélez, Álvaro Andrés, and Catalina Castrillón Gallego. "Territorio, enfermedad y población en la producción de la geografía tropical colombiana, 1872–1934." *Historia Crítica*, no. 32 (2006): 94–117.

Viloria De la Hoz, Joaquín. *Empresarios del Caribe colombiano: Historia económica y empresarial del Magdalena Grande y del Bajo Magdalena, 1870-1930*. Bogotá: Banco de la República, 2014.

Viveros Vigoya, Mara. *De quebradores y cumplidores: Sobre hombres, masculinidades y relaciones de género en Colombia*. Bogotá: Universidad Nacional de Colombia, 2002.

Viveros Vigoya, Mara. "Más allá del esencialismo: Teorías feministas, hombres, masculinidades y dominación patriarcal." In *Masculinidades y sexualidades en deconstrucción*, edited by Sonia Brito Rodríguez, Rodrigo Azócar González, Lorena Basualto Porra, and Claudia Flores Rivas, 39–59. Santiago de Chile: Le Monde Diplomatique, 2022.

Viveros Vigoya, Mara. "Social Mobility, Whiteness, and Whitening in Colombia." *Journal of Latin American and Caribbean Anthropology* 20, no. 3 (2015): 496–512.

von Schnitzler, Antina. *Democracy's Infrastructure: Techno-politics and Protest after Apartheid*. Princeton, NJ: Princeton University Press, 2016.

Wade, Peter. *Blackness and Race Mixture: The Dynamics of Racial Identity in Colombia*. Baltimore: Johns Hopkins University Press, 1993.

Wade, Peter. *Degrees of Mixture, Degrees of Freedom: Genomics, Multiculturalism, and Race in Latin America*. Durham, NC: Duke University Press, 2017.

Wade, Peter. "Espacio, región y racialización en Colombia." *Revista de Geografía Norte Grande* 49, no. 76 (2020): 31–49.

Wade, Peter. *Music, Race, and Nation: Música Tropical in Colombia*. Chicago: University of Chicago Press, 2000.

Wade, Peter. *Race, Nature and Culture: An Anthropological Perspective*. London: Pluto, 2002.

Walcott, Rinaldo. "Genres of Human: Multiculturalism, Cosmo-politics, and the Caribbean Basin." In *Sylvia Wynter: On Being Human as Praxis*, edited by Katherine McKittrick, 183–202. Durham, NC: Duke University Press, 2015.

Weheliye, Alexander G. *Habeas Viscus: Racializing Assemblages, Biopolitics, and Black Feminist Theories of the Human*. Durham, NC: Duke University Press, 2014.

West, Cornel. *Race Matters*. Boston: Beacon, 1993.

White, Richard. *The Organic Machine: The Remaking of the Columbia River*. New York: Hill and Wang, 1995.

Wilderson, Frank B., III. *Afropessimism*. New York: Liveright, 2020.

Woods, Clyde. *Development Arrested: The Blues and Plantation Power in the Mississippi Delta*. London: Verso, 1998.

Woods, Clyde. *Development Drowned and Reborn: The Blues and Bourbon Restorations in Post-Katrina New Orleans*. Edited by Jordan T. Camp and Laura Pulido. Atlanta: University of Georgia Press, 2017.

Wright, Willie Jamaal. "The Morphology of Marronage." *Annals of the American Association of Geographers* 110, no. 4 (2020): 1134–49.

Wulf, Andrea. *The Invention of Nature: The Adventures of Alexander von Humboldt, the Lost Hero of Science.* London: John Murray, 2015.

Wynter, Sylvia. "1492: A New World View." In *Race, Discourse, and the Origin of the Americas: A New World View,* edited by Vera Lawrence Hyatt and Rex Nettleford, 5–57. Washington, DC: Smithsonian Institution Press, 1995.

Wynter, Sylvia. "Unsettling the Coloniality of Being/Power/Truth/Freedom: Towards the Human, After Man, Its Overrepresentation—an Argument." *CR: The New Centennial Review* 3, no. 3 (2003): 257–337.

Wynter, Sylvia, and Katherine McKittrick. "Unparalleled Catastrophe for Our Species? Or, to Give Humanness a Different Future: Conversations." In *Sylvia Wynter: On Being Human as Praxis,* edited by Katherine McKittrick, 9–89. Durham, NC: Duke University Press, 2015.

Yanagisako, Sylvia, and Carol Delaney, eds. *Naturalizing Power: Essays in Feminist Cultural Analysis.* London: Taylor and Francis, 1994.

Yanagisako, Sylvia Junko. *Producing Culture and Capital: Family Firms in Italy.* Princeton, NJ: Princeton University Press, 2002.

Zapata Olivella, Manuel. *Por los senderos de sus ancestros: Textos escogidos, 1940–2000.* Edited by Alfonso Múnera. Bogotá: Ministerio de Cultura, República de Colombia, 2010.

Zavala, Silvio. "Los aspectos geográficos en la colonización del Nuevo Mundo." *Revista Geográfica* 29, no. 55 (1961): 51–137.

Zavala Guillen, Ana Laura. "Afro-Latin American Geographies of in-Betweenness: Colonial Marronage in Colombia." *Journal of Historical Geography* 72 (2021): 13–22.

Zeiderman, Austin. "Concrete Peace: Building Security through Infrastructure in Colombia." *Anthropological Quarterly* 93, no. 3 (2020): 497–528.

Zeiderman, Austin. "In the Wake of Logistics: Situated Afterlives of Race and Labour on the Magdalena River." *Environment and Planning D: Society and Space* 39, no. 3 (2021): 441–58.

Zeiderman, Austin. "Low Tide: Submerged Humanism in a Colombian Port." In *Infrastructure, Environment, and Life in the Anthropocene,* edited by Kregg Hetherington, 172–91. Durham, NC: Duke University Press, 2019.

Zeisler-Vralsted, Dorothy. "African Americans and the Mississippi River: Race, History and the Environment." *Thesis Eleven* 150, no. 1 (2019): 81–101.

Zimmerer, Karl S. "Humboldt's Nodes and Modes of Interdisciplinary Environmental Science in the Andean World." *Geographical Review* 96, no. 3 (2006): 334–60.

Zimmerer, Karl S. "Humboldt and the History of Environmental Thought." *Geographical Review* 96, no. 3 (2006): 456–58.

Index

Page numbers in *italics* refer to figures.

blockades, 194–97

bodies, 35, 97, 103, 213, 215; blood and arteries, x–xi; corpses, 69–70, 114, 132–33, 155; feminized, 211, 211n7; injuries and value of, 104–6, 110; labor and, 33, 126; physiological differences, 2, 3, 19–20, 161; of riverboat workers, 4, 142, 162; women as caretakers of, 155–56

bogas (riverboat workers): accidents and compensation, 104–6, 113–14, 141; armed conflict and, 135–40, 214–15; Blackness and, 125, 139–40, 143; brotherhood (*hermandad*), 187–88; crew and operations, 115–18, 140–46, *142*; depictions of, 4, 7, *31*, 158–59, 185–86; extractive economy and, 172, 205, 215; families, 171–72, 201–2; history, 125–31; homosocial intimacy and caring, 153, 161–65, 172–73; Humboldt's writings on, 180–83, 186; hydrographical knowledge, 202–4, 207, 215; inactivity, 112–14; masculinity, 2, 4, 5n3, 110–11, 152; mixed-race categorization, 36, *38*, 38–39, 185; mobility and independence, 198–202, 207; navigability plan and, 63–64; Obeso's poetry on, 190–94, *191*; physical constitution, 4, 142–43, 182, 185; regulation of, 74–75, 128–29; riverside communities and, 62–63, 194–97, *195*; safety protocols, 110–11; solidarity, 124, 187–88, 196; time and value and, 102–3; trade with locals, 94. *See also* navigation techniques

Bogotá, 24, 44, 49, 68, 125, 180; Gaitán murder, 132

Bojayá massacre, 213

Bolívar, Simón, 36, 127, 145, 184

bongos (wooden rafts), *38*, 41, 125

Bonil-Gómez, Katherine, 126

Bonilla, Yarimar, 8, 18n46

Brown, Jacqueline Nassy, 169n55

burrero (human-equine love), 150–52

Caldas, Francisco José de, 184

Camargo, Alejandro, 60n20, 212

Canal de Dique, 30, 49, 117, 133, 134, 197

canalization, 41, 55n9, 62, 117–18. *See also* dredging and channeling

Cañizares Esguerra, Jorge, 35n43

Caño Corea (Korea Canal), 137

capital accumulation, 15, 102, 117, 149n4, 159; colonial exploitation and, 149–50; by dispossession, 133–34; regimes of, 4, 11, 196, 197, 198,

200, 205; resource extraction and, 11, 59, 132, 162–63, 196

capitalism: extractivism and, 163, 172; gendered dimensions of, 159–60, 168, 172; logistical, 16, 117, 119, 153, 168; plantations and, 120n13; racial, 15, 21, 118, 120–21, 123–24, 126, 179–80, 196, 197, 199; supply chain, 85, 87n10

captains and pilots, 78–79, 108, 110, 136, 161–62, 164; duties, 115–16, 143–44; enslaved, 178n6; leaving the vessel and, 63, 114, 164; navigation skills and practices, 21, 175–80, *177*, 203–4; radio exchanges, 186–90; recruitment of, 189; salary, 199; steamboat, 130; in the wheelhouse 140, 141, 194, *195*

Cárdenas, Roosbelinda, 214

cargo, 60, 90, 100–103, *101*, 180; blockades, 194–95, 197; horse cart transport, 72; human, 120–21; liquid, 78, 108, 115, 141, 163, 205; passengers and, *65*; value and, 110; volumes, 54–55, 61–62

Caribbean coast, 4, 5, 8, 37, 49–50, 71n30, 134–35; manatees, 152; migration to, 39–40, 42; peace and violence of, 133, 139, 149; racial identity and, 41, 47n89, 116n1, 131, 149–50, 185; *raizales*, 213; Spanish colonizers and, 27, 29, 198. *See also costeños*; interior/coastal divide

caring practices, 7, 158; of fishermen, 156, *157*; performed by women, 154–56, 201–2; of riverboat workers, 2, 160–65

Carse, Ashley, 30, 85n4, 176

Cartagena, 1, 2, 44, 116–17, 133, 195; port, 30, 49, 61, 90, 109, 117, 126; shipyard explosions, 83, 84, 86–87, 95

cattle ranching, *14*, 76, 133, 158

Caycedo, Carolina, 209–11, *210*, 211n7

cédula de extranjería (foreign ID), 97

Césaire, Aimé, 12n26, 30–33

chalupas (passenger boats), 59, *65*, 65–66, 78, 166–67

champanes (wooden barges), 7, 41, 125, 180, 183, 186, 192

channeling. *See* dredging and channeling

Chimilas, 70

Chorographic Commission, 47

Chua, Charmaine, 87n6, 119, 168

circulation of goods, 16, 99, 114, 158, 186; disruptions or threats to, 85n2, 85–86, 87, 102, 109–10; fantasy of continuous, 119; importance of time, 100–102, 111, 117

knowledge systems, 18, 35, 207; hydrographical, 202–4; navigation, 143, 176–77, 185, 189–90, 192

Kobayashi, Audrey, 26

labor disputes, 95–96, 186n34, 200. *See also* unions

labor market, 174

La Mojana, 133, 134

land occupation, 134, 137, 158

La Niña, 157–58

Lesutis, Gediminas, 160n41

logistics industry, 15–16, 20–21, 85–88, 164n50; companies, 88–90; complaints and compensation, 92–94; gender and, 110–11, 159–60; hierarchies of value and, 87–88, 95; hubs and ports, *17*, *86*, 90–100, 167, 169–70; labor relations and regulatory frameworks, 95–97; managers, 110–11, 165–69; race and labor and, 87n7, 117–18, 120, 122–24, 141; risk management and insurance policies, 103–7, *104*, 114; security and training, *106*, 106–8; Venezuelan workers, 174; vessel schedules and operations, 108–14, 143–44; women in, 110–11, 169–72. *See also* cargo; circulation of goods; supply chain security

López de Mesa, Luis, 38, 42–43

Lowe, Lisa, x

Magdalena River: armed conflict and, 96, 106, 131, 132–38, 172–73, 212–15; colonial history of, 20, 29–33, 35, 124–26; commercial shipping megaproject, x, 9–11, *11*, 15–16, 20, 43–44, 54–58; disruptive activities, 93–94, 100–101; gendering, 152–56; geo-racial regimes and, 26–27, 128; Humboldt's voyage, 9, 180–84, *181*, 186; infrastructural development, 24–25, 75–76, 206; Middle (Magdalena Medio) and Lower (Bajo Magdalena), 48–49, 58, 71, 132, 155, 197; monitoring and (mis)management, 41–42, 75–77, 114; nature and race and, 8–9, 15; navigability plan, 49–50, 58–60, 63, 66, 72–73, 145; personhood and, 53, 154, 160, 165, 212; pollution, 2, 133, 205; as primary artery of trade, 4, *6*, *31*, *32*, 76, 124–25; racial mixing and, 36–40; recovery of corpses, 69–70, 132–33, 155; sediment loads, 65–66, 136–37; supernatural forces and myths of, 64, 147–50, *149*; total length, 52n1; water level, 52–53, 101, 111, 203. *See also* dredging and channeling

Magdalena River valley, 37, 47, 71n30, 190, 193; climate, 5, 158; El Banco settlement, 70–71; maroon settlements, 197–98; mixed-race workers, 39, 40, 159

malicia indígena expression, 107n23

manatees, 152

maquinistas. See engineers (*maquinistas*) or mechanics

marine infantry, *106*, 106–7, 117, 136

Márquez, Francia, 155

Márquez Calle, Germán, 149–50

Marshall, Kerry James, 29n22

Mary Magdalene, 29, 153–54

masculinity, 2, 21, 159–60, 160n41, 169n55, 176; fishing and, 155, 156; independence and, 201; of logistics managers, 168–69; productive labor and, 162, 172; of riverboat workers, 4, 5n3, 110, 164, 172–73; sexuality and, 147–48

mastery, 32, 50; over nature, 28n20, 28–29, 29n22, 30

materiality, 16, 53n10, 95

Mbembe, Achille, 87n10, 119–20

McGraw, Jason, 37, 39n63, 128, 130n66, 186n34, 201

McKittrick, Katherine, 17, 19, 28n20, 54n7, 114n25, 180n12

mechanics. *See* engineers (*maquinistas*) or mechanics

Medellín, 44, 56, 58, 68, 69, 87, 125

mestizaje (racial mixing), 9, 36–39, 46n86, 63, 70, 206; legal and political status and, 126; national identity and, 34, 36, 71, 127, 185; sexuality and, 151

Mezzadra, Sandro, 102n15

migrants, 46, 177n4; Afro-Antillean, 39–40, 40n67; Jewish and Arab, 39–42, 151; Venezuelan, 174, 189

Mississippi River, 61–62, 124, 193

modernity: capitalist, 11, 118, 119–20; Colombia and, 61, 128, 129; colonial, 12, 20, 27n16, 27–28, 30, 33, 125; infrastructures and, 33n37; liquid, 193

Mompox, 183, 190, 194

Montes de María, 133–34

Moten, Fred, 119, 122–23

mulatos, 36, 126, 183, 184n27

Mutis, José Celestino, 180

mythology, 147–50, *149*, 150n6, 152

National Center of Historical Memory, 211

National Liberation Army (ELN), 69, 84, 96, 138, 214

national unification, 34, 36, 59, 71, 127, 185

navegantes, 112, 114, 174, 187, 203–4; fights between, 164–65; freedom and mobility, 199, 201–2. See also *bogas*; captains and pilots; deckhands; engineers

Navelena, 57; collapse of, 44, 49, 79, 79–81; Magdalena River project, 56–58

navigation techniques, 146, 178n6; equipment and technologies, 175–76, 180n11; hydrographic knowledge and, 202–4, 207; Obeso's poetic references to, 191–92; race/racial capitalism and, 179–80; radio communications, 186–90; skill and intuition, 143, 176–78, 185, 189; social and spatial orders of, 176n1, 177n4, 186, 207; structures of inequality and, 196–97

Nazism, 19, 24, 42

Neilson, Brett, 102n15

New Granada, 6, 35n45, 126, 184, 197

Nieto, Judith, 156

Obeso, Candelario, 190–94, *191*, 201

O'Bryen, Rory, 126, 190

Odebrecht, 54, 80

oil industry, 80, 96, 200, 215; fluvial transport, 90, 97, 110, 112–13, 117, 163, 167; spills, 2, 205; tanker trucks, *98*, 101–2. See also Ecopetrol oil refinery

ontologies/ontological divides, 14, 20, 53–54, 68, 71; fixing, 14n32; land and water, 57–58, 62–63, 73, 148–49, 179n8; politics, 14n31, 54n6, 194; racial/raciontologies, ix, 33, 53, 142, 161, 179; subject/object, 14, 29, 33, 52–53, 78; water bodies/human bodies, 210–11. See also human/nonhuman relations; interior/coastal divide

Ortega, Francisco, 127

Ortiz, José Domingo, 70

Palacios, Leyner, 212–13

palenques (maroon settlements), 134, 197–98, 213n16

paramilitaries, 9, 69, 96, 132–34, 138–39, 158, 173

parasites, 19

Parry, Tyler, 197n55

Pastrana Borrero, Misael, 151

peace building, 10, 43–44, 84, 155, 206, 211

Peano, Irene, 169

Pérez, Felipe, 47n89

Perry, Sondra, 121

personhood, 114, 120n13, 178n5; gendered, 21, 156–58; male, 160, 165, 169, 173; of rivers, 53, 154, 156–57, 212, 215; value and, 68, 180, 190

pescadores. See fishermen

Petrobras, 80

pilots. *See* captains and pilots

plantations, 76, 118, 120n13, 133, 158, 179

pluriversality, 14n31, 54n6

Popayán, 6

potable water. *See* drinking water

power structures, 27n14, 85n5, 119, 196–97; colonial, 18, 28, 30; gendered, 159, 169n55; labor and bargaining, 21, 96, 106, 130, 144

private property, 195

protests, 12, 73, 209, 214n19

Puerto Berrío, 66–69, 155

Puerto Salgar, 44, 58, 61

Puerto Wilches, 44–49, 66

Quijano, Aníbal, 28, 119

race: Darwin on, 19; Du Bois on, 18; geography and infrastructure and, 24–26; Hall on, 16n40, 27n14, 116n2; historicizing, 34nn38–39; Humboldt on, 184n25; labor and, 21, 110–11, 116, 130–31, 141–44; logistics industry and, 87n7; purity of blood and, 36, 141n98; reconfigurations of, 205–6; slavery and capital and, 119–24; terminologies, 34; Wynter on, x, 28

race/nature entanglement, 5, 6–9, 15, 20, 28n18, 34–35, 215; disentangling, xi, 22; modern/colonial world and, 6, 27–28

racial ecologies, 7–8, 13, 53n5, 207

racial hierarchies, 9, 18, 21, 25, 60, 123–24; armed conflict and, 139, 214; *bogas* and, 126, 141, 159, 162; labor hierarchies and, 95, 104, 108, 171, 173–74; *mestizaje* and, 36–37; regional hierarchies and, 20, 46–47, 55, 127–28, 131, 184, 184n27, 185, 206; Spanish colonialism and, 34, 34n40, 36, 184. See also geo-racial regimes

racial mixing. See *mestizaje*

racism, 8, 14n31, 18n43, 43, 179, 206; armed conflict and, 213–14; infrastructures and, 33n37; institutional, 57; scientific, xi, 19, 185; structural, 214n19. *See also* white supremacy